OPEN LETTER TO EVANGELICALS
A Devotional and Homiletic Commentary on
The First Epistle of John

Open Letter
to Evangelicals

A Devotional and Homiletic Commentary on
The First Epistle of John

by

R. E. O. WHITE

WILLIAM B. EERDMANS PUBLISHING COMPANY
GRAND RAPIDS, MICHIGAN

© Copyright 1964 by Wm. B. Eerdmans Publishing Co. All rights reserved. Printed in the United States of America. Library of Congress catalog card number, 64-22024

CONTENTS

ACKNOWLEDGEMENTS

C. H. Dodd's enlightening study of 1 John in the *Moffatt Commentary* (Hodder & Stoughton) first made the epistle "come alive" for the present writer; Huther's encyclopedia of opinions in *Meyer's Commentary* (T. & T. Clark) ensured that most conceivable interpretations (and some barely conceivable) were considered; Westcott's volume (Macmillan) keeps one's exegesis sound, and William Barclay, in the *Daily Study Bible* (St. Andrew Press, Edinburgh) keeps one's feet on the ground. A. E. Brooke (*International Critical Commentary*, T. & T. Clark) provides, amongst much else, essential Hebrew and Classical background. Plummer (*Cambridge Bible*) is always stimulating, Neil Alexander (*Torch Bible*, SCM Press) is fresh and purposeful, W. H. Bennett (*Century Bible*) is too brief to be more than useful. G. S. Barrett (*Devotional Commentary*, Religious Tract Society, 1910) and William Alexander (*The Expositor's Bible*, Hodder & Stoughton) often express John's thought felicitously, and J. Ireland Hasler (*The Message of Life*, Carey Kingsgate Press) comes to the epistle with an Indian mystical background. It is, however, Robert Law (*The Tests of Life*, Kerr Lectures, published T. & T. Clark, 1909) who remains master of this epistle. "Law's book is a liberal education in Biblical theology" says A. M. Hunter. If in the following pages Law's name and words occur too frequently, it is because his treatment of passage after passage makes any subsequent commentator despair. Other books used less constantly are mentioned in the appended notes and sources. Scripture quotations are from the *Revised Standard Version* of the Bible, copyrighted 1946 and 1952 by the Division of Christian Education, National Council of Churches, and used by permission.

For help from all these, and for generous permissions to quote, the author expresses his sincere gratitude.

NECESSARY EXPLANATIONS

Introduction: *Necessary Explanations*

"THE WIND BEING IN MY FACE, tempering the heat of the sun, I had a pleasant ride to Dublin. In the evening I began expounding the deepest part of the Holy Scripture, namely the First Epistle of John. . . . Here are sublimity and simplicity together, the strongest sense and the plainest language!"

It is John Wesley speaking, and it is no accident that such a tribute to 1 John comes from an acknowledged prince of evangelical Christianity, and out of the heart of that "Evangelical Revival" which was England's version of America's "Great Awakening".

Sixteen centuries earlier, in ancient Phrygia, the Montanists had emphasised (according to F. J. A. Hort) "a strong faith in the Holy Spirit as the promised Paraclete, present as a heavenly power in the Church of the day; a belief that the Holy Spirit was manifesting Himself through entranced prophets and prophetesses; a specially stern and exacting standard of Christian morality; a tendency to set up prophets against bishops; an eager anticipation of the Lord's second coming. . . ". The lineaments of an early, if somewhat emotional, evangelicalism are here discernible, and it is revealing that F. F. Bruce can remark, as one by-product of the Montanist movement, a widening suspicion of the Johannine literature, to which Montanists so confidently appealed.

In our own time, Professor C. H. Dodd, discussing 1 John, declares that John sees "the Christian life as one of union with God upon ethical conditions . . . (and) insists that while glib talk about religious experience is a snare and a delusion in the absence of serious attention to daily conduct, a truly virtuous

9

life can spring only out of a unique relation to God, which is not, achieved by us but granted by His grace". That defines essential evangelicalism as accurately as it summarises 1 John. If Romans and Galatians have provided intellectual authority for the faith of evangelicals, it is the Johannine literature which has provided its inspiration and nourishment. For all its depth and philosophical penetration, John's Gospel is the universal textbook of practical evangelism; while beside John Wesley's high opinion of the First Epistle we may set the words of a German scholar of the last century (Hilgenfeld): that the epistle belongs to the most beautiful writings of the New Testament, and is "especially rich and original exactly in what relates to the subjective, inner life of Christianity. . . . The fresh, vivid, attractive character of the epistle consists exactly in that it conducts us with such a predilection into the inner experience of genuine Christian life". That inner experience is the central concern of evangelicalism.

(i) *Why "Evangelicals"?*

Broadly speaking, the so-called "Catholic" view sees Christianity as embodied within a divine institution, the Church; whose life is perpetuated by sacraments and hierarchy, by ritual, creed and priestly mediation; whose foundations lie in Old Testament models of theocracy and priesthood, and in the continuing tradition of the Church Fathers alongside the New Testament; and whose aim is to express through worship, witness, discipline and political action the Kingship of Christ on earth. For this purpose the Catholic Churches will seek, where convenient, the support and establishment of the State authorities, though striving to maintain spiritual autonomy at the same time.

Evangelicalism, on the other hand (as the term implies) lays its main emphasis not upon the Church but upon the gospel. It makes much of the fact of sin, the need of salvation, the obligation of world-evangelism; its immediate aim is personal conversion from self and sin to God by the power of the Holy Spirit, through acceptance in personal faith of the "finished work" of atonement wrought by Christ, and through commitment to Him, risen and ascended, as Saviour and Lord. The ground of this evangel lies in inspired Scriptures, to whose authority the Church must submit for the regulation of her own life. The true Church is an international and inter-denominational fellowship embracing all so converted.*

* See note 1, p. 223.

10

Emotionally somewhat intense, evangelical Christianity nourishes a "gospel piety" which speaks more of consecration, trust,
and divine guidance than of ethics, but which is generally
Puritan in tone and earnestness. In worship it lays much more
emphasis upon gospel preaching than upon the performance of
ancient liturgy; in organisation it stresses life and freedom more
than regularity of "orders". It values personal conviction more
highly than profession of the historic creeds; and in spite of a
certain fear that "good works" may detract from the primacy of
"faith alone" as the means of salvation, it has always been associated with active concern for the ignorant, the diseased, the
poor, suffering, oppressed, and imprisoned — not least in its
missionary enterprise.

The persistence of the evangelical interpretation of the faith,
amid temptations to closer-knit institutionalism, firmer discipline,
and more rigid patterns of faith, worship, and life, is explained
in varying phrases that usually amount to the same general emphasis. The Evangelical Alliance (founded 1846) seeks "to
promote the interests of a scriptural Christianity"; the Evangelical Revival, like the Great Awakening, sought especially
evangelistic power; the Puritans desired simplicity and immediacy
of experience; the Moravians a "simple, pure, unworldly Christianity"; the Reformation was "the revolt of genuine religion against secularisation"; the Brethren of the Common Life,
the Friends of God, the Waldensians, and the brotherhoods of
Francis, Bernard, Priscillian and the like, desired personal piety
above all else; Montanism was an attempt to revert to the primitive apostolic fervour in the face of a growing institutionalism
and secularisation within the Church.

One constant motive is undoubtedly the passionate longing to
recapture the intoxication, power, victory, and joy of apostolic
Christianity in place of the dead formalism of ritual and tradition.
Another is the search for religious certainty, directly in immediate spiritual experiences, and objectively in the inspired
record of divine revelation. A third motive of evangelicalism is the
felt need for a dynamic experience that can change human nature,
redeem sinners, and transform the world. A fourth is the recognition that *life* demands flexibility and growth; historical
continuity implies a power of inward adjustment and adaptation
to new times; universal appeal presupposes variety of expression.
Only liberty safeguards sincerity; only variety expresses vitality.

Evangelicals cannot forget that, in reply to the demand of Pharisees that the disciples conform to accept codes of piety, Jesus declared that new wine will always need new and elastic wineskins.

Johannine Christianity emphasises precisely these insights beloved of evangelicals — the fullness of individual Christian experience, the promise of the Spirit, the "abiding" of the believing heart in Christ, the assurance of cleansing through the cross, the certainty of hope, and the fellowship of believers in love.

This emphasis is especially true of the First Epistle. Nothing is here said of Church "order", or even of the Church itself in its concrete and organised life; nothing about officials or ministry — certainly nothing about priestly mediation or episcopal rule, though the latter would have been especially relevant. No attempt is made to exert any personal authority, or to require submission even to apostles: no discipline of any kind is threatened. Baptism and the Lord's Supper are assumed, but in such manner that allusion to them has been denied: no stress is laid upon them, or instruction given concerning them. The Church as an institution is simply not in sight — as it is, for example, in Romans, Ephesians, 1 Corinthians, and the Pastoral letters. Political or social obligations towards the surrounding world find no place in the counsel offered. Instead, attention is directed to personal belief and its implications for ethical behaviour and spiritual experience; to the Christian's union with God in Christ, his sonship, and eternal life; to the imitation of Christ, the dangers of worldliness, the constant need of confession and prayer; to the atonement, the eternal advocacy of Christ, and the second advent. These are all evangelical themes, while 1 John's insistence upon practical love is just such as in later evangelicalism prompts keen interest in peace and social reform.

Each interpretation of Christianity has its dangers. Evangelicalism cannot be acquitted of a tendency to subjectivism, and emotional moodiness;* to self-deception; to anti-intellectual and anti-ethical emotionalism; to excessive individualism and divisiveness; to withdrawal from civic and social responsibility, and to a want of maturity, a clinging so long to fundamentals as never to come within sight of the ultimates. Most evangelicals are aware of these temptations.

It is precisely this awareness of the values and perils of evangelicalism that directs attention to 1 John: its counsel and

* See note 2, pp. 223-224.

warnings are directly — even painfully — relevant to the besetting weaknesses of evangelicalism in every age. That is why
when we have cleared out of the way some preliminary but
necessary explanations, and worked steadily through the letter
(devotionally in the commentary, more critically in the appended notes) we shall linger to reflect on the modern message
of this most evangelical of epistles.

We shall find that John's remedy for a shallow, inward-
looking, "cheap-grace" evangelicalism is not catholicism but a
deeper, more ethical, more costly evangelicalism. So, one of the
most treasured of the practical values of 1 John is its pastoral
purpose of *reassurance*. Again and again John points to the
grounds of assurance which Christians possess, to the certainties
of the faith and the bedrock reality of our experience of God
in Christ. "Hard-hitting", "forthright", even "ruthless" in its
searching analysis and challenge, this anonymous evangelical tract
deserves as perhaps its most fitting title, "an Epistle of Encouragement".

(ii) *Why "Open Letter"?*

The letter's anonymity is matched by absence of address,
personal greetings, and reminiscences: every mark of personal
correspondence is missing except affectionate concern. Attentive
reading soon reveals that the situation addressed is one of great
delicacy: A. E. Brooke speaks of the pressing sense of danger in
the epistle: the definitions of faith are razor-sharp, the analysis
of spiritual obligation is unrelenting, and the method of argument
is an either/or confrontation which allows of no mid-way positions
between light and darkness, sin and righteousness, belief and
falsehood, God and the devil. And yet it is never explicitly
said that any identifiable person or group takes up the attitudes or
professes the doctrines which are condemned.

The reference to error is always oblique — "If we say", "Who
is the liar but he who", "Take care lest *any man* deceive you".
No one is forced into impossible situations from which it would
be humiliating to retreat: a skill and courtesy not always evident
in religious controversy. The argument is unquestionably directed
at a concrete local situation, yet not so aimed at either friend or
foe as to vindicate the one or alienate the other. The writer will
not deepen division by sharpening antipathies, however bluntly
he states the issues. The letter is open in this sense — let all
read it who will and each apply it to himself.

13

The same delicacy of approach makes the writer emphasise (ten times) that he does not suppose the readers ignorant of the truths he is laying before them; he could not appear more anxious not to give offence. He repeatedly (eleven times) affirms his affection and confidence in them, which in one so patently sincere sufficiently proves his personal knowledge of those he addresses. He knows, too, what has been happening among them, the things being said, the claims being made, how confidence has been shaken; and the readers know who writes to them. Yet nowhere is any hint given of personal authority, of apostleship, eldership, pastoral office or any other claim upon obedience: the author must placate and not command. The appeal is to the original message concerning the Lord, and to self-evident principles verified in experience — the classic evangelical argument. Pastoral concern, and an assumption of seniority, underlie the form of address, but neither is made the foundation of counsel or instruction. "That which was from the beginning", which the readers already know, is the only authority imposed.

The general relationship of 1 John to the Fourth Gospel, the second and third epistles of John, and (somewhat less closely) the Book of Revelation, is too obvious; and the tradition which associates this literature, in varying degrees, with the name "John", with the region of Ephesus, and with the years around the end of the first century is too strong for either point to need discussion. But who is "John"? Law well says of 1:1-4, "It is difficult to imagine words more studiously adapted to create the impression that the writer is one of the actual disciples of Jesus"; the phrases "That which . . . we have heard . . . have seen with our eyes . . . have looked upon and touched with our hands" take us back immediately and irresistibly into the heart of gospel events as experienced by an eye-witness. But first-hand acquaintance with Jesus was not confined to the apostles, nor was it possessed — in the ultimate analysis — only by first-generation Christians: the plural (*"we* heard") as again in 4:14, 5:18-20 (where it certainly cannot be confined to apostles) sums up the witness of all who inherit the conviction of the first generation.

That the writer means to expound the apostolic gospel is certain; that he stands very close indeed to the earliest apostolic preaching is illustrated in detail by C. H. Dodd; and that his first aim is to preserve the fellowship of the apostolic Churches is equally beyond question. Yet nothing in the epistle depends upon direct apostolic authorship to explain or enforce its teaching; and the carefully preserved anonymity, the oblique, tentative approach, the admission that the readers need no such instruction, the absence of any unambiguously *personal* reminiscence of Jesus, and the general philosophic background are perplexing if the author is the apostle John. Moreover, in face of the acute peril of the Churches he loved, the apostle John would surely be the last man to conceal his identity, and say nothing at all about his unimpeachable authority to instruct believers, derived from the Lord Himself, as one who had leaned upon Christ's breast in the hour of crucial revelation.

From a profusion of arguments and counter-arguments we may distil three probabilities: the author was (at least) a senior Christian leader among the Churches of Asia Minor, quite possibly an eye-witness of Christ; the letter was written at some time near the end of the first century; its composition probably followed the composition of the Fourth Gospel, and certainly followed the preaching of the Christian message in "Johannine" terms.

If one assumes that the reason for committing the message to writing was that it might be widely circulated, the absence of even the most general form of address presupposes a widely scattered community of varying groups and individuals. It has often been suggested that the message was originally spoken: "Substitute the word 'say' for 'write' . . . and we might imagine the whole discourse delivered in speech to the assembled Church" (Findlay)*; "a loving and anxious sermon" (Streeter); a homily, a sermon written out for several congregations (Barclay). The suggestion underlines the pastoral tone and purpose, but the intricacy and tension of the argument would demand very concentrated listening. Whether or not its contents were sometimes preached, it is now a "tract or manifesto thrown into vague epistolary form", "an encyclical, or pastoral manifesto" (Moffatt), a circular letter (Dodd). "Open letter" is the description which best combines the wide readership and the intimate personal acquaintance presupposed.**

(iii) *What Has Gone Wrong?*

Out of his personal knowledge of the situation, the author pens an argument and an appeal against division, a powerful antidote

* See note 3, p. 224.
** See note 4, pp. 224-227.

to disturbance of faith. "That you may have fellowship with us" is his immediately announced purpose; "that you may know that you have eternal life" is the final formulation of his intention in writing: stay with us — be assured — is the burden of every paragraph.

The events which created the need for that appeal are explicitly named. "I write this to you about those who would deceive you", "Many antichrists have come", "They went out from us, but they were not of us . . . they went out that it might be plain that they all are not of us." Evidently, once-loved colleagues, trusted leaders in the worship-assemblies of the local Churches, have separated themselves from the apostolic fellowship and gathered new congregations about them — with considerable success: "they are of the world, therefore what they say is of the world, and the world listens to them". Spiritual fellowship is broken, division has rent the Church, carrying away some and deeply disturbing the faith of all.

The secession is not open apostasy from Christ: the dissenters were Christian deviationists rather than disbelievers. The separated leaders and congregations still make great claims to spiritual blessing. In the typical language of evangelicalism, they "know God", are "born again of Him", are "walking in the light", are "in God" and "of God"; they "abide in Christ" and have the Spirit. John readily accepts this language to express also his own position, demanding only that it be correctly used. Moreover, in the seceding assemblies the voice of prophecy is still heard — men speaking by some spirit address the congregations — as in the apostolic groups; and it is almost as certain that the dissenters continue to observe baptism and the Lord's Supper, since John argues therefrom. The seceders claimed also to love God, and to do so more than apostolic Christians did: John nails that claim with "If any one says, 'I love God' and hates his brother, he is a liar".

Thus, though John calls the secession "antichrist", its leaders would hotly repudiate the charge, and reply that they alone were the truly "knowledgeable, advanced" Christians: it is easy to see why those who remained as yet faithful to the apostolic assemblies were so disturbed in mind, and why the author strives to reassure them of their own sufficient standing in Christ.

On the principle that the seceders must have been denying what John strenuously argues for, we may gather the general nature of the divisive doctrine from the epistle itself. (i) From the immense stress laid, in some fifteen different ways, upon the peril of tolerating sin in the Christian life it is clear that the teaching John confronted treated sin lightly, probably as something spiritually unimportant to "advanced" Christians. Not specific sins, but the seriousness of all sin, is one of John's themes, in reply to the contention that considerations of morality are "beneath" the spiritual man — the intellectual Christian. The attitude John faced is essentially that of the modern intellectual to whom morality is but social prejudice perpetuating primitive tabu. John answers fully and variously, always to the effect that "he who commits sin is of the devil".

(ii) A similar concentration of emphasis falls upon the duty of mutual loyalty and practical, detailed love (twelve times). Since he not only urges this, but argues for it, it is clear that not only intellectual pride, and the bitterness born of controversy, but something in the opposing doctrine itself, required his answer.

(iii) On no less than twenty-three occasions John refers to Jesus as Christ, the Son, the Son of God, come in the flesh, by water and blood, to possess whom is to have eternal life. The letter is written to reassure those who "believe in the name of the Son of God". The issue, plainly, is the identification of the man Jesus with the Son of God, the Christ. The unique phrases, "Jesus His Son", and "confess Jesus" point to this, in addition to the explicit "believes that Jesus is the Christ . . . that Jesus is the Son of God". In the (possibly accidental, possibly authentic) phrase of some manuscripts of 4:3, the seceders "dissolved" Jesus Christ into Jesus the man, in the flesh, who suffered, and the quite separable Christ, the Son, who did not. From the phrasing of John's assertions it is evident that he is concerned with views about Christ which challenge the fullness of the incarnation of the divine Son in flesh in Jesus, and the reality of the suffering of the divine Son in death for the world's sin.

(iv) In the epistle's 105 verses the two words for "knowing" occur forty times, once in every two-and-a-half verses; and reinforcing this is the emphasis John lays upon light and darkness, truth and falsehood, deceiving, teaching, confessing, faith, understanding. All this clearly indicates an essentially intellectualist conception of Christianity, and the probability that the ethical and doctrinal errors which had divided the Churches had intellectual, philosophical roots.

The picture that emerges therefore from the letter's contents is of the secession from once-united apostolic congregations of

Christians who, under pressure of philosophical influences, have rejected the full incarnation of Christ the Son of God in Jesus, and the full reality of His death for sin; who have come to regard ethical obligation as irrelevant to advanced spiritual experience; and who have neglected or denied especially the duty of mutual love and loyalty which is the central strand in Christian ethical thought. With great tact and gentleness, the senior Christian leader avoids directing his message to any one group or asserting any official ascendancy or authority, yet contrives to recall whoever will hear him to the original message of the apostles, and to point out the consequences of the dissenters' position with a ruthless spiritual logic that is unanswerable.

(iv) *The Source of the Trouble*

As the Church moved out of its Judaist homeland into the gentile world, she came face to face with a strange amalgam of high thinking, unbridled imagination, and specious philosophy, known to us in its many ramifications as Gnosticism. It was a "movement", a climate of thought, "an atmosphere rather than a system" (Mackintosh); it came into prominence in the first century, reached its zenith in the next, and then declined; it contrived to combine superstition, philosophical analysis, and fantasy; a semi-magical ritualism, some eastern mysticism, and emotional religiosity; a considerable power of speculation and "a wild, fanatical, and sometimes obscene cultus". Few generalisations are true of every Gnostic sect, but certain tendencies and assumptions of the movement as a whole are relevant to the understanding of 1 John.

(i) The term "Gnostic" signalises the emphasis laid upon knowledge (*gnosis*) of the universe, God, or the soul, whether attained by obscure initiation rites or by philosophical insight granted to the spiritual, the enlightened. Salvation comes by knowledge, which is more important than virtue: the saved form an intellectual aristocracy of advanced religion. John's exposition of Christian understanding is plainly relevant to this rival intellectual pride.

(ii) The fundamental insight is dualistic. Everything material is naturally and essentially evil; everything spiritual is naturally and essentially good. Thus, God is pure spirit, "the unborn and unnamed Father" (Basilides), strictly unknown (Saturnius — compare 2:22f.), and incapable of either passion or emotion. He cannot have created the world, or have any relationship with

18

it, least of all can He "love" the world. The gulf between God and the world is filled by a chain of aeons, emanations of the Godhead, in a descending series — each a little less spiritual and pure, a little more material and earthly: all the aeons together form the "pleroma", or "fullness of the Godhead". John no less emphatically than Paul (Colossians 1:19, 2:9) replies with the assertion of Christ's unique and sufficient Sonship.

In man, spirit — an effluence of the eternal light and goodness of God Himself — is imprisoned in material flesh, only to be delivered by knowledge. The Gnostic despises all matter, the world, the body: those capable of enlightenment will be saved, but the mass of men are contemptible, earth-bound creatures doomed to live in darkness. John replies with incarnation, and universalism!

(iii) Intellectual pride made Gnosticism intensely individualistic, "possessing little sense of social obligation" (Dodd), "loveless to the core" (Law). Ignatius records: "They give no heed to love, caring not for the widow, the orphan, or the afflicted, neither for those who are in bonds nor for those who are released from bonds, neither for the hungry nor for the thirsty". John's reply to this attitude is brusque: "He that loveth not knoweth not."

(iv) Morally, one reaction to dualism was to discipline and abuse the evil body to save the soul (compare Colossians 2:20f., 1 Timothy 4:3); the other was to treat all deeds done in and with the body as irrelevant to spiritual welfare. The material body cannot be made more vile: moral discipline or immoral delight are alike indifferent to the life of pure spirit. The enlightened therefore have no sin, but are "above good and evil" (Dodd). Basilides (circa A.D. 130) according to Irenaeus "bids men despise and take no account of things offered to idols, but to use them without fearfulness, and to treat as a matter of indifference the indulgence in other practices and in lust of all kinds. . .". Some Gnostics argued that the enlightened must know all things, even "the depths of Satan" (Revelation 2:24): Barclay and Moffatt mention traces of the idea that even in God Himself the darkness of evil is comprehended (contrast 1:5). To this moral indifferentism, John is especially merciless.

Gnostic ideas had infiltrated into pre-Christian Judaism; Colossians, Timothy and Revelation show their presence in Asia Minor during the second half of the first century. To Gnostics, Christianity seemed a new "mystery" religion, offering in "faith" a fresh enlightenment, and in the sacraments a new saving magic; on the Christian side were "ill-informed converts ready to re-interpret the faith in terms of modern thought" (Dodd). What Neil Alexander calls the widespread tendency among Christians to "go Gnostic", and Barclay describes as attempts to "improve" the gospel, to make Christianity intellectually respectable, con-stituted the Church's greatest peril to date.

For any attempt to graft Christian faith onto Gnostic premises was bound to involve evasion of basic Christian truths, especially concerning the relation of God to the world, the incarnation of the divine Son in flesh (to the Gnostic an incredible idea), and the atonement for sin wrought through divine suffering.

In general, Gnosticism's re-interpretation of the gospel repre-sented the humanity and suffering of Christ as simply unreal. He appeared among men "unborn, incorporeal, and without form, seen as a man in appearance only" (Saturnius) — exactly as God ap-peared in Old Testament theophanies. The Leucian Acts of John (circa A.D. 160) asserts that sometimes when John would touch Jesus he found nothing substantial or tangible before him, and that when Jesus walked He left no footprint. A spiritual emanation of the one true God, perhaps the lowest in the chain of aeons, Jesus could never (on the Gnostic view of matter) be-come true man, or die. "If He suffered He was not God; if He was God He did not suffer". At the crucifixion another was sub-stituted, Simon of Cyrene or Judas Iscariot, while the divine Christ talked with John at a safe distance, mocking the ignorance of His enemies.

Against all this, Ignatius (a decade or so after John's epistle) makes Jesus say, "I am not a bodiless spirit", and writes: "There is only one Physician both carnal and spiritual, born and unborn, God become Man, true life in death, sprung both from Mary and from God, first subject to suffering then incapable of suffering — Jesus Christ our Lord". Elsewhere he stresses that Christ was "truly born, ate and drank, was truly persecuted under Pontius Pilate, was truly crucified, and truly died. . . . If as some godless men, that is unbelievers, say, He suffered in mere appearance (be-ing themselves mere appearances) why am I in bonds?" Much in the Fourth Gospel, and in 1 John, is plainly directed at the attempt to explain away the reality of incarnation and of the gospel *history;* it is not impossible that this "phantom" theory has shaped the language of 1 John 1:1-4.

More relevant still to the understanding of 1 John is the particular form of Gnostic re-interpretation associated with the name Cerinthus. This accepted the real, physical manhood of *Jesus,* but distinguished between Jesus — born of Mary and Joseph as the Messiah of the Jews — and the divine Christ, either an aeon or the Holy Spirit, who did not *become* flesh but allied Himself with the man, Jesus, at the moment of baptism (descending in the form of a dove), and (being incapable of suffering) left him before the cross. The Gospel of Peter (circa 130) explains the cry of dereliction as "My power, my power, why hast thou forsaken me?".

The much repeated story of John's encounter with Cerinthus at the Ephesian baths preserves the tradition of the senior leader's wrestling with Cerinthianism. 1 John 5:6 — Jesus "came by water and blood . . . not with the water only but with the water and the blood" — leaves little doubt that it was the Cerinthian type of teaching which the writer had in view. The denial that "Jesus is the Christ" (2:22) points the same way, since by the time of 1 John, the only other interpretation, the Jewish denial of Jesus' Messiahship, could "possess little more than antiquarian interest". So do 4:2, and 15: Law expounds the "exquisite precision" of 4:2 — "come" implies pre-existence; "has come" points to the abiding fact; "in" means permanent union with "flesh", ("into" would have suggested Cerinthus' temporary association only); and the union is realised in the self-identical person Jesus Christ, so that the confession required is the "confession of Jesus", not of some proposition about Him.

If the view of Cerinthus was that the Holy Spirit descended on the man Jesus, then there is added significance in John's statement that "the Spirit is the witness" (and no more), immediately following a reference to Christ's baptism (so John 1:33). If Brooke, Bettenson, and Guthrie are right that "the teaching of this heretic had a decidedly Jewish flavour", then the strange mingling of moral neutralism with reverence for Jewish Law in 3:4 may be explained. And John's insistence upon moral obligation is also explained in the light of the attitude to morality associated with Cerinthian Gnosticism: the alternative explanation, that John is addressing a Church of the second generation that has grown lax about sin through simple backsliding, is difficult to reconcile with the warmth of affectionate encouragement, the tenderness of John's concern, and the absence of such accusation, which mark the letter.*

* See note 5, pp. 227-229.

We must not allow later systematisation of Gnostic thought to control exegesis of 1 John, but there is little doubt that it was the infiltration of ideas and speculations of a generally Gnostic type and a specifically Cerinthian pattern which had occasioned the serious secession which 1 John confronts. E. F. Scott points out that when Colossians was written such ideas were recognised as dangerous, and by a generation later than 1 John the Church would be putting forth all its energy to destroy them; but there was a stage between when instruction and explanation such as that in 1 John might recapture minds drifting towards Gnosticism and reassure the wavering that they did already possess the truth, and with it eternal life.

For Gnosticism undermined at once the Christian gospel, ethic, and fellowship. As Mackintosh says, the sharp separation between a Christ not truly human and a Jesus who is not divine, apart from its indifference to history and its foundation in cosmic rather than ethical ideas, left it wholly uncertain whether the Redeemer "came from the highest God or not. . . . Ambiguity on this point disqualified Gnosticism as a substitute for a faith that clung to history and in that history found very God". Law remarks that the Gnostic spirit and temper are never dead, and Hasler recalls meeting two Indian Spiritualists excited over "a new discovery regarding the personality of Jesus" which turned out to be Cerinthianism. Similarities with modern theosophy and with Christadelphian tenets are patent, and the very close relation of Gnosticism to Christian Science is equally obvious. Dodd likens the distinction made by Cerinthus between Jesus and the Christ to the religious value which some moderns attach to "the Christ-idea" as distinct from "the Jesus of history". Others will feel that the modern fashion of "demythologising" the Christ of history, in order to fit what is eternally valid in the New Testament story into the categories of a scientific world-view, using evolutionary theory in place of the ancient cosmology and existentialism in place of the ancient dualism, is merely a modern attempt to repeat the Gnostic experiment.

So long as Gnostic sophistries and "new" moralities hold fascination for religious minds, so long will 1 John's recall to "that which was from the beginning" retain for Christian hearts its sharp relevance and searching power.

Part One:

DEVOTIONAL INTERPRETATIONS

1: *The Word of Life*

That which was from the beginning, which we have heard,
which we have seen with our eyes, which we have looked upon
and touched with our hands, concerning the word of life — the
life was made manifest, and we saw it, and testify to it, and
proclaim to you the eternal life which was with the Father and
was made manifest to us — that which we have seen and heard
we proclaim. . . .   1:1-3*

An extraordinarily tangled and condensed opening sentence indicates
the writer's personal position, his immediate purpose, and (in the
next words) his deepest motive.   He desires to be heard simply
as a witness, with others, to the original and authentic Christian
message: names and personalities are irrelevant.   Instead of "We
. . . who heard and saw . . . proclaim", the curiously indirect "That
which . . . we have heard . . . we proclaim" focuses attention
upon the message rather than the messengers.   Similarly, because
to define parties is to make explicit positions and loyalties which
must then be defended to save face, John writes to all who will
read, though well knowing that some need his counsel more than
others.   Nevertheless, his position and theme are left in no doubt:
he writes as a witness to the original message of life.

"WHERE IS THE LIFE we have lost in living?" cries T. S. Eliot,
voicing the deepest of all individual needs — recovery of a

---

* Readers will remember throughout that the interpretation offered is
defended in notes at the end of the volume where disputable matters and
others' opinions are discussed. See notes p. 230 and on 1:1-3, pp. 231-233.

25

quality of life that has clear meaning, driving purpose and satisfying depth within it and a hope ahead. Perhaps our generation
has more excuse than most to feel with Santayana that life is no
spectacle or feast but a predicament. All our determination to
"live it up" does not suffice to kindle that exuberance of joy,
that overflowing zest for every challenge and opportunity, that great
souls have known. For many of our contemporaries, the way
to the tree of life has been barred by scepticism, obscured by misunderstanding, overgrown with social habits alien to true happiness;
some already taste in youth the fruit that embitters all the after-
days with disillusionment and cynicism, many with high privileges
of education and culture still ask with the rich young president of
the synagogue where they may discover life that satisfies. John
has an answer.

(i) *Life's Quality* — The Gospel had been written "that men
might have life", the epistle "that they might know" that they
possessed it. This is "what he promised us": He came that men
might have life abundant — "brimming over", of a fullness not
limited by human resources and strength; life imperishable, so
that they "never die"; life eternal — "timeless", of a quality not
belonging to time and earth at all. John expounds this new life
in moral, intellectual, emotional and immortal dimensions as at
once profoundly ethical, radiantly enlightened, spiritually empowered, and triumphantly everlasting. Its essential quality lies,
however, in its newness, vitality, freshness, growth, activity, power,
and victory — for it is divine.

Thus to pass out of death into life is salvation. This is the
broadest definition which the New Testament offers of God's gift
to man in Christ. It includes the blessedness of life under God's
reign, which is the promise of the synoptic Gospels; the free justification before God which Paul emphasises; the salvation or total
health which Luke describes; the unbreakable covenant with God
which Hebrews expounds; and the manifold gift of grace in
which Peter exults: gathering all up in the widest term of all —
God gives us *life*.

And eternal life is no mere enrichment or adornment of normal
human energies, still less indefinite extension in time of ordinary
human existence. It is new, from above, imparted to man by God
in a new birth, so that those who share it become children of His
family, partakers of life divine. Essentially, John says, eternal
life consists in knowing the only true God and Jesus Christ whom
God has sent: but "knowing" here is not to be limited to intellectual

comprehension — it is a "knowing the Lord" which involves personal acquaintance, companionship, obedience, trust, the exploration in all life's changing circumstances of His unchanging character and grace. In crude, mechanical modern metaphor it means plugging in to God and knowing divine energies flood the veins of feeling, stimulate the nerves of action. In the ancient organic figure, it is being engrafted in the Vine through which divine life flows to the furthest tip of every branch. What this produces in character and experience we might well guess from its Source — but we need not guess: it was manifested in Christ.

(ii) *Life's Source* — It is a large part of the Bible's distinctive message that life originates in God. With God is the fountain of life — this, says Westcott, is the last limit of human thought. The most important truth in Genesis is that life, and the conditions that make life possible, stem from the purpose and the power of God; God breathed into man's nostrils the breath of life, and man became a living being. The God of the Old Testament is beyond all else *the living God,* in contrast to the dumb and lifeless idols of the heathen.

And this is the most important truth, too, in Christ's name for God — "the Father — the living Father" (John 6:57). The Father has life in Himself (John 5:26): of no-one else *at all* can that be said. In other words, God *is* Spirit (John 4:24) — and to what a parched and life-drained soul was that gracious reminder given that God is vital, inexhaustible, self-existent Personality, the very spring of new life to all who seek refreshment! For it is the property of life to communicate itself, and in one of the very greatest of His words Jesus so defines the gospel: "As the living Father sent me, and I live because of the Father, so he who eats me will live because of me" (John 6:57).

And so John defines the word of life. That life which in the beginning was in God, "with God", or more accurately "(turned) towards the Father" as its source and home, has flowed forth in Christ: "God gave us eternal life and this life is in his Son. He who has the Son has life". The Christian's new life *must* be rich and full, victorious and everlasting, just because it flows from everlasting fountains in the changeless self-existence of the living God!

(iii) *Life's Manifestation* — John's message must seem incredible until we start where he starts — at Bethlehem. "This life is in His Son", and inseparable from Him. When the Word became flesh, the life inherent in the Word (John 1:4) was re-

27

vealed, embodied, and imparted. John's four separate statements
— "we heard", "we have seen", "we have looked [steadily] upon",
"we touched" express a developing climax of certainty, a growing
intimacy, culminating perhaps in the invitation of the Upper Room
after Easter — "handle me, and see". Divine life could only be
experienced by wondering, incredulous men as it became audible,
visible ("with our eyes" stresses the factual, objective reality,),
tangible (having the finger-tip reality Thomas had demanded) and
comprehensible — being contemplated, pondered "with that careful and deliberate vision which interprets its object": and so it
became in Jesus. But the four modes of apprehension are again
summed up in two — "that which we have seen and heard" as
though the visual images were paramount in recollection, and the
sayings and commandments paramount in authority, in apostolic
memories.

So Jesus is the divine Life uttered in human terms (which may
be the meaning of "the word (or: Word) of life"). He is the
life, and the life-giver, because He perfectly embodied, eloquently
expressed, and freely communicates divine life to all who believe.
It follows that he who has the Son has life.

(iv) *Life's Witnesses* — Yet the historic manifestation of the
divine life in Jesus must remain confined to one generation unless
those who saw Him bear witness and their witness is believed. The
authority for their witness is their personal experience: the several
stages of their personal apprehension become qualifications for
leading others into understanding. The writer is not primarily a
teacher of truths, not like Luke "a sedulous investigator and re-
corder of the facts as certified by the most trustworthy witnesses"
(Law: Luke 1:1-4) but himself a witness. The distinction is important also for ourselves. The idea of "witness", or of confessing
or denying Christ, occurs seventeen times in these five chapters: the
Fourth Gospel rehearses the witness borne to Christ by the Father,
the works, the Spirit, and records as the final commission of the
disciples — "Ye are my witnesses". The communication of life
can only continue as the witness to it is faithfully sustained in
succeeding generations. Imparting facts is not enough: we must
share life.

Though the basis is personal experience, the witness of which
John speaks is nonetheless collective and corporate. In "we
testify", William Alexander remarks, the "we" is the plural of
modesty: "it rises into majesty in 'we proclaim' ". The spokes-
man of the gospel is the vehicle of a shared experience — he does

well to remember that; his "we" expresses Christian solidarity in a common certainty. More than one man's personal memories lay behind the apostolic message, and their conviction had been inherited now by second generation Christians also: we know through how many further generations the Fact of Christ has exercised its saving power.

Thus, though the authority lies in experience, the witness is very far from being the assertion of individual opinion. The process of authority is threefold: we hear, see, ponder, handle the fundamental historic facts about Jesus and the Life He manifested amongst men, so making *discovery;* we have known Him, been forgiven, overcome the world, have been made strong, have come to love the brethren, and thus we "know", so reaching the conviction bred of personal *experience;* so we proclaim, and the word kindles life — the message we heard from Him, which is no lie (2:24, 27) authenticates itself in those who believe.

Truly, the "word of life".

2: *Spiritual Fellowship*

> . . .that which we have seen and heard we proclaim also to you,
> so that you may have fellowship with us; and our fellowship
> is with the Father and with his Son Jesus Christ. And we are
> writing this that our joy may be complete.   1:3, 4*

The tangled opening sentence continues, so providing in one of the
most sweeping and condensed gospel-summaries in the New Testament, a definition of (i) the content of the gospel as the manifestation of eternal divine life in Christ; (ii) the authority of the
gospel in the shared experience of the historical Jesus through the
ongoing Church, issuing in a declaration of the truth divinely
authenticated afresh in each generation; (iii) the fruit of the
gospel, in the fellowship of those who share the divine life through
Christ and the joy it imparts. But meanwhile, John has with the
utmost tact affirmed his own authority to speak in the delicate
contemporary situation in the name of the original gospel; he has
stated his concern that Christian fellowship be unbroken by defection or schism; he has insinuated already, in seemingly inno-
cent but actually loaded phrases, the burden of his differences with
the out-goers — that Jesus as the Son of God, Jesus the Christ,
Bearer and Vehicle of the divine gift of life, who was no phantom,
but heard, seen, pondered, handled, is integral to the authentic
message and to the fellowship arising therefrom; and he has
nevertheless softened this early thrust at his undefined opponents
by immediately asserting his entire goodwill in writing, his desire that the joy of all be unimpaired by discord or division. Not
at all a slight achievement for any single sentence!

* Notes on 1:3, 4, p. 233.

AS THE DEEPEST of all modern man's individual needs is the recovery of life of satisfying quality, so the most desperate of all modern social needs is the rediscovery of community. Something much safer, more lasting, more immune to accidental tensions and to blunders than a mere balancing of self-interest, or the immobilising of mutual antagonisms by deterrent fear, is essential if human society is not to be destroyed. Almost equally urgent is the need to rediscover the roots of individual wholeness and happiness in social cohesion and loyalty, if human hearts are not to be starved of significance and affection. John is again near to the centre of our need in naming immediately after the thirst for life the hunger for fellowship.

(i) *It is the nature of life to "flow"; of spiritual life, to overflow.* It is wrong, or at least superficial, to represent the fellowship of Christians as a duty: it is a fact. John passes immediately from asserting life to asserting fellowship, because the sharing of life creates fellowship — and can do no other. Life cannot be channeled: to confine it is to stifle it: and all solitary confinement is a living death. "None of us lives to himself", says Paul, implying as clearly that the soul that is "to itself" is dead. For the same reason Paul (and the whole New Testament) strongly condemns sins against Christian fellowship — lies, bitterness, the unforgiving spirit, rivalry and the like — because denial of fellowship is the denial of the one life that binds all in the family of God.

For the inevitable result of life manifested and communicated is life shared. Our fellowship is with the Father and with His Son in a community of life that *must* embrace everyone else within that fellowship. "The life that is shared exists only as shared . . . the life of the Church is the divine life disclosed in the incarnate Christ" (Dodd) — and that divine life is indivisible. To possess life is to be brother, sister, to all who possess it: to deny the kinship is to repudiate the gift of life.

(ii) *The fruit of the overflow is community* — "koinonia". Living religion has always created groups — from the "disciples" gathered around the prophet Isaiah, and the "fearers of the Lord" who spoke often together in the barren days of Malachi, to the disciples whom John the Baptist taught to fast and to pray, and the various communities of Jewish devotees who formed the brotherhoods of Pharisees, Essenes, and the Dead Sea sects. So Jesus gathered about Him the nucleus of the Church, binding them by commandment and by a memorial Supper to stand together: and when the Spirit came upon them on the day of Pentecost one of the earliest manifestations of His power was the entirely new depth and scope of spiritual community that came into being — even to a sharing of goods and a supplanting of family ties by those of Christian loyalty. The impulse to meet and share together has never left the Christian heart: the most individualistic evangelical groups still fashion some form of brotherhood and occasionally establish close-knit communities. Even in extreme interpretations of the evangelical principle, where all other forms of Church life are rejected, there remains a "Society" of Friends.

So long as the faith held derives from the teaching and Spirit of Jesus, so long it must be so. The idea of a life-sharing community, which is much more than a human association of the like-minded, a mutual insurance of common interest, and much more too than the sum of its several parts and members, is essential to Christianity. Christ came to reconcile, to reunite the family of God's prodigals, to bring us — together — to God, in one body by His cross. The thought is everywhere in the New Testament, but especially, and characteristically, in the word *koinonia.*

Originally a commercial term, signifying joint-partnership in business (as in a fishing vessel), or co-ownership, the word retains this shade of meaning when Christians are called "fellow-heirs" with Christ. But the more usual associations in the New Testament are with organic metaphors — Vine and branches, the Body and its members, the Communion of the Lord's Supper, and the Father and brethren in the family of God. It is used of the Christian's partnership in the Son, in the body and blood of Christ, in the sufferings of Christ, in the Spirit, in faith, and in eternal life.

Such is the rich and many-sided "fellow-ship" of the communion of saints, a life-in-community at wholly new depths and finding wholly unexpected avenues of expression in succeeding generations. And this, John declares, is the effect of sharing together in the divine gift of life as it was manifested and communicated through Christ. That his readers may preserve fellowship is one purpose of his appeal: for schism spells spiritual decay, and division reveals death.

(iii) *The marks of community are fellowship with God and mutual joy.* "Our fellowship is with the Father and with His Son Jesus Christ": John is concerned to emphasise the identity of Jesus with the divine Son and Christ as the necessary basis of the apostolic fellowship, but in so doing he also underlines the important truth that our human fellowship as Christians is nourished, sustained, protected and enlarged only as each Christian remains in the secret, inward company of the Father and the Son. Alienation from God always underlies alienation from one another: and the comradeship and loyalty that binds believers together is different from anything else on earth precisely because it takes its nature, colour, and durability from the deeper, unseen relationship of believers to their Lord. That is why, throughout the epistle, John finds in the presence or absence of this love and loyalty towards the brethren an infallible indication of the soul's true relation to the Father Himself.

The other mark of Christian community is joy — the felt experience of *koinonia*. The glimpses which Luke affords of the inner life of the early Church are always characterised by gladness and song, thanksgiving and joy: and for John too, joy has a special importance in the life of the Christian body. It is the purpose of Jesus for His disciples (John 15:11), and His clear promise (16:20, 22). Nor is it surprising that of the New Testament's hundred references to Christian joy, thirty-seven concern the gladness to be found in the fellowship of Christian colleagues.

In the present passage however this joy is overshadowed, it is not entirely "full". For there are those (John hints) who are not wholly within the fellowship of the apostolic circle: some have already "gone out", others waver. So he writes to promote stronger fellowship among those that remain, to establish the waverers, perhaps to recapture some of the seceders: and all this, that the joy of all may be unimpaired. "If one member suffers, all suffer together", says Paul: it is obvious of the physical body, less obvious but no less true of the body spiritual. So the loss of any impoverishes those who remain; John would preserve the circle intact, that all may rejoice together. That is an ecumenical attitude in which "Christ's prayer (John 17:11) and John's purpose are one and the same" (Plummer).

Divine life manifested, communicated, shared, enjoyed — that is the theme of the word of life.

3: *God Is Light*

> This is the message we have heard from him and proclaim to you, that God is light and in him is no darkness at all. If we say we have fellowship with him while we walk in darkness, we lie and do not live according to the truth;   1:5, 6*

Since he writes to promote fellowship, John at once declares the conditions on which alone that fellowship can exist. The manifestation just affirmed bears upon its surface a message, that God is holy, and they who would have fellowship with Him must live in the light of His holiness. Thus John lays down the first and fundamental principle of the counsel he will offer, that religious experience and daily conduct, mysticism and morality, faith and ethics, are in Christianity inseparable. In doing so he again hints at the direction towards which his thought is aimed, by using — and possibly correcting — a phrase familiar to the Gnostics themselves.

LIGHT IS A UNIVERSAL religious symbol because it is, and it represents, a universal human need. The metaphor has always fascinated the eastern mind: it speaks no less powerfully to minds of the west today. For a horror of great darkness haunts our time. It varies in degree from the so-well-named "shadow of a doubt", through the twilight of a reverent (if indolent) agnosticism, to the outer darkness of a lifeless, limitless, and apparently lightless

* Notes on 1:5, 6, pp. 233-234.

Space, and on to the final darkness "when all the labours of the ages, all the devotion, all the inspiration, all the noonday brightness of human genius" reaches its destined extinction in the vast death of the solar system and "on man and all his race the slow sure doom falls pitiless and dark" (Russell).

It would be unfair to suggest that many modern thinkers prefer darkness to light: but a universe mindless, purposeless, meaningless and menacing, which is what modern materialists delight to offer us, is bound to be unrelieved by any heartening beacon of reason, morality, comfort, or hope. In such a context the apostolic message is trebly appropriate, relevant, and timely: God is Light, and a rational, moral, purposeful universe reflects His glory; Light is come into the world, in the face of Jesus Christ, and he that followeth shall not walk in darkness. We refuse the philosophic pose of the stiff upper lip and the closed eyes: we build on far better than "unyielding despair": we sing with prophets and angels, shepherds and saints, "Arise, thy light is come, the glory of the Lord is risen upon thee!"

(i) *The statement* that "God is light" belongs (as it were) midway between "God is Spirit", which expresses God's essential Being as personal, timeless, immaterial, self-existent, and "God is love", which characterises God's unvarying attitude in all relationships. "God is light" connects no doubt with much that is simply metaphorical in Zoroastrianism, Platonism, and Jewish thought. Philo wrote the phrase, but his next words almost retracted it, the Jew in him fearing its apparent equation of God with an abstract quality or a created object (Neil Alexander). The flaming sword of divine holiness that forbade re-entrance to paradise, the reflected glory on Moses' face, Ezekiel's vision of the lightnings, Christ's own transfiguration, the Seer's vision of the ascended Christ, and Paul's experience at Damascus, all stand in the same tradition of language with the psalmist's praise "The Lord is my light". An unbearable blaze of unshaded, unapproachable radiance, which serves to hide by sheer brilliance, is an apt symbol — indeed the only possible one — of divine "glory".

In Johannine thought, however, the meaning of this language is more psychological than pictorial. The light-darkness metaphor is one of John's most frequent themes, and it has intellectual, moral, and emotional applications. Intellectually, light is the truth by which men "see" to walk without stumbling, to work in the daytime, to perceive where they are going. Not to possess light is to live blind. To follow Christ, however, is to possess the light of the world, the light of life, "enlightenment". In this sense it is possible to speak of light as "testified to" and "believed in": it is truth functioning as intellectual illumination.

Morally, men who are "in the light" see the real nature of their sins, and some choose darkness to avoid this self-exposure. Christ is the light of moral judgement (John 9:39); to receive the light is to be morally transformed (so 2 Corinthians 4:4-6). He who hates his brother is in darkness, he who loves lives in light. On this side John is nearer to Paul's use of this metaphor: Christians are children of the light and of the day, and must put aside the conduct that is fit only for hours of darkness; "the fruit of light is found in all that is good and right and true". The agelong conflict of good and evil can be stated as a wrestling of light with darkness — and the light is not eclipsed.

Emotional overtones naturally cling to these terms: to be in the divine light is to be transfigured (compare Luke 9:29, 2 Corinthians 3:12, 18); to be blind, to love darkness, to claim to see while refusing light, is to be utterly lost, desolate, helpless. So Judas, leaving the light of Christ's presence, and of the apostolic fellowship, to "go out" to betray, passes "into night".

To all who look back to Jesus this is axiomatic — the most elementary truth that we learned of Him: that God is light, and dwells in "the pure severity of perfect light". Christ *is* the divine light, the truth and holiness of God breaking into the world's darkness, as the outshining of the Father's glory. The light of the knowledge of the glory of God shines, as Paul said, in the face of Jesus Christ. As in Him the divine life was manifested, and communicated to men, so also in Him the divine light was focused, revealed, and beamed upon our shadowed world.

John's premise is affirmed first positively, then negatively, for clarity and emphasis: no other light burns so steadily — stars pale, the moon wanes, the sun suffers eclipse, but with "the Father of lights" there is no variation, or shadow due to turning (James 1:17), and (against some Gnostic speculation that God must embrace both good and evil to comprehend all experience) John states categorically "in him is no darkness at all". If John is taking up, to echo, a Gnostic phrase, nonetheless he is but reasserting the central theme of prophetic religion — that the Holy One of Israel, the high and lofty One who inhabits eternity, whose name is Holy, is of purer eyes than to behold evil, and cannot look upon wrong.

(ii) *The argument* which John bases upon this fundamental premise is equally factual and inescapable; denial of it is therefore not moral inconsistency, or simple hypocrisy, but downright falsehood — "we lie". "Whereas for Gnostics", says Neil Alexander, " 'God is light' is merely a mystical notion to get lost in, for John it immediately spells God's absolute ethical demand." It follows by necessity from the nature of God as truth and holiness that to have fellowship with Him is to be set within the radiance of that searching light. It is to *walk in the light* (1:7); to "live and move" (Moffatt; the term walk, as throughout the Old Testament, embracing the whole of moral conduct) in the constant light of divine scrutiny, permitting nothing shady, shameful, or hidden from God, to retain a place in our interest, action, or affection. It is to *be in the light* (2:9) in the more inward sense of letting thoughts and emotions, imagination and desire, also be irradiated by the divine light — a spiritual psychiatry that brings into the daylight of the divine presence all that we strive to hide even from ourselves. It is to *remain in the light* (2:10), despite the humbling, painful results. Far easier to evade the glare, to shelter within the shade of convenient trees (Genesis 3:8), to let devotion become perfunctory, worship impersonal and formal, distinctions blurred by argument, conscience insensitive through inattention! Easier, too, to be satisfied with outward religious conformity and to seek less and less the immediate presence of the Most High, lest the secrets of our hearts should be revealed.

What is quite impossible, John says, is to have fellowship with the Light and walk, deliberately or carelessly, in darkness. To profess to have such fellowship, and yet to hug the dark, is both an intellectual and a moral lie: it is to utter falsehood, and not to practice truth. "For John, the truth is not something simply to know, but something, known, to do" (Neil Alexander). And it is not enough to say the inconsistency *ought* not to be: John declares it *cannot* be. Only the pure in heart see God; without holiness no man can see the Lord, and only they whose faces are toward the light can know the fellowship of the Father. "For what partnership have righteousness and iniquity?" asks Paul, "or what fellowship has light with darkness?" In the contention of John and the question of Paul, the whole Christian protest against the pagan divorce of religion from morality is crystallised — and a solemn warning sounded, which will echo through this epistle, against deceiving oneself about spiritual experiences devoid of ethical significance.

To fall occasionally and painfully into sin is not the same as to walk deliberately and persistently in self-chosen and self-justifying darkness. For the former experience there is provision in the mercy of God: for the latter attitude, only the light that exposes, the glory that reveals itself in judgement (John 3:19).

4: *Walking in Light*

> . . .but if we walk in the light, as he is in the light, we have
> fellowship with one another, and the blood of Jesus his Son
> cleanses us from all sin. If we say we have no sin, we deceive
> ourselves, and the truth is not in us. If we confess our sins, he
> is faithful and just, and will forgive our sins and cleanse us
> from all unrighteousness. If we say we have not sinned, we
> make him a liar, and his word is not in us. My little children,
> I am writing this to you so that you may not sin; but if any
> one does sin, we have an advocate with the Father, Jesus Christ
> the righteous; and he is the expiation for our sins, and not for
> ours only but also for the sins of the whole world. 1:7 — 2:2*

From the agreed axiom — "God is light" — and the rather less
readily agreed corollary, that to claim fellowship with God and
walk in darkness is falsehood, John proceeds at once to describe
upon what basis fellowship with God becomes possible, nevertheless, for sinning men. He defines too the attitudes on man's part
which exclude such fellowship altogether, in particular those denials
of sin's seriousness and responsibility in which some Gnostic
Christians indulged. His argument, moreover, is made to turn upon
precisely those conceptions of Jesus — as God's Son, as shedding
His blood, as "the Righteous One", as dying in expiation of sin —
which also the dissenting groups have questioned. Yet still no
direct opposition is named or implied: "with great gentleness he
puts the case hypothetically, and with great delicacy he includes
himself in the hypothesis" (Plummer).

* Notes on 1:7 — 2:2, pp. 234-236.

ADAM HIDES HIMSELF AWAY from the presence of God among the shades of the garden; Isaiah cries, "Woe is me! For I am lost; for I am a man of unclean lips . . . for my eyes have seen the King, the Lord of hosts!". "Who shall ascend the hill of the Lord? And who shall stand in his holy place?" asks the psalmist, and offers the daunting reply, "He who has clean hands and a pure heart . . . .". When vouchsafed the vision of the divine, Moses at the beginning of the Bible must take off his shoes, and John at its end falls prostrate as one dead. Even in the presence of the gentle Christ the woman of Samaria blurts out her past, Zaccheus passes sharp judgement upon himself, the woman of the city weeps out her shame, and Peter pleads, "Depart from me, I am a sinful man, O Lord!". Scribes and Pharisees, too, shrank sometimes from the presence of Him in whom the holiness of God confronted and exposed the sins of men.

So Paul distils the essence of unvarying biblical truth when he declares that God "dwells in *unapproachable* light". Yet the Bible as clearly, and as unvaryingly, affirms that God will dwell with men and be their God. How may that be?

> *Eternal Light! Eternal Light!*
> *How pure the soul must be,*
> *When, placed within Thy searching sight*
> *It shrinks not, but with calm delight*
> *Can live, and look on Thee!*
> *Oh, how shall I, whose native sphere*
> *Is dark, whose mind is dim,*
> *Before the Ineffable appear,*
> *And on my naked spirit bear*
> *The uncreated beam?*

Again John has an answer: sinful men may know the fellowship of the holy God because God Himself has made threefold provision against sin, upon two simple but necessary conditions.

(i) *The twofold condition* concerns man's own attitude toward sin. The intuitive reaction of a man conscious of wrong is to accuse others and excuse himself: if he cannot deny it altogether, he will minimise his sin, multiply extenuating circumstances, appeal to the accommodating opinion of the majority, and finally declare he could not help it. Until repentance unmasks him to himself, the one thing he will not do is "come to the light, lest his deeds should be exposed". Yet until he does just that, and sees his action and himself in the light of God's judgement, *he cannot be saved.*

To walk in the light is, quite simply, the opposite of Adam's hiding away from God. It is the submission of our daily behaviour, deliberately and persistently, to the light of God's holiness and truth. In part this means subjecting all conduct to the scrutiny of Christian ethical principles. But it involves something more immediate and personal: an honest self-examination in God's presence, in which the heart consciously bows before the judgement of the Most High and dares to expose the soul to the divine X-ray —

> *Search me, O God, and know my heart!*
> *Try me and know my thoughts!*
> *And see if there be any hurtful way in me,*
> *and lead me in the way everlasting!*

We walk in the light "as He is in the light" who was, and ever is, in the radiance of His Father's presence, delighting always to do the Father's will.

Such self-judgement in the presence of God must not be reduced, however, to a "devotional" mood of self-accusation and inward tension. Behind John's phrase here lie the many Johannine references to Jesus as the Light of the world, and the associated invitations to follow and believe His light, to submit to the light's exposure, to walk in daylight and not stumble, keeping His commandments, to live as those who watch for the light of the dawn, to work while it is day, and to wait for the goal that shines ahead — seeing where we are making for. Gathering these rays of the truth together, we can soberly assess how far each day we have walked "in the light" — that is, in the light of His presence, of His judgement, of His will, of His hope, of His purpose and of His promise. So seeing ourselves in His light, not our own, we can offer up each day for the Father's approval — or forgiveness.

For such self-exposure to divine light must result in frank and frequent confession, both that we *have sinned* in many separate acts, and that we *have sin* within ourselves. "The plural 'sins' is significant", says Robert Law; "confession must descend upon particulars — conscience does not deal with abstractions." And A. E. Brooke compares "to have sin" with "to have faith" as like principles which work within the soul to form the character. To acknowledge that sin does in fact contribute to the kind of person we are, is to admit serious and humiliating fault. Nothing is here said of the form such confession should take: the usage of the word, and the undoubted apostolic practice of confession of sins at baptism suggest that John has in mind open admission of wrong before men as well as private confession in the presence of God.

To claim a sinless record, or to repudiate our responsibility for sin — as some of those did who had left the apostolic circle — is, John says, mere self-deception. Such attitudes prove that truth has no place in our character — "is not in us". Moreover, they contradict the divine testimony concerning us, making God a liar, and demonstrating clearly that His word, the gospel of redemption from sin, is not yet in control of all our thought.

John is as anxious as any one that his readers leave sin behind: he pauses in his argument to say so. Yet sinlessness is not achieved by self-deceit, evasion, or false claims; it can only be approached progressively by self-exposure to the light, and humble confession to the Father. These are the inescapable twin conditions of our fellowship, as sinners, with Him who is light, and of all our experience of His grace.

(ii) *The threefold provision* which God has made against sin embraces cleansing, expiation, and an Advocate. Admission into fellowship, in spite of sins discovered and confessed, is the essence of forgiveness, which has to do especially with the personal relationship which sin has broken. Welcome replaces banishment, favour cancels condemnation — the flaming sword is lowered — and we have access, by faith, into this grace wherein we stand. The consequences of sin may or may not be removed: if still they must be faced, then now, after forgiveness, faced with the help of God, they become a salutary discipline. What matters is that God is for us, that our heart is at ease with Him, that pardon has brought us peace. The miracle of restored relationship — and it is no less — is the central marvel of conversion.

But to it John adds cleansing from all actual unrighteousness — the continual, progressive removal of defilement itself. The act of confession possesses a cleansing, psychological power, but this is not all that John has in mind. God does not forgive, and leave us as we were: His discipline, His light bearing upon our newly sensitive minds and hearts, and above all the constant experience of fellowship with Him, produce a cumulative and unceasing refinement of conscience and sanctification of character that makes sinners into saints. Forgiveness and cleansing *together* comprise Christian salvation.

And both are related to "the blood of Jesus, His Son". He is the means of appeasement, of propitiation or expiation, concerning our sin (2:2, compare 4:10). John's language is plainly sacrificial, even more clearly than in John 6:53, 54, 56: the expiatory offerings of Judaism, and perhaps of paganism, illumine the meaning, and it is to be assumed that the circle of ideas reflected in "the Lamb that takes away the sin of the world" (John 1:29), and in the whole Johannine representation of the death of Christ as *the* passover Lamb, lies behind the phrases. Jesus "appeared to take away sin" (1 John 3:5); He "laid down His life for us" (1 John 3:16); and now He Himself, and not only His death, remains the expiaticn for all sins, as the cleansing also is a present continuous process in Christian life. Nor is this saving sacrifice valid only for some small coterie of "knowing ones" initiated into sacramental secrets: "He is the expiation for the sins of the whole world".

God's provision of cleansing and Sacrifice is crowned by the gift of an Advocate — a pleader, intercessor, "a friend of the accused called to speak to his character or otherwise enlist sympathy in his favour". The title Paraclete is used of the Holy Spirit in John's Gospel (14:16, 26; 15:26, 16:7) and is translated in RSV as "Counselor", with presumably the American legal overtones which would belong in British Courts to "barrister" or "Queen's Counsel". Westcott, who reviews the usage of the word, cites in illustration: "We must find a more powerful advocate by whom the emperor will be brought to a favourable disposition towards us", and "he who fulfils one precept gains for himself one advocate, but he who commits one transgression gains for himself one accuser". He contends that in epistle and Gospel the meaning is Advocate — "one who pleads, convinces, convicts in a great controversy, who strengthens on the one hand and defends on the other". Though the word is used of Christ only here, "another advocate" in John 14:16 implies it and Paul (in Romans 8:34) states the truth explicitly: Christ "at the right hand of God . . . intercedes for us".

The letter to the Hebrews expresses the same faith in characteristic fashion: Christ has "entered into heaven . . . to appear in the presence of God on our behalf", a merciful and faithful High Priest, ever living to make intercession for us. In Hebrews, also, the intercession and the atonement for sin are well-nigh united in one common conception, as in John; and the emphasis in Hebrews upon the qualifying sinlessness of the High Priest is echoed in John's title for the Advocate, "the Righteous One". We do not appear alone in the Courts of the Most High: we have not to make confession, or plead our own cause, unaided: He who by nature (God's Son) and by right ("the Righteous One") has unhindered access to the right hand of God *represents us*. However the metaphors and analogies baffle imagination, the message for our hearts is clear — we sinful men, confessing, are admitted to the fellowship of the everlasting Light, through the righteous Son.

Finally, John emphasises that this threefold provision against the consequences of sin has been made by God because He is faithful and just — faithful to His unchanging purpose of salvation and His gracious promise in the gospel, just in accepting the expiation for sin wrought through the death of Jesus. Presently John will add love as the source of expiation: here justice and faithfulness are elements in the character of light, upon which the whole passage is proceeding. Brooke recalls the covenant of God with men in Old Testament thought, and well remarks, "It is probable that throughout the Bible this idea of God's faithfulness to His covenant in spite of man's unfaithfulness, is the primary significance of the righteousness of God".

So, that very holiness and truth which might be thought to banish sinners irretrievably from fellowship with Him who is light, becomes in the new situation created by expiation and confession the sure ground upon which sinners are accepted, forgiven and cleansed.

> *There is a way for man to rise*
> *To that sublime abode:*
> *An offering and a sacrifice,*
> *A Holy Spirit's energies,*
> *An Advocate with God.*

5: *Claims and Credentials*

And by this we may be sure that we know him, if we keep his commandments. He who says "I know him" but disobeys his commandments is a liar, and the truth is not in him; but whoever keeps his word, in him truly love for God is perfected. By this we may be sure that we are in him: he who says he abides in him ought to walk in the same way in which he walked.

2:3-6*

The assumption of the preceding verses, that spiritual experience is morally conditioned, is now twice restated, without metaphor. To say that Christ is the expiation not for our sins only but also for the sins of the whole world spotlights the distinction between "us" and "the world", between those who know God in Christ and those who do not. Yet even this knowledge, like the claim to fellowship with God, may be counterfeited: here also we may deceive ourselves. The only proof that we have really known God in Christ is the moral one: or — if we prefer mystical to intellectualist terms — the only proof that we are "in Christ" is that we walk as He walked. The bearing of the argument on the high claims of the seceders is obvious, but they are still not singled out: the "if we say" of chapter 1 becomes "He who says" in 2:4, 6 — a shade more definite — as John moves carefully towards the direct accusation of "Who is a liar but he who says . . ." of 2:22.

* Notes on 2:3-6, pp. 236-237.

EVANGELICALS ARE OFTEN UNPOPULAR, among Christians and non-Christians alike. "Broad-minded" believers dislike the scrupulous Puritan conscience that too often condemns by habit and may harden into mere self-righteousness. Robust extroverts distrust the constant "poking about" among motives, feelings, and "inner experiences" that too often goes with "spirituality". Not only dogmatism, but assurance and conviction are out of fashion — except in science — and when the believer speaks with earnestness of the things he knows to be true, or seeks to persuade another to share the same assurance, he seems, to those whose faith is no more than a wistful hope, to be lacking in humility of mind.

Claims to know the truth, to know God, to have received divine guidance, to be forgiven, to be living in the fellowship of the risen Lord, are consequently often dismissed as cant, and the blessed assurance of the true disciple appears to the outsider and the half-Christian as the worst form of arrogance in the least fitting place — in religion.

Not infrequently, of course, charges of pride and dogmatism are true and justified. Assurance and humility are not always found hand in hand. And sometimes the high spiritual claims are not substantiated by the quality of life accompanying them. Evangelicals commonly make much of knowledge, the holding of orthodox beliefs, and the understanding of sound doctrine; and they value the spiritual discipline of regular worship, prayer, and Bible study: yet evangelicals themselves are suspicious of mere creeds and scholarship on the one hand, of appointed religious exercises, rituals and fast days, on the other. They perceive, what the world itself also guesses, that there is wide difference between "head-knowledge" and knowing the Lord, between "doing the actions" and abiding in Christ.

It is an obvious, and serious, weakness of evangelicalism that "knowing the Lord" and "abiding in Christ" are matters concerning which it is perilously easy to be deceived, and to deceive oneself. "Deep teaching" is often mistaken for deep experience, and religious emotion for spiritual life. It is evident that among John's readers, including those about whom he was most anxious, catchwords like "I know Him" and "I abide in Him" were current hallmarks of spirituality, and John insists that language correspond to reality. Otherwise, "the claim, unsupported by its requisite moral guarantee, is underlined with the writer's 'roughest and blackest pencil-mark' as the statement of a liar" (Law).

(i) *The evidence of knowledge is obedience.* The real test of what you know is how you live. That is as true of the scientist, the artist, the economist, the psychologist, as of the Christian. Professed insights that do not control behaviour are exposed as mere theoretic opinions, and not convictions, the professional jargon of the charlatan. John indeed goes further: only by obedience to the truth we say we have, can we ourselves be sure we are not misled. The test we usually apply to ourselves is that of feeling — the feeling of sincerity, of joy and peace and confidence. John affirms that we know whether we have truly arrived at an understanding of the gospel, and the knowledge of the Lord, by its practical effect upon ourselves, in the creation within us of the desire and the will to obey His word.

This was the Master's own test of religious reality. "Beware of false prophets, who come to you in sheep's clothing but inwardly are ravenous wolves. You will know them by their fruits." It was His test of the truth of religious talk: "Not every one who says to me, Lord, Lord; shall enter the kingdom of heaven, but he who does the will of my Father. . .". And it was His test also of religious claims: "On that day many will say to me, 'Lord, Lord, did we not prophesy in your name, and cast out demons in your name, and do many mighty works in your name?' And then will I declare to them, 'I never knew you; depart from me, you *evildoers'* ".

In another great saying Jesus underlines the converse of this close relationship between knowing and doing: obedience becomes the condition of understanding more. "My teaching is not mine, but his who sent me. If any man's will is to do his will, he shall know whether the teaching is from God or whether I am speaking on my own authority."

It must be so. For Him whom we claim to know is everywhere in the gospel presented to us as the Christ, the Lord: to confess Him Lord is the saving confession that makes a man a Christian, upon that confession the Church is built, and towards the universal acknowledgement of its truth all the endeavour and hope of Christian hearts is directed (Romans 10:9, Acts 16:31, Matthew 16: 16f., 2 Corinthians 4:5, Philippians 2:9-11). This is "to know Christ", according to New Testament teaching — as the risen Lord whose right it is to command, whose example is our ideal, whose will is our law, whose love for us evokes an answering love for Him, whose death on our behalf leaves us gladly but unpayably in debt to Him. But to know Him thus *means* to obey Him; and to obey Him, so far as we already know Him, is the condition of knowing Him more perfectly.

Whoever claims, therefore, to "know Christ" and yet does not "watchfully" keep His commandments, is (again) stating what is patently false. He thinks he is spiritually wise, knowledgeable, instructed: but he does not yet know the elementary principle of Christianity — that Jesus is Lord. He is uttering what is strictly untrue: but more than this, he himself is a liar, in that the truth he boasts of knowing is not a ruling force within him.

On the other hand whoever does keep the word of Christ, even though he makes no great claim to spiritual understanding, shows by his obedience that in him love towards God has reached its full maturity and fulfills its end. We expect John to say that "whoever keeps His word, in him truly is *knowledge* perfected", but that would be asserting far too much, and playing directly into the hands of those who made knowledge and not character the primary matter in religion. In a very similar passage (1 Corinthians 8:1-3) Paul just as neatly avoided pandering to the Corinthians' shallow intellectualism. For both apostles, loving obedience is the only proof that we know Jesus as living Saviour and Lord.

(ii) *The evidence of abiding is imitation.* In some apostolic circles, as in some modern evangelical groups, strictures upon "mere knowledge" would be especially welcome. Then, as now, "not many wise according to worldly standards" were found within the Churches; and an intellectualist Christianity which aimed at the university campus and forgot the foolish and barbarian, would be a travesty of apostolic evangelism. Equally important, the immediate certainties of mystical experience exercise a great attraction over many minds; Christian and Gnostic alike expressed a true and powerful longing when they aimed at some direct and personal awareness of the divine.

For this immediate mystical experience of God in Christ, the apostles used the language of "indwelling" — Christ in us and we in Christ. Throughout the New Testament, the Christian is described as a man "in Christ", almost as frequently as a man who "believes": Peter uses the phrase once, John at least a dozen times, Paul well over 160 times, and Luke once. Such wide currency shows the phrase belonged to the original tradition of Christian thought, and its place in Johannine teaching is evident from the repeated use of "abide in Me" in the treasured discourses of John 13 to 17.

The Christian was "baptised into Christ", incorporated into the

Body of Christ, and lived "in Christ" as his new world, the very atmosphere of his new existence. "In Christ" there was no condemnation; "in Christ" we are alive unto God; if any one is "in Christ" he is a new creature; Christians can do all things "in Christ"; "in Christ" we are always led in triumph and blessed with every spiritual blessing; the dead "in Christ" shall rise first, and "in Christ" shall all be made alive. Meanwhile the spring and centre of ongoing Christian life, and the secret of Christian progress, was to "abide in Him". Little wonder that many preferred this form of words to that which emphasised knowledge: here, surely, was certainty, spiritual reality, a profoundly creative and empowering experience of the divine, through Christ.

Indeed so: but how do we know that we *are* in Him? John is again ruthless in his reply. Mystical experience, like pretensions to knowledge, can only be proved genuine by appropriate behaviour. "He who says he abides in him ought to walk in the same way in which he walked." For to be "in Christ" *implies* similarity, conformity, imitation, in the sense of community of life and interests and aim. The phrase can have no other meaning than the moral identification of life with the Lord "in whom" we live — and this is true whether we find the theological background of the phrase in the idea of a corporate "Son of Man", in the figure of the "Body of Christ", in the Vine and its branches, or in the nearer, simpler metaphor of Christ as the surrounding atmosphere of the Christian's existence.

Screwing up one's feelings to a pitch of prayerful earnestness is not the same as being "in Christ". John's test is relentless: the imitation of Christ, walking as He walked, purifying oneself as He is pure, walking in the light as He is in the light, keeping the commandments and abiding in His love as He kept His Father's commandments and abode in the Father's love, is the sole reliable evidence that we draw our life from Him. The imitation of Christ is a constant theme of apostolic teaching. God makes all things work together that we might be conformed to the image of His Son; we are changed into the same image, from glory to glory, even as by the Spirit of the Lord; the ministry is given to the Church for the perfecting of the saints until we all come to the measure of the stature of the fullness of Christ; when He appears we shall be like Him. Perhaps John's expression of the theme is as searching as any: only by walking as He walked do we show that we abide in Him, and have received His life into our hearts.

John's ethical rigorism does not falter. Three claims to spiritual experience and prestige have now been reviewed: to have fellowship with the light, to know Christ, to abide in Him; and each is subjected to the same fierce test of consistent conduct. To walk in the light, to keep the commandments, to walk as Jesus walked, alone provide the credentials that substantiate such claims and give them useful meaning. Knowledge and mysticism have their place in Christianity; but their place is to make men Christ-like, in heart and mind, in spirit and attitude, in character and conduct. High intellectual and mystical claims without correspondingly high moral attainments are just "spiritual" humbug.

6: *He Who Ever Hates Is Lost*

Beloved, I am writing you no new commandment, but an old commandment which you had from the beginning; the old commandment is the word which you have heard. Yet I am writing you a new commandment, which is true in him and in you, because the darkness is passing away and the true light is already shining. He who says he is in the light and hates his brother is in the darkness still. He who loves his brother abides in the light, and in it there is no cause for stumbling. But he who hates his brother is in the darkness and walks in the darkness, and does not know where he is going, because the darkness has blinded his eyes. 2:7-11*

With yet another expression of pastoral affection, John denies any intention to impose new obligations, other than those always inherent in the apostolic gospel; but he reminds his readers of the Master's own "new" commandment, because by this, too, they can judge just where they stand, as the age of darkness passes and that of light advances. That command was to love one another: some who say they are in the light are in fact obviously still in darkness, since they hate their brethren, and only they who love are truly enlightened, see where they are going, and stumble not. Almost insensibly the distinction between those who belong to light and those who still belong to the passing age of darkness, is further defined, and a fourth test of spiritual standing is suggested: but still no direct accusation is made — though the consciences of some readers must by this time have been growing uneasy!

* Notes on 2:7-11, pp. 237-240.

51

OF ALL THE BITTER lessons of the twentieth century none is more plain than this: that victory is not enough, that revenge solves no problems, that resentment finds no way forward into peace, and enmity nursed blinds him who nurses it, even to his own highest good. National hostility, racial rivalry, class hatred, ideological bitterness, family quarrels and personal feuds, all mend nothing: they only intensify and complicate the problems that evoke them, leading into deeper confusion and still more intractable situations. It is an elementary principle of social wisdom, but like most elementary principles easily forgotten, sometimes too obvious to be observed: He who hates his brother is in darkness, always, of necessity; he moves and walks in confusion of relationships, blundering, not understanding; he does not see where he is going, what lies ahead, or where his attitudes will come out; the darkness of an unloving heart gets into the mind, the conscience, the eyes and the very soul. Hate blinds men to facts, to people, to reality, and to all good sense.

Good will, on the other hand, is itself enlightening. The *will* to reconciliation, to serve, to understand, to be just, so very, very often resolves the deepest problems of relationship. Love will find a way, though not of course without great thought, experiment, initiative, sacrifice. Love so frequently finds solutions where ill-will saw only insoluble conflicts of interest. "It is because self-seeking governs men that life becomes so entangled. Love is that power of moral understanding which, almost with the certainty of instinct, discovers the way through the maze to those 'good works which God hath before ordained that we should walk in them' " (Law).

Such observations seem now trite and obvious. But it has taken a lot of human suffering to teach us what John said in thirty words.

Anxious still not to arouse pride or offend, John repudiates any thought of imposing a novel demand, inventing some new gospel requirement — too many are embroidering the apostolic gospel as it is. The rule he has been insisting upon, that profession shall be matched by practice, faith evidenced by works, is an "old commandment" — part of the gospel from the beginning. All the same, speaking of commandments, he will remind them of the *new* commandment, belonging essentially to the new age which now steadily advances, the commandment new from Him and new also to them: to love one another. This is the law of the age of light, the mark of the children of light, that true light which, since

Christ, is already shining. By it you may distinguish those who
are truly in the light, and those who merely think and claim they
are. For — whatever his pretensions to enlightenment — he who
lacks love is living in the dark, moving around in darkness, stumbling, lost, and blinded. There *is* no darkness deeper than hate.

And there is no hatred darker than religious hate. John's concern as he writes is with that which we — to our shame — too
often accept as inevitable: division and discord among brethren
claiming the same faith and allegiance. The fostering of Christian fellowship remains his primary aim, and the schisms and de-
fections of the Asian Churches haunt his words. Theological
controversy, especially when accompanied by claims to great
spiritual superiority, breeds prolific and deep division: even the
word hatred is not too strong for some of the invective, passion,
obduracy, and pride, that have marked the Church's domestic
quarrels, or for the persecution and violence that some Christians
have offered to other Christians during earlier "Christian" centuries.

Nor is the cold indifference of some Christians towards their
brethren in other Churches far removed from this. The stubborn,
unreasoning suspicion that condemns all attempts towards unity
and fellowship among the divided disciples of one Lord, glorying
in rather than regretting the solid difficulties that keep them apart,
is not much better than hatred. Says W. H. Bennett, "Love towards all fellow Christians as Christians, even when they differ
from us in doctrine, ritual, Church organisation, and discipline,
is a duty which, even today, the Church seldom ventures to preach
and rarely attempts to practise".

John has in mind as he pens this trenchant paragraph the attitude of the orthodox towards the sectaries, of the misguided and
proud-hearted seceders towards the apostolic fellowship, of the
"knowing ones" towards the common herd of "unenlightened"
Christians, and of all who allow disagreement in religious opinion
to poison personal relationships. It matters not that he claims to
be in the right, to "enjoy a fuller light" upon Christ, to be in the
one true Church, to be faithful to the old, fundamental gospel
truths: if he hates his brethren he is in darkness, "groping in the
blackout", benighted, lost, and blind. Perhaps saddest of all, he
cannot foresee where his state of mind will bring him.

And he is in consequence still in the pre-Christian era! For
him, the Day of Christ has not yet dawned. Although in fact the
darkness of one age is passing away and the light of a new day is

53

breaking — *true* light, not the false glimmer of a specious philosophy — yet, the man who cannot get along with his Christian brethren is clinging to the old regime, living still, within his heart, in the gloom of Christless yesterday. For, from the very beginning, this has been the character of the Day of Christ, this the new commandment which from the start we heard from Him: that we love one another. To hate is to prove yourself pre-Christian. You have not yet begun with Christ; for you the world's night still holds sway; for you Bethlehem's star has shone in vain. The light of the world has failed to irradiate your life, nor has His love sweetened your soul. He who has not love has not Christ: for this is His commandment — that we love one another as He has loved us. No less!

7: *The Evangelical Experience*

> I am writing to you, little children, because your sins are forgiven for his sake. I am writing to you, fathers, because you know him who is from the beginning. I am writing to you, young men, because you have overcome the evil one. I write to you, children, because you know the Father. I write to you, fathers, because you know him who is from the beginning. I write to you, young men, because you are strong, and the word of God abides in you, and you have overcome the evil one.
>
> 2:12-14*

In the phrase "He who says he is in the light and hates his brother" John has moved towards clearer definition of the ideas he is opposing, and in a few verses more he will proceed to unmistakable description and sharper exhortation: but he breaks off first to recapitulate yet again his pastoral purpose, and to disarm all suspicion and hostility with a passage — "thrust like a wedge into the middle of a paragraph" — essentially apologetic, and conciliatory. His impulse to write does not spring from doubt of their standing in Christ: rather, it is because of their knowledge and experience that he can so appeal to them! They have entered into an evangelical experience too precious to be thrown away for doubtful and divisive intellectual theories. At the same time, in describing this experience, John lays foundation for argument to come.

* Notes on 2:12-14, pp. 240-242.

IT IS NOT EVANGELICALS ALONE who make much of religious experience. Everyone for whom the religious quest is more than an escapist dream, for whom religious thought is more than an academic hobby, acknowledges that finally the quest and the creed must mediate to the individual an experience of God, must create within him moral impulses and resources that transform character, must illumine his way and enhearten his endeavours — or be condemned as hollow and idle make-believe. Evangelicals doubtless make more of this subjective test of religious truth than do some other Christians, for whom tradition or the ecclesiastical institution would have equal importance: but no one in earnest about religious questions would fail to recognise that doctrine must vindicate itself in experience in the long run.

A foremost theologian affirms that the appeal to religious experience has been characteristic of the Christian thinking of the nineteenth and early twentieth centuries; the eager collection of data from the widest "varieties of religious experience", and the creation of a whole new science, "the psychology of religion", testify to this; while the new emphasis laid upon the fundamental unity of all Christians in "an experienced fellowship with God through Christ" is one of the discoveries of the ecumenical impulse.

Nevertheless, the appeal to experience is no modernist discovery. A true appreciation of just how much Christ has given us and done for us is the surest of all safeguards against slipping away from faith to some superficial substitute, and this argument is used within the New Testament. When Paul would shock the Galatians into a sense of their peril in turning to "another gospel", he demands of them, "Did you receive the Spirit by the works of the law, or by hearing with faith? . . . Did you experience so many things in vain?" When the Hebrew Christians stood in danger of letting slip the things they had heard, they too were forcibly reminded of their experience — of being enlightened, of tasting of the heavenly gift, of being partakers of the Holy Spirit and tasting the goodness of the Word of God, the powers of the Age to come — lest they too should flirt with unbelief to their own immeasurable impoverishment.

And so John, even as he affirms his confidence in his readers' experience of Christ as the main reason for writing to them at all, yet contrives to remind them how much is at stake if they turn away from the things they have heard at the beginning — how much they stand to lose if they secede!

At the same time John provides an unexcelled definition of that experience of Christ, valid for all time. The dangers involved in presenting "spiritual experience" as "evidence" for doctrines, or status, are obvious. Any emotion associated with religious places, occasions, relics, rituals, music, or persons, may be called "a spiritual experience". The aesthetic satisfaction provided by ornate religious ceremonies is very often so described, and so is the contagious mass-emotion generated by well-handled crowds in some "revivalist" crusades. The appeal to experience can thus degenerate into emotion for emotion's sake. Similarly, it can be used to justify extreme fanaticism, as minds of a more intellectual cast are "driven" by immediate, unarguable, "personal convictions" of what is right and true.

It is plainly essential to determine what constitutes "Christian experience", in all its variety, if the argument based upon it is to be sound and useful. Before we accept as genuinely Christian experience any individual's testimony to special insights, emotions, visions, or convictions, it should be demonstrated that they are in harmony with Christian ethics, consistent with — and arising out of — the divine revelation in Christ and the scriptures, and such as others can share — no entirely private experience commends itself as part of the universal gospel. And the experience should persist, at least in its effects for truth and goodness in the life of him who experiences it. But such cautions and conditions do not compare with John's matchless analysis of the believer's experience of his Lord.

(a) All Christians have known forgiveness: all have found in Christ the Fatherhood of God. This is said to all readers — for all who believe are children of the Father. Forgiveness is the initial gift of the Christian gospel. Starting from the presumption that "all have sinned, and come short of the glory of God" — that indeed the most powerful, and perhaps the most prevalent, impulse toward Christian faith arises from a sense of guilt and helplessness in the struggle with evil — the good news of Christ is the news of free pardon to all who repent and believe. With that call to repentance and faith Jesus began in Galilee, moving amongst men with the assurance "your sins are forgiven . . . her sins, which are many, are forgiven . . .", declaring that He had come to seek and to save the lost, announcing the joy in heaven over one sinner repenting, and the welcome that awaited every returning wayward son. He came to give His life a ransom for many; He established in the service of the Supper the covenant of pardon through His blood, and explained His death as necessary that repentance and remission of sins might be preached in His name. His life as "Friend of publicans and sinners" found fitting climax in the prayer that penetrates all the meaning of the cross — "Father, forgive them. . .".

This free forgiveness to the penitent Jesus sets against the carelessness that forgets "unless you repent you will all likewise perish"; even more often He sets it against the laborious attempts of those who — whether in pride or in despair — strive to earn God's favour: "Come to me, all who labour and are heavy-laden, and I will give you rest". Paul is entirely right, therefore, in making justification ("acquittal") by faith the open door to every spiritual blessing — to access into gracious fellowship with God, to peace and joy, and to hope of divine glory, to an experience of the Spirit as shed abroad in the heart. And so is Barth: "The way of the Christian is derived from the forgiveness of sins. . . . This is the point at which the Christian man obviously looks back on the way from which he originates".

"*Father,* forgive them. . .": "While he was yet at a distance his *father* saw him, and had compassion. . .". The first, and always the deepest, reflection of the Christian upon his own forgiveness is that God is for us, in spite of sin; that God is love, caring and redeeming; that, in the word Jesus used so often and so joyfully, God is Father. The name — filled with all its Christian content — includes all that is essential of the Christian's knowledge of God: His kingly majesty — the Father in heaven; His providential care — the Father knows you have need; His world-redeeming purpose — it is the Father's good pleasure to give you the kingdom; His reconciling plan — the Father sent the Son to be the Saviour of the world; His personal tenderness towards men — the Father Himself loveth you; His gift of immortality — in the Father's house are many rooms.

The world has conceived God in many guises: Moloch and Mars, Jupiter, Neptune or Bacchus, Shiva, Juggernaut, Buddha, Allah, Thor and Odin; "the best poet" (E. B. Browning), a "skillful Mathematician" (Sir Thomas Browne), "the unconcerned Spectator" (Bacon), "an unutterable sigh planted in the depth of the soul" (Richter), "the President of the immortals" (Hardy), "the most significant mind of our generation" (Wells), "the force not ourselves that maketh for righteousness" (Macaulay), "the great mathematician" (Jeans), "the Eternal" (Judaism). The Christian discovers Him to be Father — the God and Father of our Lord, Jesus Christ; Him from whom all fatherly-relationship in heaven and earth is named. And so discovering, he finds in God his rest, his joy, and everlasting hope.

The joy of forgiveness through the love of the Father is the most fundamental of all definitions of Christian experience.

(b) Within this twofold birthright of all the children of God there are differences of application according to circumstance and need. Some children of God are "fathers" — senior Christians of matured faith, among them responsible leaders in local groups — the "Elders", or presbyters. In them, the blessings of the gospel have matured as "good wine kept until afterward". John writes to them because they have known "Him who is from the beginning" — a phrase which echoes 1:1 and 2:7, and evidently refers to Christ; it would have no particular significance here as a title for God, whereas the incarnation of the Logos, who was from the beginning, is the crux of the faith John writes to defend. Moreover, the continually advancing, unfolding, inexhaustible exploration of the significance and glory of Christ is precisely the supreme blessing of the maturing Christian life. The author of John's Gospel had special reason to know the immeasurable enrichment won by years of pondering the story, and exploring the personality, of His Lord, until from every word and action he beheld His glory, full of grace and truth.

"We look to mature experience for a largeness of view, a calm, untroubled depth of conviction, a clear-eyed judgement upon life, which youth cannot have" (Law). "From His fullness have we all received, and grace upon grace", it takes time and widening experience for that incoming tide to fill the bays and inlets of the individual life. The spiritual wisdom and depth of knowledge that only come with lengthening spiritual experience are the especial blessing of the mature.

Youth, on the other hand, rejoices in its strength, and most of all in its strength for conflict, in the joy of victory. "The difference of 'fathers' and 'young men' answers to that of the 'thinkers' and the 'soldiers in the Christian army', and to the two main applications of the faith: as a spring of wisdom and . . . a source of strength" (Westcott). As the reward of the fathers is advancing knowledge, the fruit of experience, so the reward of the young men is victory, the prize of strength.

To be an "overcomer", in the language of Johannine Christianity, is to deserve the highest award of Christian valour. To "overcomers" at Ephesus was promised the privilege of eating of the tree of life in the midst of the paradise of God; to those at Smyrna, not to be hurt by the second death; to those at Pergamum, to eat of the hidden manna; to others was promised authority, the freedom of heaven, an unchanging memorial in the eternal Temple, a place beside the highest Throne. So also in Pauline thought, to be led in the train of Christ's triumph, more than conquerors through Him that loved us, was the peak of Christian experience. For in that first century, no less than now, the Christian calling was a call to battle and the Christian life a ceaseless war against fightings within and fears without, against unbelief and the enemies of the cross of Christ, against spiritual wickedness in high places, against principalities and powers and the rulers of the darkness of this world. The joyous discovery of the young, therefore, was the experience of victory, the finding in Christ of the cause to fight for and the strength with which to struggle, and the undying hope that refuses to acknowledge final defeat, but holds we fall to rise, and are baffled to fight better.

Apposite though the commendation is to younger men — and a faint Greek pun underlines it — yet it is not of their own natural strength or animal spirits that John is thinking, which would be no match for the evil one: but of a conferred and implanted strength — "the word of God, which abideth in" them. Law finely remarks that "the Word of God as the weapon by which all temptation is to be met, is one of the great commonplaces of scripture"; it immediately recalls the "sword of the Spirit", the Word "sharper than any two-edged sword", and the strategy of Jesus Himself in the wilderness temptation. The young men "conquer because they are strong, and they are strong because God's word is ever in their hearts" (Plummer).

The old in their stored experiences and the young in their tested strength represent the truth and grace overflowing from Christ that enrich the lives of all who believe, adding to forgiveness and the knowledge of God as Father, the joy of moral victory and the advancing exploration of the riches of Christ, as youth mellows to maturity. And in these four great gifts of the gospel — forgiveness, the knowledge of the Father, victory, and unceasing enrichment, the characteristic notes of Christian "religious experience" are to be found.

(c) Yet all can be surrendered by disloyalty, by letting slip the things once heard and believed. Forgiveness was "through His Name" — and the name is but shorthand for the whole character and work of Christ, the incarnate Son. Yet the true

"Name" of Christ was being denied by the opposing groups. The knowledge of the Father — John will shortly show — depends logically upon unclouded faith in the Son; the blessedness of accumulated understanding of Him who is from the beginning is forfeited if we deny that He was from the beginning, leaving only a mere man, or worse — a phantom! The strength of the young men depends on the abiding within them of the Word of God — not exchanged for some new-fangled theory!

It may well be that the form of John's appeal owes something to division between 'fathers' with their longer experience and reflection, and 'young men' with their impetuous contempt for fine-drawn theology: but either may stand in danger of leaving that fellowship in which they first were blessed, and going out with great excitement and a flourish of intellectual trumpets, to some desert place that shall prove barren, unsatisfying, impoverished, and forsaken of blessing. So even as he records his confidence in the experience they have known, John warns of the dire loss involved in giving up the apostolic faith. All Christian experience is experience *of Christ*: it must be distorted, corrupted, lost, if we move away from that gospel which centres wholly in Him.

8: *Rock Against the Drift*

> Do not love the world or the things in the world. If any one loves the world, love for the Father is not in him. For all that is in the world, the lust of the flesh and the lust of the eyes and the pride of life, is not of the Father but is of the world. And the world passes away, and the lust of it; but he who does the will of God abides for ever.　　　2:15-17*

Before the conciliatory pause, John had mentioned the "New Commandment" to love one another, made more urgent as a test of spiritual standing as the old age of darkness passes away and the new day of light advances.　The passing of the darkness will however carry away with it the sphere of darkness, the world and all its ways that are not of God.　Thus a complementary duty arises — *not* to love the transient world, but to cling ever more closely to the unchanging will of the Father.　Thus again the mind is prepared for the sharpened distinction between the faithful apostolic groups and those whose intellectual compromise with the thought-fashions of the world reveals that they are not "of the Father".

ISAIAH HAS A WONDERFUL PICTURE of the power of one great character to stand erect against the slow deterioration of a time, the force of personality that resists within itself the drift of a whole generation:

* Notes on 2:15-17, pp. 242-243.

> *Each will be like a hiding-place from the wind,*
>   *a covert from the tempest,*
> *like streams of water in a dry place,*
>   *like the shade of a great rock in a weary land.*

George Adam Smith here interprets memorably. Where the desert touches a river valley or oasis, wind-blown sand in continual state of "drift" is the real cause of infertile soil and blighted growth. But where a rock rears above the sand the picture changes. After the early rains, in the rock's lee some blades will spring and soon a tiny garden. "How has the boulder produced this? Simply by arresting the drift." So, "deadly forces, blind and fatal as the desert wind, sweep down human history": and mankind's true heroes are those mighty souls who set their backs against the destroying blasts, and in whose shelter other men grow free, adventurous, and strong.

Yet the strong man himself needs something immovable to cling to. Jesus answers Isaiah with the parable of a soul itself built upon the sand and carried away with the stormdrift; and another built upon a rock, stoutly resistant to all spiritual weather, unmoved by all the complex pressures of a tempestuous time.

(a) An age in transition from darkness to light (verse 8) must of necessity see the end of much that has seemed permanent. The light of the new Day reveals the flimsiness of what had seemed so real and enduring. The human "economy" passes away: the whole organised life of society in so far as it has developed by its own resources, under the compulsion of its own interests, and independently of the will of its Creator and King, carries within itself the seeds of mortality, the inner inconsistencies that must prove fatal. The world's treasures pass away, succumbing as Jesus prophesied to moth and rust and the thieves of time and death. All that matters to the world — what is sensually gratifying, what is outwardly magnificent and imposing, what ministers to arrogant pride and boastful superiority — passes away. The desire of such things itself dies, as appetites that are sated pall, and even fashions in sinning change! The world passes away, "the elements melting with fervent heart", to make way for a new heaven and a new earth.

And at length man passes away:

> *All flesh is grass,*
>   *and all its beauty is like the flower of the field.*
> *The grass withers, the flower fades,*

> *when the breath of the Lord blows upon it;*
> *surely the people is grass.*

A deeper drift threatens man's existence than the changing fashions of thought and the fluctuation of all human hopes, the instability of human institutions and the inconstancy of society's aims. Mutability and frailty are reinforced by mortality and judgement in John's solemn sentence: "the world passes away".

All this is clearer because the age itself is passing in the progress of the divine programme. Already "it is the last hour". To cling to the world is therefore to pass away with it: to love it, so as to build one's life upon it and focus one's affections, loyalties, and aims upon it, is to court insecurity and cultivate frustration. It is not adaptation to the drifting sand, but adhesion to the unshifting rock, that confers permanence and strength, and provides the shade in which weaker souls can shelter. And, in the final analysis, that rock, too, is Christ.

(b) For over against all that passes is set simply the doing of the will of God. If we recall Isaiah again,

> *The grass withers, the flower fades;*
> *but the word of our God will stand for ever. . . .*

and add Peter's contemporary interpretation: "That word is the good news which was preached to you", we ought perhaps to count the gospel revelation among the things that endure, along with faith and hope and love. But such distinctions are mainly academic: John is thinking of persons, and this alone confers permanence upon personality — alignment with the divine and enduring will. In such a man, the everlasting gospel does its work, abiding faith and hope and love are perennially enshrined, and the enduring purpose of God lifts humanity to the unmeasured perspectives of eternal life. Amid all that drifts and changes, decays or is destroyed, the will of God is the "interior castle" wherein the menaced soul finds refuge, security, and the secret of undying hope. "He who does the will of God abides for ever."

(c) The consequent detachment from the world and the things in the world, which John counsels, rests upon two reasons, one of loyalty and the other of simple sanity and common sense. Loyalty is involved: because to love the world is to fail to love the Father. The things most characteristic of the world's life — lust, ostentation, and pride — are entirely alien to the Father's mind, utterly opposed to His purpose and rule, wholly lacking that love which is His nature. Within the world's sphere of unreconciled activity· and unredeemed enjoyment, "the things of God" struggle for survival and mastery among "the things of the world", and in that situation a man must declare his allegiance.

"He that is not with us is against us," Jesus had said, and "No man can serve two masters". "The world is crucified to me", declared Paul, "and I unto the world." James is as incisive as John: "friendship with the world is enmity with God". It all sounds ruthlessly black-and-white, but "the Church had no choice — it could bear its witness only by separation from pagan society" (Dodd). Yet after two thousand years of Christian influence, life in a leavened society calls still for wise discrimination, clear judgement, and keen conscience. To support, encourage, patronise, enjoy, finance, draw profits from, or defend things that owe their existence and continuance to renunciation of God, is to be no friend of God: "love for the Father is not in him". And F. W. H. Myers puts John's underlying concern — accommodation to the world's ways of thinking, even about Jesus — into a noble modern protest —

> *Whoso has felt the Spirit of the Highest*
> *Cannot confound nor doubt Him nor deny:*
> *Yea, with one voice, O world, tho' thou deniest,*
> *Stand thou on that side, for on this am I.*

But the issue is no less one of sane self-preservation than of loyalty to the Father. For to build on sands that drift is to invite disaster: to love things that are bound to pass is to determine beforehand, with open eyes, that the heart shall at last be left barren and bereaved; to lay up as one's only treasure that which moth and rust and burglary will take from you is to ensure a final bankruptcy. The world has no future, says John, nor have they who love it and live for it. On the other hand, to build already on the foundation of the world to come is to build for ever; to steer one's thought by, and set one's heart wholly upon, the age of light that is advancing, is to inherit the kingdom that cannot be moved.

Thus, the passing of the darkness and the advance of light imposes the moral imperative of the "new commandment"; the transitoriness of the world imposes the obligation not to cling to it or follow its ways. In other words, the urgency of the last days demands that Christians love each other more and the world far less!

9: *The Logic of Denial*

Children, it is the last hour; and as you have heard that antichrist is coming, so now many antichrists have come; therefore we know that it is the last hour. They went out from us, but they were not of us; for if they had been of us, they would have continued with us; but they went out, that it might be plain that they all are not of us. But you have been anointed by the Holy One, and you all know. I write to you, not because you do not know the truth, but because you know it, and know that no lie is of the truth. Who is the liar but he who denies that Jesus is the Christ? This is the antichrist, he who denies the Father and the Son. No one who denies the Son has the Father. He who confesses the Son has the Father also. Let what you heard from the beginning abide in you. If what you heard from the beginning abides in you, then you will abide in the Son and in the Father. And this is what he has promised us, eternal life.   2:18-25*

At long last the opposition is defined, and much already said falls into place in the closest possible argument: the contrasts, emphases, allusions, reminders, of the previous verses are now seen to be immediately relevant to a Church some of whose former leaders have defected to Gnostic groups and deny the incarnation they once professed.   The defection merely exposes a prior inward alienation (19) and proves the apostolic warning of a lying Antichrist.   Still there is no personal condemnation: the words fit those who so choose: but the consequences of denial are described with a spiritual logic not to be evaded.

* Notes on 2:18-25, pp. 243-245.

66

THE DIFFICULTIES OF BELIEF are sufficiently known. The good fight of faith has perhaps never been more arduous, nor has simply holding on to truth required more courage. It is not the weak-minded who believe: the weak-minded give up, and surrender their faith! The cost of *unbelief* is not always so accurately reckoned, and sometimes when it is hard to retain one's faith, the high price of letting it go is a steadying reflection.

An eloquent Welsh preacher expounded the costly implications of "The fool hath said in his heart, There is no God" in a long, sad soliloquy on his "wasted" life. Setting the mood of reluctant loss of faith, he began to remove one by one the pulpit furnishings, talking to himself meanwhile of the lost values. Hiding away the Bible, he murmured over its treasured passages, recalled its association with conversions and crises, with sickbed and marriage and death; removing the hymnbook he hinted at the thrill of adoring worship, the buoyant praise, the humbling gratitude and tender penitence of its poetry and music; putting away the pulpit cushion he recalled great sermons that redirected lives, and a long life of Christian testimony. So he set resolutely aside the pulpit flowers, and with them all the radiance shed on nature by the Father's love; the pulpit chairs, with their memories of children saying anniversary pieces and grave old men full of wisdom, faith, and prayer; and finally he stepped down the pulpit stairs, talking with himself of the years spent in patiently, stumblingly, but lovingly proclaiming a God now "disproved" — and slowly, leaving the pulpit bare and empty, he walked to the Church door.

Turning with his hand upon the latch, he whispered into the astonished silence, "Do you want them back?"; and three thousand shouted as one "Yes — Aye — Yes!" Returning, he replaced everything, quietly, impressively, without a word, and as he laid the Bible again upon the cushion, he opened it and read — "Comfort ye, comfort ye my people, saith your God."

It is John's argument too. Denial is easy, smart, and self-inflating: but *can we afford to let faith go?*

(a) The word, and the idea, of "Antichrist" doubtless struck John's readers with the sense of horror which it has carried ever since. "The devil's own messiah" was to be the mark of the last hour of the age of darkness, the final and most dreadful manifestation of evil, the climax of blasphemy, the acme of defiance against God. It would come as a sharp shock to be told that those who had left the apostolic circle, in pursuit of some "advanced", "more intellectual" version of Christian thought, were in fact embodying the dreaded spirit of "Antichrist".

To some it would appear an extreme, exaggerated charge, but John insists that his readers know it as well as he. To deny that Jesus is Christ is to be anti-Christ, not only by the literal meaning of words but by denying the very claim of Jesus upon which the whole Christian faith is built. To deny this is to contradict all He stood for, to oppose all that God in Christ intended. It is to set oneself against everything truly Christian by cutting the ground from beneath every principle, standard, assumption and hope upon which Christian civilisation has been erected.

Unwilling to pay that price for unbelief, many deny the logic of their own denial: they prefer to pick and choose what shall be accepted, what denied — rejecting the miraculous, the superhuman, the too-high moral standards, the too-humbling message of redemption, the unique and eternal divinity of Jesus, but trying to hold on to the Christian valuation of persons, to freedom and charity, and to some undefined human hope. It will not work. If Jesus was wrong about who He was, He is wrong about everything — a naive fool, a fanatic, a megalomaniac or a deceiver — it makes little difference, if we cannot anyway trust His own self-estimate, the testimony of those who knew Him, and the message of the Word of God through Him. All who have followed Him have been misled, the whole Christian vision is a perilous mirage, all Christian enterprise is built on lies and foolish obsessions, and the world is in deeper darkness than it knows — if Jesus is not the Christ of God, the Saviour of the world.

(b) There is involved in such denial, moreover, a certain self-revelation of a most unwelcome kind. Difficulties of belief are one thing: the final surrender of belief is always as much a moral betrayal as an intellectual defeat. It argues a certain inner reserve, a lack of the spiritual certainty which true experience of God bestows. "They went out from us, but they were not of us; for if they had been of us, they would have continued with us; but they went out, that it might be plain that they all are not of us."

Something very similar is implied in the parable of the True Vine. The branch that fails to abide in the Vine, becoming inwardly severed from the trunk by some want of living adhesion and union, is first borne farther away by its own weight — "thrust forth" — then pruned away by the Husbandman, then finally removed to be burned. The public removal only reveals and climaxes the private and secret separation. So John says of the seceders: "these false teachers had not renounced the truth, for the truth they had never possessed. They had not fallen from the communion of the Church, for to the communion of its inner life they had never really belonged. . . . It was only the hatching of the serpent's egg" (Law). That they had, to all outward seeming, both possessed the truth and shared the fellowship, and still maintained the claims and the outward forms of the gospel, in no way disproves John's diagnosis: secession, on such an issue, only reveals how little they had ever really known. On the other hand, John can say to those who read, "you know the truth, by the inner certainty of a divine initiation — you need no one to show you where falsehood lies: hold to the truth you have received, the conviction you have already won".

Few surrender their faith with deliberate and open admission of their failure to maintain spiritual discipline and a faithful fellowship with the Light: always there is some attempt at self-vindication, some pretence at inevitability, at "not being able to help myself"; often there is a claim to overwhelming intellectual difficulties created by mental or educational superiority. Yet the truth remains: to give up believing reveals more about our inner disloyalties than we usually care to have known.

(c) John presses the logic of denial upon a third point which, once said, seems obvious, but which doubtless the seceding party would strongly contest. It seemed a minor matter to dispute the particular terms to be applied to Jesus, to deny Him this or that title as the definition of His person and authority, while holding professedly to all else in spiritual life and experience. So many would argue still. John declares this cannot hold either. For to deny the divine Sonship of Jesus is to surrender our only real clue to the nature of God: if Jesus is not Son, then God is not Father. Here again, not only do the terms themselves carry this implication, being strictly relative: in addition, the only evidence for God's Fatherhood is Christ's revealing Sonship. Thus, "no one who denies the Son has the Father: he who confesses the Son has the Father also"; this was the purpose of John's emphasis that our fellowship is with the Father and with His Son.

The argument is but the application of Christ's own words: "No man knows the Father except the Son and anyone to whom the Son chooses to reveal Him. . .". Christ's answer to Philip's plea, "Show us the Father" was clear: "He that hath seen me hath seen the Father. . .". Far more than some modern "Christians" realise, the whole circle of Christian understanding of God is

centred upon the person of Jesus; to doubt His uniqueness, authority, and divine glory, is to doubt all we most readily take for
granted in His teaching about God. That is why Unitarianism
proves so often the parent of agnosticism.

True, this argument had a sharper nuance for John's readers
than for us, in that the alternative to "the God and Father of
our Lord Jesus Christ" was for them Zeus, Mars, Venus, Bacchus,
Dionysius — the whole disreputable tribe of unworshipful deities
who claimed the first century's adoration — or else some philosophic abstraction, some fleeting intellectual gleam charged with
hysterical emotion induced by hynoptic rites. Yet it remains true
also for us that if Jesus be not the Son, in the bosom of the Father,
and so uniquely able to reveal Him, then the Fatherhood of God is
a nebulous, sentimental idea, unsupported in nature, history, or
much of non-Christian personal experience. If we retain God
in our thought at all, it will be in far different terms — as Fate, or
malicious Destiny, or the irrational blind Force that defeats our
ideals — and with very different moral and social consequences.
Much more probably, however, if we surrender the Sonship of
Jesus, we shall destroy faith altogether.

(d) And so it is, finally, (John argues) with spiritual experience
as a whole. The promise of eternal life is bound up with that
which you heard from the beginning. If that abides in you, you
abide in the Son — both as to faith and in daily experience — and
so also you abide in the Father: and this is what eternal life *means*.
"This is life eternal — to know Thee, the only true God, and
Jesus Christ whom Thou hast sent." To deny the Son, and so,
intentionally or not, to deny the Father, is to lose eternal life
itself. The question of the eternal security of believers is not
here really relevant, since John holds that defection from the
apostolic fellowship only reveals what has always been true of
these "deniers": he is drawing out the consequences of their
own position. For this is certain: to surrender the full faith of the
original apostolic testimony concerning Jesus is to lose all that
"eternal life" means, of fellowship with God, of abundant living,
of adequate resources, of immortal hope. These are *gospel* gifts:
to reject the gospel is to choose again the barren and hopeless life
of men "without God, in the world".

It may sometimes be hard to go on believing, in an intellectual
climate whose currents run counter to faith: but the price of denying is more than any heart can ever want to pay.

10: *The Inner Light*

I write this to you about those who would deceive you; but the anointing which you received from him abides in you, and you have no need that anyone should teach you; as his anointing teaches you about everything, and is true, and is no lie, just as it has taught you, abide in him. And now, little children, abide in him, so that when he appears we may have confidence and not shrink from him in shame at his coming. If you know that he is righteous, you may be sure that every one who does right is born of him.   2:26-29*

Resuming the reassuring remark just interjected — "You have an anointing from the Holy One and all know . . ." — John declares that the readers really need no one to instruct them, either self-appointed "advanced" teachers or apostolic seniors! It is only because of persuasive seducers that he ventures to address them. Christ's anointing once taught them, and still continually teaches them, concerning the truth or falsehood of all things; and in spite of the denials of the antichrist, it is utterly reliable. So they should abide steadfastly in Him to whom it testifies. This is the more urgent as the last hour draws to His coming: that they might be confident, not ashamed, at His presence. But if that anointing teaches them anything at all — as that Jesus is righteous — then they know already how to distinguish seducers from true teachers: similarity proves sonship — he who does righteousness has been born of him. So the whole argument that Christian experience and Christian character go always together is rounded off, and the theme of the next section introduced.

* Notes on 2:26-29, pp. 245-246.

IT IS AN ASSUMPTION of New Testament Christianity that all normal men can perceive truth when it is presented to them; therein lies the responsibility of hearing the gospel. Jesus ever appeals to the innate sense of truth which can — if we will — discern the meaning of His parables and epigrams. On one revealing occasion He contrasts the popular ability to read the signs of the weather and the changing seasons with the spiritual blindness that fails to notice the working of God's hand. "Why", He once asked, "do you not judge for yourselves what is right?"

"The spirit of man is the candle of the Lord." It would seem that this profound doctrine of the inward illumination that distinguishes man from the brutes underlies the description by the Fourth Gospel of the eternal Logos as "the true Light that enlightens every man". It certainly underlies Paul's references to the knowledge of God, and of His law, written on Gentile hearts; and his conception of evangelism as "commending the truth to every man's conscience in the sight of God".

Yet the Christian himself has still further inward illumination — he has received the Light of the World, so that he needs not to walk stumbling through darkness; and the light itself is within him, an anointing and enlightenment within his own soul that is the gift of Christ — the "Anointed One". By this gospel illumination the light of rational and moral nature is gloriously completed and superseded.

Plainly this does not confer omniscience upon the believer — "compared to this papal infallibility would be a trifle!" (Law). But it does confer an inner sense of truth, "an intellectual conscience", by which the genuine and the false may be distinguished; just as, without implying complete and infallible moral knowledge and insight, conscience itself yet knows intuitively good from evil and right from wrong. Instruction, warning, exhortation, as in this epistle, still have their place: John cannot mean "you have no need that anyone teach you *anything*". But they had no need for others to do their thinking for them, to show them what was false, and what was true. Christian experience itself makes for "senses exercised", and the prayer for wisdom and spiritual understanding is one that we need continually to offer, that we may discern the things that differ and approve that which is excellent. Nevertheless, the ultimate witness to Christian truth lies within the Christian heart: the appeal is always, "You all know . . . you know the truth when you hear it, if you will but pause, and think, and be loyal . . . ".

Dogma imposed by authority, the overbearing spiritual tyranny which demands unquestioning intellectual obedience to *ex cathedra* pronouncements, has no place in John's scheme of Christian thought, nor in the whole New Testament. "Let every man be fully persuaded in his own mind": only that free and total assent gives faith any meaning, any moral power, any intellectual honesty.

(i) *The call, then, is to steadfastness* in the truth once so seen. Whether the anointing consists in the gift of the Spirit at Christian baptism or in the knowledge of the original gospel, it must be faithfully adhered to. Christians must abide in it: even more important, and in consequence, they must abide in Him of whom it tells. This is the antidote to heresy, the cure for all mental confusion.

Thought rooted in the original gospel, life rooted in Christ, ensure that what is intellectually specious and morally perilous will be detected and refused, even when the full issues are unclear and the answering arguments do not come readily to mind. This is the truth within the Quaker doctrine of the inner light, though John would root it very firmly within the apostolic message concerning Jesus. It has to do not with knowledge but with discernment, not with theoretic understanding concerning religious things but with the living of the Christian life and the exercise of Christian loyalties. Spiritual safety — and enlightenment — lie for the Christian not in scholarship but in saintliness. The true follower of Christ, however humble, however ungifted with mental agility and acuteness, *abiding in Christ* does not walk in confusion, "tossed to and fro and carried about with every wind of doctrine": he finds light enough to walk by, a lamp at least for his feet and a light sufficient to illumine his path.

(ii) *The exhortation to abide* in the truth and in Christ is set (like the appeal not to love the world and the warning concerning antichrists) in the strengthening light of the age that is advancing, in the brilliance and glow of the advent hope. In that final, revealing denouement, our group-loyalties and party-labels will matter nothing beside our standing in His presence — either *assured* or *ashamed*. These are essentially words of personal relationship, concerned not with our record or our reward, but with His approval or frown. Assurance, boldness, is by derivation and essential meaning "freedom of speech", the openness, the absence of inhibiting fear, that betokens true friendship and mutual confidence. "It is the splendid word which denotes the citizen's right of free speech, the masculine privilege of courageous liberty; it is the tender word which expresses the child's unhesitating confidence in 'saying all out' to its parent" (William Alexander). Assurance at His coming, assurance before God (3:21), assurance in the day of judgment (4:17), and assurance in prayer (5:14) are promised by John to those who resist attempts to lead them astray from the truth, who abide in Him in whom they have believed, to the end.

The alternative is confusion of face, the sense of over-whelming shame in His presence. The real question is not whether those who trifle with new doctrines and take lightly old obligations can face their former friends, but whether in the end they can outface the Lord — or be "shamed from Him at His coming".

(iii) *Nor will it serve* to plead the difficulties of finding one's way amidst the deep things of advanced Christian thought, or to shift the blame upon the divisions among the teachers, the confused counsels of the varying sects and groups who claim allegiance. If the spiritual anointing teaches you anything, you know at least the character of God, as Christ the righteous has revealed Him. And it takes no great intellectual power to draw the obvious practical conclusion: that everyone that does righteousness is born of God. By that simple touchstone the readers can find their way in the present confusions; the moral test, yet again, suffices as evidence of truth. The children of God are like their Father.

Beneath this argument lies of course the typically Hebrew assumption of native similarity between father and son, expressed in the idiom that makes "child of" an adjective of quality. As the peacemakers, and those who love their enemies, and all whose love acknowledges no boundaries, are said by Jesus to be "children of your Father which is in heaven" because they reflect in themselves the divine character, so on the other side the children of the devil sin, and lie, as "their father" does. Resemblance proves relationship; Abram's children will do the works of Abram, and share his faith; God's sons, imitators of God as dear children, will reflect God's righteousness. John will have other tests by which to know the true child of God: he that believeth . . . every one that loveth . . .; but the basis is always the same: faith in us answers to the faithfulness of God, righteousness in us reflects the divine righteousness, love in us is God's love shed abroad in our hearts, bestowed upon us. The rule for the discernment of seducers is plain — "like father, like son".

In these days it is perhaps especially difficult to claim such sureness and clarity of Christian opinion as John assumes, about true and false teaching, valid and invalid loyalties. The immature are led astray, the mature so easily become spiritual "knowalls", obstinate, proud, unteachable. The only possible security is to abide in the gospel and in Christ, and there humbly, without great intellectual or spiritual pretensions, to cling to the things most surely believed, to follow with all fidelity the inner light of the Spirit and the word, to remember that we must stand in His presence at the last — and that whatever is truly of God, whether people, teaching, conduct, or movements, will be Godlike.

11: *The Moral Force of Hope*

> See what love the Father has given us, that we should be called
> children of God; and so we are. The reason why the world
> does not know us is that it did not know him. Beloved, we
> are God's children now; it does not yet appear what we shall
> be, but we know that when he appears we shall be like him,
> for we shall see him as he is. And every one who thus hopes in
> him purifies himself as he is pure.   3:1-3*

The moral implications of the experience of God as light give
place, somewhere around 2:29, 3:1 to the social implications of the
experience of God as love — but precisely where is hard to decide.
The idea of passing darkness and advancing light of 2:8 echoes in
the "now . . . shall be" of 3:2; "when he appears" of 2:28 recurs
in 3:2; the contrast between love of the Father and of the world,
of 2:15, is recalled in the thought that the world does not recognise the children of God — itself a phrase prepared for in the
"born of him" of 2:29; "walking as he walked", "doing righteousness as he is righteous" now become "pure as he is pure"; the
present passage thus gathers up effectively much that has preceded.
Yet 2:29 is an excellent title for the following paragraph. Membership in God's family becomes the dominant theme: to be loved,
to be God's children, and to await the Advent, all carry solemn
implications of spiritual endeavour. For sonship implies no less
moral obligation than fellowship with the light — especially as
we shall one day stand in the presence of the Son. And this is
true of every Christian: the moral slackness of so-called advanced
Gnostic thought has no place in apostolic certainty — or hope.

* Notes on 3:1-3, pp. 247-248.

IT IS ONE OF THE GLORIES of the Christian gospel — too obvious and· familiar to be noticed — to have achieved the final definition of the relation of men to God. The Creator and His handiwork, the King and His subjects, the Holy God and His chosen people, the Shepherd and His sheep, are all metaphors both useful and true: but none describes adequately the nature of God, or of men, nor the intimacy of their relationship in biblical faith. Jesus Himself contrasted the servant, who implicitly obeys what he is told without sharing the confidence of his Lord's reasons and intentions, with friends who stand much nearer in mind and heart. But the grandest, most adequate, and most intimate image is that of the divine family — the Father in heaven, the children who rejoice in His life and love.

Old Testament faith had groped toward this. "As a father pities his children, so the Lord pities those who fear him." "When Israel was a child, I loved him, and out of Egypt I called my son." "Yet it was I who taught Ephraim to walk, I took them up in my arms." "You are the sons of the Lord your God." But in the revelation through the Son the truth shines clear: "To all who received him, who believed in his name, he gave power to become children of God. . . . In Christ Jesus you are all sons of God, through faith." And by that root-metaphor of divine-human relationship every part of Christian life comes to be described — trust, prayer, brotherly love, discipline, imitation of the Father, forgiveness, redemption of prodigals, work, the Christian goal, and the eternal hope of home-gathering in the Father's house.

(i) *Three degrees of certainty* about sonship are present to John's mind: we are *called* God's children, we *are* God's children, and we shall, in due course, be *recognised* as God's children by others. What a man is "called" has special significance for John. There is wide difference of status, for example, between being called servant and being pronounced friend. So with the words "You call me Teacher and Lord; and you are right. . . . You shall be called Cephas. . . .He who is called Christ. . . . The man called Jesus. . . . He called them gods" John continually underlines the importance attached to names as indicating nature, character, or status.

For any man the most wonderful name of all is "child of God": to be so called is evidence of surpassing grace, and this John bids us reflect upon, with a unique apostrophe expressing "astonishment and admiration" (Plummer). Such is the exalted purpose harboured for us by the amazing love God has "bestowed" — for His is love not only shown but given, in concrete and specific privilege and blessing. It is sonship granted by grace through faith, to those with no claim to such favour: God has called us His children — that in itself is love unutterable.

But we have more than the name; we are God's children in fact, and now. In Johannine thought this follows of necessity from our new birth, not of the will of man but of God — our being born "again" or "from above", of water and the Spirit. The breathtaking conception of life with divine origin and derivation lies behind each use of "Father" for God in John's writings. The full thought runs: God has given us eternal life in His Son; having the Son we have life, and the life we have is that of sons, as children of the living Father; its advent in our experience is new birth — regeneration; its issue, life eternal.

John will presently offer evidence for this inward certainty of relationship, but to the child of God himself no evidence is necessary: as Paul says, the inner witness of the Spirit of God's Son within the heart, whereby we cry "Abba, Father", is the immediate basis of Christian certainty. We know "by the Spirit he has given us" is John's echo of the same thought. We are not waiting for fulfilment of the gospel promise concerning what we shall be called; we have it now, and know it: we *are* the children of God.

The final degree of certainty is the public recognition of what we are, the evidence to others. For this too John will offer evidence by which the child of God may know his brethren. Recognition by the world is another matter. The deep distinction holds, between the darkness and the light, between those of the world and those of the Father. The world did not know Christ — the unique and only-begotten Son: can we then be surprised if it does not acknowledge us? We share His rejection — and this in itself is a sign that we share His sonship. The world treats us as it treated Him: what clearer proof could we ask that we are truly "of Him"?

(ii) *Yet our present certainty* does not exhaust the purpose of divine love toward us: words cannot express or define all God has prepared for those who love Him. This much we know, that present experience is the "earnest", the promise and guarantee, of more. And especially of this, that when the full purpose of God is at last unveiled, and Christ appears, we shall share His likeness, seeing and reflecting Him perfectly, as He is.

Christlikeness is, as we have seen, the supreme goal of the Christian on every page of the New Testament, and it is implied in almost every statement of Christian experience or aspiration. It is the very meaning of sonship to be like our Father in heaven, as it is the purpose He has predestined for those whom He has called; it is the goal of Christian growth to reach the full stature of Christ, as it is the fruit of all true worship that beholding "as in a glass the glory of the Lord" we should be changed into His likeness. To have the mind of Christ, to grow up into Him in all things, to show forth His virtues — in such perfection God's great end for us attains completion. "The manifestation of the sons of God", in glory, as sons, is the plan of God for Christian hearts!

And so here, the goal of Christlikeness is an essential element in Christian hope. Our present approximation to His image must become perfect identification when He comes, and (as Paul implies, in his reference to being changed into His image as we behold His glory) there is some profound inner connection between the spiritual insight and vision that reads aright the mind of Jesus and the moral and mental growth that reflects the image of His character. "As the whole body, the face, above all the eyes, of those who look towards the sun are *sunnied*" (Bengel) — "even as the planets, when they face the sun, are clothed with its radiance" (Law) — so we shall be perfectly like Him when we see Him as He is: and we shall be satisfied when we awaken in His likeness.

(iii) *The hope of His appearing* is at once an inspiration and a deep, steadying comfort, assuring as it does of the final vindication of Christian truth and faith, the final triumph of the Lord we love. Yet here it is the moral power of hope which John underlines. The advent truth is not all consolation. It imposes high standards of preparation, and a living sense of an impending judgement far more searching than our own. As Law points out, John's tone is not that of exhortation but of fact: "to strive after His purity is the inexorable test of having the hope of His glory". The long forward look, which takes account of consequences, which keeps in mind the harvest to be reaped, tends always towards moral vigilance and a tender conscience.

It is not only out of despair that we are "saved by hope", but out of indolence, and carelessness, and a slumbering obedience. To "set on Christ" this hope of standing in His presence unashamed, to fix on Him our forward gaze and look eagerly for His appearing, is to know that nothing must impede one's spiritual progress towards His likeness, nothing of impurity mar the spotless image of Himself that He would reproduce in us. No evangelical doctrine has more powerful and practical moral stimulus than the doctrine of the advent.

So once again the divine life cannot be divorced (as some still suppose) from moral excellence. As "God is light" involves our walking in light, so "God is Father" involves our bearing the image of His sonship, in whose presence we shall all appear. To be God's child, and to wait for the full manifestation of what sonship means at the advent of the Son, is daily to approximate to His likeness. Ethical indifferentism is as impossible within the divine family as it is within the divine light. The moral implications of sonship are obvious — "You therefore must be perfect as your heavenly Father is perfect"; the moral implications of the advent hope ring in the ears that heard the words of the departing Lord — "Blessed is that servant whom his Master when he comes shall find so doing . . . whom the Master finds awake. . . . *You must be ready*".

12: A Spiritual "Who's Who"

Every one who commits sin is guilty of lawlessness; sin is lawlessness. You know that he appeared to take away sins, and in him there is no sin. No one who abides in him sins; no one who sins has either seen him or known him. Little children, let no one deceive you. He who does right is righteous, as he is righteous. He who commits sin is of the devil; for the devil has sinned from the beginning. The reason the Son of God appeared was to destroy the works of the devil. No one born of God commits sin; for God's nature abides in him, and he cannot sin because he is born of God. By this it may be seen who are the children of God, and who are the children of the devil: whoever does not do right is not of God, nor he who does not love his brother.   3:4-10*

Children of a holy God must needs be holy: the obverse of "Every one . . . purifies himself" 'is plainly "Every one who commits sin", and the implied contrast of 3:1-3 with those who are *not* God's children and who do *not* cherish the purifying hope, calls once again for clear definition. The whole series of spiritual claims is reassembled and tested by the severest ethical realism: no accusation is made that the seceding party fails to meet the tests, but principles are again enunciated that leave no doubt where every one claiming to be Christian — advanced or otherwise — really stands; and the "he who doeth", as well as the deception, (2:29, 3:4, 7, 8, 9, 10) shows whom John has in mind. The whole paragraph condenses in the sharpest way the ethical position of the secession, as 2:18-25 condensed its theological position, and argues unanswerably the conclusion that character alone betrays status — adding the particularising "rider" that only love of the brethren proves divine relationship, as the next step in John's indictment.

* Notes on 3:4-10, pp. 249-251.

ONE UNTRUMPETED VICTORY of the Christian faith is best exemplified in the sharpest accusations of her critics. The least defection from the highest moral standards, on the part of Christian leaders, the slightest inconsistency between teaching and practice, professed faith and personal behaviour, is held to "prove" there is nothing in religion. The cardinal sin of Christians is "hypocrisy" — understood as the failure to be what you claim to be — and it is held to be unanswerable evidence that Christian claims are false and the gospel an illusion.

In the modern western world, some might lay their main emphasis upon less ethical elements in religion, such as emotion or ritual; some might profess to believe that ethics needs no religious foundation or sanctions; many perhaps persuade themselves that the best of both worlds may be assured by preserving a perfunctory religiousness alongside a fairly lax moral attitude. But very few would accept or defend the complete divorce of religion from morality, or contend any longer for the view that belief and behaviour belong to separate compartments of human responsibility. Hence the seemingly self-evident and unanswerable argument, that poor-living Christians suffice to disprove Christianity.

Yet this universal association of true religion with high morality is itself a novel assumption, an insight very far from being self-evident, which we owe mainly to Jesus Himself, and to that highly ethical religious tradition out of which Christianity sprang. It was not the Mystery Religions alone, or Gnostic speculation, which saw no necessary connection between spiritual excitement and moral aspiration, between ecstasy and ethics, between vast claims to have been initiated into divine secrets and being taught to tell the truth, to live purely, to do justly, love mercy, and walk humbly with God.

Much of pagan idolatry was inextricably associated with prostitution and drunkenness, with cruelty and fraud — as the titles of the gods and goddesses, and the fame of their shrines, sufficiently show. This is as true of Greece and Rome as of Egypt, Assyria, Babylon, or India. Paul's picture, in his letter to the Romans, of contemporary society in moral decay makes no accusation of widespread atheism, but rather blames a prevailing religiousness which had no ethical foundations. In Israel both lawyers and prophets had waged ceaseless war against this separation of religion from morality, exalting the glory of God in ethical terms — as holy, wise, good, the God of judgement and mercy —

and reiterating alongside every promise of divine blessing, every invitation of grace, the inescapable conditions of repentance, sincerity and obedience without which all blessing and grace must fail. John the Baptist reasserted this correlation of ethics and faith, and the Master Himself in sermon and parable, in epigram and example, bound the two together in an ethical faith and vision that settle the matter once and for always. It is true that in one great stream of Christian tradition ritual and asceticism seem sometimes to overshadow the importance of honesty, purity and love, as in the other "simple faith", or pride of spiritual knowledge, sometimes dispense with the moral requirements of the gospel. Yet both exaggerations are obvious departures from that identity of true faith with the holy living which Jesus demanded.

Paul drew the Christian conclusion without qualification or evasion: "the unrighteous will not inherit the kingdom of God . . . neither the immoral, nor idolaters, nor adulterers, nor homosexuals, nor thieves, nor the greedy, nor drunkards, nor revilers, nor robbers. . .". But the Bible's bluntest word upon the subject of religion and morality is this paragraph of John's. Here, the claim of some Gnostics that "their superior enlightenment placed them above the moral law, that they were neither the better for keeping it nor the worse for breaking it" (Plummer) is clearly in mind. John's reply is to provide a simple guide to the spiritual peerage, a useful handbook by which to assess all claims to possess divine ancestry — a spiritual "Who's Who"! "By this it may be seen who are the children of God, and who are the children of the devil: whoever does not do right is not of God, nor he who does not love his brother."

(a) To this end, various claims to spiritual status, experience, and lineage are here assembled, in what may be recognized at once as an especially "evangelical" terminology. Claims to "abide in him", to "have seen him", to "know the Lord", to be "righteous" (justified by faith), to be "born of God", "the children of God", to be "of God", — these are watchwords of gospel teaching in each generation. Such phrases lay the emphasis of Christianity, not upon social or personal morality, nor upon a chosen philosophic position, nor upon membership in a continuing Christian institution, nor upon the performance of required sacramental or liturgical acts, but expressly upon faith-attitudes and emotional experience, upon inward relationship to God, upon justification, new birth, and knowledge of Christ.

That such claims are near to the heart of New Testament

83

Christianity, and in harmony with Christ's own demand for repentance, and faith, and inward surrender to the rule of God, is scarcely open to question. Nor can it be doubted that all else in Christianity — morality, philosophy, Church-membership, sacrament or ritual — derive whatever value they possess from the "evangelical" experience of God. But here lies the difficulty. For this inward and spiritual experience is, of all things in Christianity, the most easily mistaken, the most frequently counterfeited. What *is* the proof that a man deeply and truly knows God?

Neither violent emotion, nor tears, nor the insistent and loud profession of faith, nor "signs following" in the shape of ecstatic "tongues", nor healings, nor physical convulsions, nor spasmodic penitence, nor indeed any observable evidence whatsoever, can guarantee a genuine experience of God's presence and power. Feeling and fervour alike can be dangerously misleading as "proofs" of spiritual life: Corinth possessed such manifestations more than most Churches, and needed badly to be taught more trustworthy judgments of what were genuine and what counterfeit "experiences".

Paul's "more excellent way" of assessing the presence of the Spirit was the way of Christlike love: John's test is twofold, righteousness and love. Only a divine quality of living *proves* that the life finding expression is of God.

(b) This, which ought to be self-evident to anyone with the Gospels in his hands, John argues from several grounds.

First: he establishes the principle that sin is not to be lightly dismissed as mere aberration, insignificant, morally unimportant. As Law well says, too often the sinfulness of sin is wrapped around with euphemisms and circumlocutions — but "all sins have sin in them: one little lie has in it that which would subvert the throne of God and extinguish the light of heaven". Sin is defiance of divine rule — *lawlessness* in a universe where, rightly, God's writ runs. Thus John exposes sin's nature from the side "on which its absolute antagonism to any fellowship with God appears most unrestrictedly" (Huther). Sin is an activity essentially anti-God and cannot be ignored, minimised, or explained away.

Second: tolerance of sin contradicts the purpose of the incarnation. "You know that he appeared to take away sins." The fundamental intention of God's act in Christ — to get rid of sin — rules out once and for all the weak acceptance of sinfulness in those who profess to be saved by His coming. "Indifference to sin, in whatever degree, on whatever pretext, is the direct negation of the whole purpose of Christ's mission . . ." (Law): one cannot accept Christ and oppose His purpose at the same time!

Third: in Christ Himself no sin is found, and the sinlessness of Jesus establishes the standard of Christian discipleship. His perfection makes carelessness in Christians a direct affront to the Lord they profess to love. That is why "no one who abides in him sins", and why "no one who sins has either seen him or known him".

Fourth: the profession of righteousness — "justification" by faith — demands, in all consistency, an actual righteousness of life, according to the standard of righteousness seen in Christ. To be "accounted righteous" by the mercy of God (which is to be "justified"), and to *be* righteous are not the same thing — else no sinner could ever be saved! Yet one cannot claim the righteousness of Christ —

> *Jesus, Thy blood and righteousness*
> *My beauty are, my glorious dress;*
> *Midst flaming worlds, with these arrayed,*
> *With joy shall lift up my head!*

— and at the same time practice unrighteousness! That would be to acknowledge the need of it, and deny the necessity of it at the same time. The "theoretic fallacy" is especially perilous here. For words, and most of all abstract words, exercise a subtle tyranny over the mind, and must be reduced to *things* before truth is served. *Righteousness* means actually doing whatever is right; *sin* is doing wrong. And Jesus Himself had said, "Unless your righteousness exceeds that of the scribes and Pharisees, you will never enter the kingdom of heaven".

Fifth: sin is of the devil — always has been! — "from the first" (Brooke). "The devil sins on principle", says Barclay. And "the reason the Son of God appeared was to destroy the works of the devil". He would break up and destroy "from its foundation the whole system and establishment of evil that dominates human life" (Law), and they who follow Him are committed to that cause. Christ undoes the work of Satan, and "sin undoes the work of Christ".

Sixth: — and incontestably — the child of God, having God's life (or nature, or seed) within him, cannot sin: all that is of God and all that belongs to sin are essentially and for ever opposed: what derives from God is holy, sinless, perfect — and God's life in us can never sin. "The divine nature, to whomsoever it is imparted, is righteousness; therefore the test of possessing it is *doing* righteousness" (Law). The new life-principle, the formative element of the new man and the determinative factor in the new life, being from God just does not sin! "Christians who sin forget themselves" (Gore). Whatever compromising, harmonising, or "realistic", hedging qualifications we wish to pile upon that stark statement, we need take care we do not end by blaming God — or God's life in us — for our failures to *be* what we *are*. There is a time when Paul's word is simple truth: "it is no more I that do it, but sin that dwelleth in me" — though we remain responsible for that indwelling sin, and for giving it opportunity. Yet when we are ourselves, truly children of the holy God, nourished and dominated by the divine life He has implanted through His word and Spirit — *then,* we cannot sin. To say we are often something else, and something far less, does not alter this truth — nor excuse us.

There is not much more that can be said about the Christian's sin than that! Sin is "simply inadmissible", says Findlay; when it occurs, it is simply inexcusable. By its own nature, by the incarnation, by the sinlessness of Jesus, by all the claims to righteousness, by the origin of sin in Satan and by the origin of our life in God — sin is intolerable. John's conclusion is proven six times over — "By this it may be seen who are the children of God, and who are the children whose life derives from the devil. Every one who does right is born of God (2:29); whoever does not do right is not of God". It's as simple as that.

(c) It is all very water-tight, logical, uncompromising. Yet the specious arguments that claim emotion, knowledge, "spiritual experience", as sufficient evidence of a divine work within the soul, and that depreciate the need of obedience, character, Christlikeness, must be remembered — and the ease with which, in so many sects and movements on the fringe of Christianity, ecstasy or visions, nervous convulsions and miracle-working, superior theosophy, or some unregulated intuitional "guidance" have been erected into proofs of grace.

It is all the more confusing because deep emotion, thrilling and creative insights, astonishing answers to prayer, wonderful experiences of divine healing, deepened spiritual understanding, and the certainty of divine direction of one's life, are all genuine and precious accompaniments of Christian salvation. The Christian life that lacks these things will be shallow and poor indeed. But the only sure, unchallengeable, unshakable proof of Christian grace is Christlike character. "To believe in Christ and to believe in sin, to love Christ and to love sin, to live in Christ and to live in sin, as one's element, is as unthinkable as that one should face north and south at the same moment" (Law).

The children of the divine family reveal their parentage by their quality. By this it may be seen who are the children of God. By their fruits you shall know them.

13: *Family Distinctions Pursued*

For this is the message which you have heard from the beginning, that we should love one another, and not be like Cain who was of the evil one and murdered his brother. And why did he murder him? Because his own deeds were evil and his brother's righteous. Do not wonder, brethren, that the world hates you. We know that we have passed out of death into life, because we love the brethren. He who does not love remains in death. Any one who hates his brother is a murderer, and you know that no murderer has eternal life abiding in him. By this we know love, that he laid down his life for us; and we ought to lay down our lives for the brethren. But if any one has the world's goods and sees his brother in need, yet closes his heart against him, how does God's love abide in him? Little children, let us not love in word or speech but in deed and in truth.   3:11-18*

Sin is lawlessness, and the essential law is that of love: so the sharp distinction between genuine and spurious just defined in terms of sin and righteousness is now redefined in terms of love and hate. A right relation to men supplements a right relation to God as evidence of true spiritual life. The claims examined are now somewhat differently expressed ("passing out of death into life . . . having eternal life . . . possessing God's love") but the vigorous practical test remains as first framed in "the original message"; unless it be met, self-assurance is mere self-deception. Once more, the seceders are not said explicitly to fail the test: but secession, jealousy of others' good, failure in loyalty and charity, speak for themselves.

* Notes on 3:11-18, pp. 251-253.

"WORDS, WORDS, MERE WORDS, no matter for the heart", complains Troilus. "Oaths are but words, and words but wind", retorts Butler. In an age of advertisements and propaganda distrust of eloquence is deepened a thousandfold. Especially, perhaps, in that wordy business, religion — so very liable to overflow in talk, evaporate in argument, and satisfy itself with learned definitions of high principles!

John's rigorous practicality protests, "let us not love in word or speech, but in deed and truth". His impatience with abstractions has already given a concrete content to the principle of righteousness by adding the defining clause "as He is righteous"; now he would define as plainly what the law is which true children of God obey. What else could it be, but the message heard from the beginning, that we should love one another?

Thus the distinctive family-likeness of the children of God is resolved, first, into a law-abiding, sin-hating obedience; and secondly, as its most fundamental expression, into love of the brethren. Love becomes the clearest demonstration, both to ourselves (14) and to others (15), that the claims we make are justified.

Christian love is, on the one hand, the plainest evidence that we possess *divine life* — have passed from the death of sin to life in God, enjoy already the life in Christ which is eternal. For the life which is given us by the Father in His Son is no empty "principle of spiritual existence", but *life* of a particular quality, whose very pulse is love. "In the cross of Christ we catch, focused in one vivid moment, the eternal quality of creative life", said Streeter, and this is John's point. Unless the divine life reveals in us its characteristic nature, we have no proof of its presence at all. He who does not love makes clear thereby exactly where he stands: he "remains in death".

Christian love is, on the other hand, the surest proof that we possess the *divine love*: for that, too, is self-evidencing within the soul that has received it, and its evidence lies in the creation of love — in love "shed abroad", as Paul says, within the heart. "The natural state of man is selfishness, which involves enmity to others whose claims clash with those of self: to love others proves that this natural state has been left behind" (Plummer). Consequently, "there is no clearer proof of the great transition from death to life than love of the brethren: but the absence of such love is not only the absence of such proof, it is the proof that the transition has not taken place" (Law).

This further test of where men stand is stated in clear contrast to two prevalent attitudes, each rooted in Gnosticism, and each still with us. One is a fanatical jealousy over religious differences that nourishes antagonism towards fellow-believers in the name of "convictions"; the other accepts theoretically the evangelical principle of love, but never gets beyond theological theory to living fact and daily charity.

(a) The former contrast, obviously relevant to John's overriding purpose to foster Christian fellowship, is the whole point of the sudden and odd reference to Cain and Abel. For the outstanding features of the Cain story are hatred between *brethren* and hatred engendered on *Religious* grounds. The address, "brethren" (in 3:13), as Westcott says, "contains an implicit argument", for it is precisely the rift within the Christian family which makes the readers' situation closely resemble that of the ancient fratricidal tragedy.

In this context, "hatred" and "murder" seem violently exaggerated terms. But to John's black-and-white mind the attitude of Christians who cut themselves off from fellowship with other Christians on grounds of intellectual pride and self-righteousness, amounts to a total denial of love just where, by all arguments, it ought to be affirmed. For this attitude John's word is hate, and for the identification of hatred with murder John has the overwhelming support of the Sermon on the Mount (Matthew 5:21-22).

The Cain story is extremely obscure, and shows every sign of having been revised by Jewish scholars in the interests of later Judaist ideas. But John's meaning is clear: the cause of this "brotherly hatred" lay in differences about worship and the jealous claim to superiority before God — "because his own deeds were evil and his brother's righteous". This archetype of all murder was — a religious dispute! To John's mind the situation in the Asian Churches, in which brother denied spiritual life and fellowship to brother, reflected precisely the same evil principle and deserved the same condemnation. If the Gnostic teachers already used the Cain story for their own purposes (as seems possible) then the use of this illustration is all the more apt. The sudden question "And why did he murder him?" has the air of a hackneyed topic of debate familiar to the readers. In any case John's point is plain: intellectual and spiritual pride that destroys brotherhood in Christ is — murder. Among the Asian Churches, every man belongs either to the circle of Cain

— with hate and death for company: or to the circle of Christ, and love, and life eternal.

John makes three comments on his own illustration. Cain is of the evil one, not born of God, or abiding in God, but one of the "children of the devil" (of verse 10). So are all Cainites. Secondly: it is an axiom of apostolic Christianity that no murderer has eternal life abiding in him. To deny life is to forfeit life (so Romans 1:28-32, Galatians 5:21, 1 Corinthians 6:9, 10). Thirdly: if we can meet such a spirit, of hatred and life-denial, among "Christian" brethren, what wonder is it if the world hates us! The world which is "not of God", but is "passing away", is scarcely likely to sympathise with Christians: "the moral descendants of Cain and of Abel are still in the world and the wicked still hate the righteous" (Plummer). As Westcott remarks, the hatred of the world is in a certain sense natural: but hatred may find place among the brethren — "there are Cains in the new family". Shall we expect unbelievers to treat us kindlier than professing fellow-Christians? This parenthesis on the inevitable dislike of the world for the Christian, besides sharpening the contrast with hatred among the brethren, prepares in the most subtle way for a point to be made later — the popularity of Gnostic teachers among those who are of the world! But John's immediate meaning is that love alone distinguishes the true children of God.

(b) The other contrast in which John sets this principle, the contrast between theoretic assent and practical charity, is likewise highly relevant to the readers' circumstances. Nothing, certainly, is wanting to their knowledge! *We know* the commandment that we love one another. *We know* that we have passed from the sphere of the world, with its darkness, its hatreds, its hastening doom, because we are found within the fellowship of God's children, and love the brethren — loyal membership of the apostolic community is itself evidence of spiritual life. And all this *we know* because we learned at Calvary not only the love God has for us, but the very meaning of love itself.

He laid down His life for us, and we plainly ought to lay down our lives for the brethren — not secede from them, denigrate them, cut them dead. The interpretation of the cross in terms of love, and the implied obligation that we in turn should love, are inseparable from any sound evangelical doctrine of the atonement. "All that Christ was and did says to men this one thing: 'Love one another'. . . . No one can learn the gospel without learning this" (Law). So there can be no question that the profession of love, in creed and promise, is required of well-instructed Christians.

But all this does not guarantee love within the heart. Only one thing does: that when we have this world's goods, ("enough to live on" — NEB), we shall not contemplate a brother's need with philosophic detachment, as did Gnosticism, but shall freely and at once open the floodgates of compassion — and one's hand and heart — toward him. It is of little use to believe great principles about giving one's life for the brethren if we will not even share with them the means to live! John will have nothing of lip-service, of abstract altruism: love *means* love-in-action. "We must above all beware of crediting to ourselves as love what is but the mouthing of well-sounding phrases, the play of imagination upon lofty ideals, or the thrill of merely emotional sympathies. We are apt to regard our appreciation of those ideals and our susceptibility to those emotions as entitling us to a high place in the moral scale — to feel as if we had paid every debt to love when we have praised its beauty, felt its charm, and experienced its sentiment" (Law).

So John scorns mere talk about loving and demands the deeds and truth of love as alone evidence of spiritual life. Exactly so had Jesus faced one who sought to inherit eternal life with the demand to sell — give — follow. Whatever professions of faith we make concerning the cross, however eloquently we portray the principle of vicarious love as the new basic thought of Christianity, it is in daily concern, gift, and attitude, towards all sorts and conditions of men, that we show how much we have understood, how deeply we have experienced, the love of God. We do not purchase salvation by charity, but we are not saved without it. To be forgiven much is to love much, and not to love is to abide in death: but to love is *to do*.

Thus the mutual loyalty of fellow-Christians, expressed in acts of fellow-feeling and concern, is exalted into a test of the reality of religious life. "The ethical criterion for 'religious experience' upon which the writer has insisted again and again, is made quite precise and grounded firmly in fundamental principles: charity is the touchstone" (Dodd). "By this all men will know that you are my disciples, if you have love one for another". And by this *we* know, too, that we have passed from death to life, because we love the brethren. It is doubtless equally clear to all who see aright that whoever has not love abides in death.

A solemn word for a divided Church!

14: *Spiritual Encouragement*

By this we shall know that we are of the truth, and reassure our hearts before him whenever our hearts condemn us; for God is greater than our hearts, and he knows everything. Beloved, if our hearts do not condemn us, we have confidence before God; and we receive from him whatever we ask, because we keep his commandments and do what pleases him. And this is his commandment, that we should believe in the name of his Son Jesus Christ and love one another, just as he has commanded us. All who keep his commandments abide in him, and he in them. And by this we know that he abides in us, by the Spirit which he has given us.   **3:19-24***

Who can confidently withstand John's uncompromising assertions of the ideal — uncondemned by his own heart? Yet confidence *is* possible. God is greater than our heart, more merciful in judgement than we sometimes are. And there are plain, straightforward questions to which we can without pride or faltering give honest answers, and so be reassured. No need, then, to run to the seceders for encouragement! Yet John's encouragements are given in terms that lend themselves to further elaboration of the issues at stake, so preparing for yet clearer exposition of apostolic truth.

RELIGIOUS CONTROVERSY IS ENJOYABLE for argumentative minds and pugnacious temperaments. It provides occasion for vigorous self-assertiveness and spirited contention which can yet be "justified" as valour for the truth, courageous defence

---

* Notes on 3:19-24, pp. 253-254.

of "principles". Among more tender, and perhaps more earnest, souls religious controversy is often the cause of very painful heart-searching, self-distrust, dismay. So the defection of once-trusted leaders and the loss of Christian friends inevitably unsettled John's readers, while the uncompromising rigour of his definitions and tests of spiritual genuineness must have constrained many of them to ask with the earlier disciples, "Who then can be saved?"

This is why the epistle is full of reminders, appeals, and reassurances, by which troubled hearts may be encouraged. The wistful hope of ultimate salvation which is all so many modern Christians possess, is not the prevailing tone of apostolic Christianity. Certainty, assurance, and abounding joy, mark their faith. In spite of all his ethical incisiveness, "we know" is a keynote of John's testimony no less than of Paul's, and the challenge of heresy, the claim of a spurious "religious experience", did not lead to any abatement of his certainty, but rather to its clearer affirmation. It was imperative — for mature character, for stout resistance to evil, for strong endurance, for strenuous evangelism — that believers tolerate no inward doubts, harbour no evil heart of unbelief, but reassure their hearts in confidence before God. It is imperative still.

Yet that reassurance will itself be only self-deception unless it be clearly and firmly based where alone confidence can safely build. Feelings, motions of the spirit, orthodox opinions, pugnacity of profession, all are insufficient evidence of grace when we seek reassurance about ourselves in the very presence of God. The heart knoweth its own misgivings, and the more earnest the wish to serve the Saviour, the more sensitive the conscience will be to the kind of self-examination John has been conducting. Far too often for spiritual comfort, "our hearts condemn us".

Such undermining misgivings would be reinforced, for many of John's readers, by their inward sympathies for those now revealed as "not of God", children of the devil, of the order of Cain. For though John has not condemned parties or individuals, the effect of his analysis is to define loyalties uncompromisingly.

In view of all such self-questioning, and every genuine self-doubt of earnest hearts, John first insists "how much kinder is God to us than we are willing to be to ourselves" — to borrow Anthony Trollope's phrase. "God is greater than our hearts" — greater in judgement and in mercy, in understanding and in love. We need sometimes to recall that "if we are faithless, He remains faithful, for He cannot deny Himself"; and that "there is therefore now no condemnation for those who are in Christ Jesus". "If God is for us, who is against us? . . . Who shall bring any charge against God's elect? It is God who justifies; who is to condemn?"

If proud hearts need humbling, and those who think they stand must take heed lest they fall, sometimes humble hearts need lifting up to the full assurance of faith, and hearts fearful and prone to fall need the gracious promise that "God shall make him stand". There is no sin in being downcast — but there is in want of faith: the only real defeat is in despair, and none need despair with a faithful, patient God.

Nor is this all. Law says: "The question under consideration is not one of merciful judgement, but solely one of *evidence* as to whether we are, or are not, 'of the truth'". But surely this is the essence of merciful judgement: that God, knowing all things, does not — like our accusing hearts — take notice only of the inconsistencies and failures, the battles lost, the weak evasions of our duty, the faltering faith: He takes note equally of the struggle and the attempting, the prayers and penitence and shame, the "going out into the night and weeping bitterly" that proves how passionate is the loyalty we yet cravenly denied.

No clearer illustration of John's meaning could be given than the unforgettable scene beside the lake when Jesus taxes Peter with threefold denial of his so proudly professed love — and Peter, grieving, appeals to *all* Christ knows — not the denials and the cowardice only, but the tears and the torment and the deep regret, and the love that longs to do better, that pleads for opportunity to try again. God, knowing all things, is fairer, and more merciful, than we are sometimes ready to believe. "The perfect knowledge which belongs to God", says Barclay beautifully, "is not our terror but our hope".

Yet might not even this, again, be self-delusion? Can we be sure that God's being greater than our hearts does not really mean that He sees through our self-encouragement and knows the secret faults behind the presumptuous assurance? John's answer is to list once more plain and practical tests by which we can examine ourselves, to see whether we are holding to the true faith.

(a) "By this", for example, by the deliberate doing of what is right (3:4-10) and the practical loving of the brethren (3:11-18), we can assess our own position. We know, without illusion or hypocrisy, whether the love of right is — or is not — a principle of our inmost striving, whatever our success. We know, without self-pretence, whether or not love prompts us to Christlike thought and action, however worthy of the prompting the final performance may be. If such impulses of righteousness and love arise within our nature, we may be sure they are not of us but of God; they are evidence that we have been born of the truth of the gospel, and that — to some extent at least — we are abiding in Him. The self-accusation of conscience is answered by the realistic confession that in us, in our flesh, dwells nothing good, that

> *Every virtue we possess,*
> *And every conflict won,*
> *And every thought of holiness,*
> *Are His alone,*

and that self-knowledge becomes our deep assurance that whatever of righteousness and love we find within us is proof of God's dealing with our hearts. Once more ethics, and not emotions, are the sign: we apply to ourselves the tests that earlier were proposed for others. And by the love of right, and of the brethren, which He has given us, we know — despite all failures in performance — that we are His.

(b) Another test is possible, for our own assurance only, and not for the examination of others: that we find prayer fruitful, and our requests acceptable with God. Our "confidence" — basically, again, freedom of speech — will most naturally express itself in prayer: and once more John's affirmation leaves us breathless: "we receive from Him whatever we ask."

Of course, John is not dealing with theoretic questions about the efficacy of prayer: he is counselling hurt and disturbed souls unsure of their own standing before God. Such have no thought of how much they can get from God, of how far they can stretch that "whatever we ask" to their own advantage. They remember to whom prayer is offered, on what conditions of obedience and faith, and in whose Name: they pray from hearts eager to be accepted with God. Such prayer prevails, in the sense that the heart set upon what God chooses, and prefacing its requests ever with "Hallowed be Thy Name, . . . Thy will be done", *cannot* be disappointed, whatever God's reply may be. Such find prayer infinitely rewarding, not simply for the specific answers it gets, but for what it *is,* the enjoyment of God's presence in the conversation of the soul.

96

"When a good conscience gives us boldness towards God, our prayers are granted, for children in such relations to their heavenly Father cannot ask anything which He will refuse" (Plummer). The same profound understanding of prayer, as proceeding from an obedient and abiding heart and therefore assured of answer, lies within the promise, "If you abide in me, and my words abide in you, ask whatever you will, and it shall be done for you. . . . Whatever you ask in my name, I will do it". When "the sole object of the believer is to do thoroughly the part which has been assigned to him, his petitions are directed to this end, and so are necessarily granted" (Westcott). The once-blind beggar of Jerusalem had seen this much: "If any one . . . does his will, God listens to him". Brooke cites a noble Jewish saying: "Do His will as if it were thine, that He may do thy will as if it were His".

The Christian who has approached this experience, even fitfully, knows assuredly that grace has been at work in him; he knows he has already received more divine favour than he can ever explain.

(c) Yet a third test of one's own spiritual standing is the will that delights to obey, the deep, earnest desire to please God. Perhaps John here only develops the thought implied in "By this" of verse 19, which looks back to the keeping of the commandments in 4:10; but it becomes a little more definite now, and more personal. This again is clear evidence of grace within the soul, even though weakness of will or confusion of mind makes our obedience uncertain, or immature. The *will* to obey is the crucial matter, though the confusion of mind need not be so great as we sometimes excuse.

For the twin commands here named, to believe greatly and to love sincerely, really cover the whole duty of the Christian man. To "believe in the name of his Son Jesus Christ" ("the full title is a compressed creed" [Westcott] and as Law suggests very probably a reminiscence of the baptismal formula, Acts 8:16, 19:5) and to love "just as he has commanded us", may be large and far-reaching ideals, but they are not obscure or perplexing. They coincide exactly with Paul's great definition of what "avails" with God: faith working through love. And we *know* whether we are anxious to obey these divine injunctions, or simply careless about them; we cannot really deceive ourselves as to whether we *want* to please God thus. We may be deeply disappointed that we do not more consistently succeed: but

"Lord, I believe — help Thou my unbelief" was a confession of *faith* acceptable with Christ, and Peter's dogged "Thou knowest that I love Thee" — asserting, still, great love alongside admission of great failure — was not spurned as hypocrisy, but accepted for what it is — the love that struggles with its own fears and weakness and will not give in.

And if the will to obey is present with us, then it is God who is at work in us "both to will and to work for his good pleasure." All who keep His commandments, honestly endeavouring to do His will and please His heart, surely abide in Him, and He in them (24). Feelings come and go: the *will* to obey still proves our standing in grace when fear and despondency undermine our confidence, and tears of penitence hide God's face.

(d) Almost as an afterthought John adds a fourth ground of reassurance: "We know that he abides in us, by the Spirit which he has given us," — *has given,* as a definite and memorable moment of our lives. Once again the last phrase of a paragraph strikes the spark which the following verses will fan to flame: for this experience of the Spirit again needs careful assessment. But possession of the Spirit, by whom our whole nature has been renewed, of whom answerable prayer is born, through whom the word brings life to the soul, by whose empowering Christian witness and work proceed, is John's fourth sure sign of divine favour. If there is any evidence at all of God's Spirit in our lives, then we know for certainty that God has begun His good work in us, and will perfect it until the day of Christ.

By the accepted principles of righteousness and love; by the experience of rewarding prayer; by the will to obey and possession of the Spirit, we can be sure that we are accepted with God. Yet none of these rests on our own merit, or deserving, or understanding — they rest on the grace of God toward us, on the work of God within us, on the wonder of the love and mercy that is far, far greater than our judgement of ourselves, and will not let us go.

So humbly, thankfully, we lift up our hearts.

15: *Criteria of Power*

Beloved, do not believe every spirit, but test the spirits to see whether they are of God; for many false prophets have gone out into the world. By this you know the Spirit of God: every spirit which confesses that Jesus Christ has come in the flesh is of God, and every spirit which does not confess Jesus is not of God. This is the spirit of antichrist, of which you heard that it was coming, and now it is in the world already. Little children, you are of God, and have overcome them; for he who is in you is greater than he who is in the world. They are of the world, therefore what they say is of the world, and the world listens to them. We are of God. Whoever knows God listens to us, and he who is not of God does not listen to us. By this we know the spirit of truth and the spirit of error.

4:1-6*

John has named last among the grounds of Christian reassurance the possession of the Spirit. But others also claim the same divine inspiration, and appeal to their "success" as evidence of their claim. It is necessary therefore to test all inspiration as to its origin and quality, and in proposing two such tests, John again plainly defines the basic theological difference between the apostolic churches and the seceding group, and sharpens beyond all compromise the dividing lines between "them" and "us". It is no longer "he that . . . whoever . . ." but "we are of God . . . they are of the world", while the confession that Jesus Christ has come in the flesh is shown to be the inescapable distinction between those who are of God and those whose inspiration is of antichrist. If the spirit in us makes this confession, it is of God and we know thereby that God abides in us (3:24b).

* Notes on 4:1-6, pp. 254-255.

THE PROBLEM OF POWER haunts evangelicals everywhere. Above all other divine gifts, we hunger for revival, a surge of spiritual energy that shall rekindle life at the heart of the Church and bring conviction, conversion and hope to a fretful and frightened world. Convinced that the gospel is the word for our time, we long for a fresh baptism of the Spirit who shall set the word free and drive the word home. We need the direct, divine inspiration which shall banish our fumbling, fearful attempts to speak a good word for Jesus and confer the unparalleled boldness, eloquence, authority, conviction and passion of Pentecost upon all who witness to the truth. We read enviously the stories of Wesley, Finney, Moody, Spurgeon, and the whole glorious line of silver-tongued advocates of grace, who could move hearts, win assent, break stubborn wills, and see lives transformed under the spell of the saving word. We covet earnestly such inspiration for ourselves.

And we covet success. Almost inevitably we measure power by numbers, by attendances at campaign rallies and audience-statistics for religious radio, by recorded conversions and congregational "constituencies" and denominational totals and the size of the pressure-groups accessible to our persuasion. Since the aim is a world for Christ, the enthronement of Jesus as Lord over all hearts and all realms of influence, it is hard to see how we can measure our progress by any other means than by estimating how far His name is known, by how many new lives His claim is being acknowledged.

Yet how perilous is the process! A political demagogue propagating some neo-pagan creed of materialism and greed, violence and revenge, will display a passionate eloquence, a personal conviction, an intellectual and emotional force that kindles in his followers a near-hysterical enthusiasm, such as few evangelists have attained. An ecclesiastical pontiff, wielding almost absolute authority by dogmatism and fear, can count his ardent followers in millions. A visionary* will produce an inspired translation of golden plates exhibited by an angel, and thereby persuade a quarter of a million to endure great hardship and establish a new frontier settlement. Some inner impulse in a mind deliberately made vacant, some manifestation assumed to be from beyond the grave, will evoke enormous generosity, costly and passionate propaganda.

The same techniques of psychological persuasion, the same deployment of emotional rhetoric, dogmatic repetition, uncritical

100 * Joseph Smith (Mormon)

suggestion, and disparagement of reason, will stir a racist mob or an evangelistic convention! And the same tests of popular appeal, audience reaction, nationwide "following" measure the success of a sales campaign, a political publicist, a television idol, a baseball team, or a "famous" preacher.

Clearly it is not enough to be inspired, or inspiring, to be passionate in manner or to catch the ear of the crowd, in order to prove oneself a true servant of the kingdom of God, endowed with His Spirit. The seceding teachers of John's day could lay claim to both credentials of power — persuasiveness and popularity. They had been leaders within the apostolic fellowship; they manifested abilities accepted as the valid apostolic gift of prophecy, speaking directly under the inspiration of the Spirit; they carried with them in their dissent a great following of eager admirers, and soon gathered about them many others who welcomed and responded to their advanced philosophic creed (verse 5). Inspired men with wide popular support: yet they were not of God.

The criteria of power must obviously be defined with care. Inspiration can come from many quarters — "Test for source!" "Do not believe every spirit, but test the spirits to see whether they are of God; for many false prophets have gone out into the world" — "men speaking apparently under an inspiration as real as that of any Christian prophet, and yet proclaiming doctrines . . . radically unchristian" (Dodd). A "spirit of error" is abroad, essentially antichristian, yet masquerading as the Spirit of truth and of God.

The claim of the pseudo-prophet faced Christianity from the first. The "wolf clothed as one of the flock", the false prophets who in the last days would "lead many astray", "false christs and false prophets" who would "show great signs and wonders, so as to lead astray, if possible, even the elect", occur among the warnings of Jesus Himself. Bar-Jesus, whom Paul found at Paphos, is described as "a magician, a Jewish false prophet". It is essential to realise that here the word "prophet" is not lightly used: it presupposes inspiration; and the hysterical cries induced by "seances" of certain pagan sects as evidence of divine "possession", are referred to in 1 Corinthians 12:2-3. Ecstatic, inspired utterance was an accepted sign of the presence of the Holy Spirit, both in the gift of "tongues" and in the ministry of the "prophets", who spoke forth in the Christian assemblies the mind and word of God concerning the affairs of the group. So, in the book of Revelation (16:13, 14; 19:20; 20:10) the false prophets of the

101

Roman Imperial religion are "demonic spirits, performing signs . . . deceiving. . .".

The implied problem of distinguishing false from true inspiration is defined in the Bible as early as Deuteronomy 13:1-5. There, a "prophet . . . or a dreamer of dreams" giving "a sign or a wonder" but counselling idolatry, is to be rejected forthwith. The test is the fundamental doctrine of Judaism — monotheistic faith — and by the truth the inspiration is to be judged. At Corinth, some were troubled because under (otherwise indistinguishable) inspiration, certain "prophets" — either beyond conscious control, or possibly in the synagogue next door (Acts 18:7), or at some pagan seance — cried out "Jesus is accursed" with all the earnestness and evidence of "possession" which the Christians themselves accepted as manifestations of the Spirit. Barclay well comments: "these perils came from the very fact that the early Church was so vividly and vitally alive". Paul's prescription is plain: apply the test of the original baptismal confession: "I want you to understand that no one speaking by the Spirit of God ever says 'Jesus be cursed!' and no one can say 'Jesus is Lord' except by the Holy Spirit". The fundamental doctrine of Christianity is the Lordship of Christ, and again by the truth the inspiration is to be judged.

And John's test is the same: the fundamental doctrine involved a true incarnation, and by this again the inspiration of the false prophets is exposed. "By this you know the Spirit of God . . . the spirit of truth and the spirit of error . . . the spirit of antichrist . . . every spirit which confesses that Jesus Christ has come in the flesh is of God, and every spirit which does not confess Jesus is not of God. This is the spirit of antichrist." John does not yet elaborate this decisive definition of the apostolic faith, the confession of a true incarnation of the divine in truly human form: but he affirms it with the utmost clarity as the fatal distinction between apostolic and seceding groups and between their respective inspiration. The confession of Christ is indeed the touchstone of everything truly Christian; by it all that pretends to divine authority may be sufficiently tested.

But if "inspired" eloquence, or manner, or personality, is no proof in itself of divine enduement, neither do popularity, success with crowds, effectiveness in the use of mass media of communication, provide any reliable criterion of true spiritual power. Jesus had said very plainly, "Woe to you when all men speak well of you, for so their fathers did to the false prophets" — condemning for all time every attempt to measure truth by counting heads, or spiritual success by the number of adherents gained. The seceding party, with their specious religious theosophy, was evidently exceedingly popular, and the smaller apostolic companies viewed with concern and probably with envy the "success" of those who had "gone out". The Pastoral Epistles, 2 Peter and Jude, show similar distress over the great popularity of distortions of the gospel, compared with the more limited appeal of the truth.

John's comment echoes Jesus. So far from popularity being any guarantee of truth, or index of real power, it is likelier to accompany falsehood. "They (the false teachers) are of the world, therefore what they say is of the world, and the world listens to them." The world loves to hear the echo of its own wisdom and ways; "success with the pagan public John could only regard as proof of a fundamental affinity with paganism" (Dodd); for "the world loveth its own". But what the world likes is not necessarily the truth of God: the voice of the people is — the voice of people!

This has an air of the grossest intellectual and spiritual snobbery: a self-justifying assumption that the excellent of the earth must be few — and we are among them! Yet remembering the high standards of John's statement of the gospel, can this be avoided? He who does not want the truth of God will go to no great inconvenience to attend where it is taught: the more searching the demands, the fewer who will be eager to meet them. The dictum of Jesus cannot be evaded: however desperately we long to see the crowds flock to our evangelical assemblies, it remains true that "the gate is narrow and the way is hard that leads to life, and those that find it are few".

It is not pride, but inescapable moral and intellectual principles, that make Christian minds suspect any appeal to popular success — the opinion of the majority — as the credential of divine truth and evidence of divine blessing. Christians cannot forget what the majority once shouted in Jerusalem! And the principles that give pause possess the highest authority: "If I tell the truth, why do you not believe me? He who is of God hears the words of God; the reason why you do not hear them is that you are not of God. . . . Every one that is of the truth hears my voice". Truth sifts its audience: "he who does what is true comes to the light" — and only they that have ears attuned will hear. It will sift John's readers, too: "We [apostles and those loyal to them] are of God" — you are too, if you accept that which was from the be-

103

ginning, the Christian message. As "the test of spirits lies in the witness to the incarnation", so "the test of men lies in the recognition of the truth" (Westcott).

If it be asked how, then, shall the multitudes ever be won and saved, John's answer is exhilarating. This is an issue, he says, between Christ and Antichrist, truth and falsehood, God and His enemy. Who can doubt where victory lies? "Little children, you are of God, and have overcome them; for he who is in you is greater than he who is in the world." Even now, "the darkness is passing away, and the true light is already shining". Already Christ has been manifested to destroy the works of the devil, and the young men are strong through the word of God, and have overcome the evil one. John is no pessimist. The world passes away, but he who does the will of God abides for ever.

Truth may be unpopular, but it will stand. Before it, all that is Antichrist will go down in final defeat. The God who is greater than our own accusing hearts in wisdom and in mercy, is greater also than the forces of error and falsehood in the world, that lead so many astray (3:20, 4:4). Already in principle, and in the readers' own resistance to heresy, truth has conquered: and they who are of the truth will live to rejoice in the victory of Christ.

16: *Love's Theology*

Beloved, let us love one another; for love is of God, and he who loves is born of God and knows God. He who does not love does not know God; for God is love. In this the love of God was made manifest among us, that God sent his only Son into the world, so that we might live through him. In this is love, not that we loved God but that he loved us and sent his Son to be the expiation for our sins. Beloved, if God so loved us, we also ought to love one another. No man has ever seen God; if we love one another, God abides in us and his love is perfected in us.   4:7-12*

John has been saying that one test of true inspiration by God's Spirit is loyalty — the loyalty that listens — towards those who are of God and who confess Jesus as Christ come in the flesh. That loyalty, at a Christian intensity, is love: and such loyal love among Christians is all the more necessary now that divisions are forcibly defined. The theological and experiential *necessity* of such love is therefore now ruthlessly asserted: only in those who themselves love is the saving purpose of God's love being achieved. Evangelical faith and active love are demonstrably inseparable: sound doctrine here marches with sound ethics or falls by the way! With almost aggressive clarity John pinpoints the two affirmations on which apostolic faith insists, as against the dissenting groups — a real incarnation and a really atoning death — and these comprise at once the fundamental evidence of the love of God for men and the unanswerable argument why men should love each other.

* Notes on 4:7-12, pp. 255-257.

ASKED BY A YOUNG LAWYER concerning the greatest —
most comprehensive — commandment in all religion, Jesus re-
plied "Thou shalt love. . .", and this remained unchallengeably
the law of Christ, His final injunction to those who followed Him,
and the basis of that last judgement of which He warned the
world.

Paul, having learned from Christ, makes love the fulfilling of
the whole law, deducing from it every moral obligation and attractive virtue. "Faith working by love" is the essence of what
"avails" in the gospel of Christ, and without love all that passes
for spiritual eminence — tongues, prophecy, knowledge, faith,
philanthropy, martyrdom — is profitless, an idle pretence.

The skilful analyst of Christian character who penned 2 Peter 1
made love the crowning stage of that moral development which
begins with faith's vision of the ideal in Christ and moves there-
after by a spiritual logic of its own towards the perfection of
life in Christlike love.

John, as we have seen, has emphasised more than once that
love is the sole dependable evidence that we have passed from
darkness to light, from death to life; that we are "of God", or
have God's love abiding in us. Now however John goes further
than all in interpreting Jesus. As, according to the Master, there
is no discipleship without love; as according to Paul, there is no
working faith, no experience of the Spirit, without love; as according to 2 Peter there is no growth in character without love; so
John here declares, without love there is no gospel — no gospel
believed, no gospel to be believed.

(a) Four sharply stated reasons support this contention. First,
that love is of God — derives from God. "The origin of love lies
beyond humanity" (Westcott). A balance of mutual interests,
or the compromise of competing selfishness, usually urged upon the
basis of "enlightened self-interest", is the nearest the unchristian
world can get to love. True love of man and woman is noble, and
at its best surely of God, who made us male and female; but its
natural and physical concomitants distinguish it — and parental
love, too — from the love which Christ commands. The splendid
love of friends, likewise, is involved with mutual attraction, the
recognition of worth and common enrichment: wonderful as it is,
it is yet something different from the Christian law. In Christian
eyes "the less we like an individual the more need there is to love
him" (Hasler). Love for the unlovely, and for the unloving, love
universal, prodigal, sacrificial, eternal, is something supranatural,

suprahuman, beyond the reach — even beyond the comprehension — of the unevangelised world. It is strictly and exclusively "of God", a manifestation of the divine nature, only found in the Christian gospel. "Human love is the moral nature of God incarnate in man" (Law).

It follows, secondly, that "he who loves is born of God". God's life and character necessarily manifest themselves in those who are His children. Like the former definition of who are born again, this follows from John's strongly realistic sense of what it means to derive one's life from God. Merely emotional, or intellectual, or doctrinal, or sacramentalist, or mystical conceptions of new birth will not satisfy John — nothing but the evidence that the divine quality of the new life is revealing itself in the daily conduct and bearing of the new-born. As God is righteous, they who do right are born of Him; as love is of the divine nature, so those possessing that nature will show it by loving.

Thirdly, and pressing the point yet further, John adopts the language most loved of his opponents. On the basis that "like is only known by like", John asserts there is no knowledge of God apart from love; and he stresses this pertinent argument both positively and (lest his readers fail to see its relevance to themselves) also negatively and exclusively. In the moral realm, insight and understanding wait upon sympathy and appreciation: only the forgiving understand forgiveness, only the merciful appreciate mercy, only to the pure is purity conceivable. And they alone know God who are willing to learn love, for the loveless heart has never understood what God is like. God's power, eternity, majesty, wisdom, judgement, may be perceived, and feared: but they will not be understood, and God Himself will not be known, except we love. "He who loves . . . knows God. He who does not love does not know God"; it is as plain as that.

For fourthly, most startling of all, John is prepared to say without qualification, that God is love. *That* is why love is divine, why to be born of God involves loving, and knowing God requires a loving mind. God *is* love: as love is a personal relationship, the statement assumes divine personality, and so includes the Gospel's declaration "God is Spirit"; as love worketh no ill, rejoiceth not in iniquity, fulfils the whole law, it is seen to be but the glow of beauty on the face of holiness — and so John's statement includes, again, the earlier affirmation that God is light. But Judaism and Greek philosophy had learned that God is Spirit; Judaism and Zoroastrianism had learned that God is light. Only

Christianity, lifting each statement in either hand into the radiance of the divine glory in the face of Jesus Christ, saw them coalesce in the profoundest of all religious affirmations — that one truth "worth all languages in earth or heaven" — God is love.

John means it is the nature and property of God to be merciful, bountiful, faithful, abounding in grace, over-flowing in loving-kindness, patience, and tender-heartedness, dealing with us in steadfast righteousness and strongly seeking ever our highest good. God is unlimited, immeasurable, and inexhaustible good will. Providence, forgiveness, comfort, redemption, are not things God does; they express what God is, and will ever be. Neil Alexander well quotes Dodd: "All God's activity is loving activity. If He creates, He creates in love; if He rules, He rules in love; if He judges, He judges in love". He cannot help it: for God is love.

So Christianity dares to proclaim in an age of unleashed power, of ruthless reason, of unsentimental science, in a world of impersonal forces and empty spaces and appalling dangers, that the heart of reality is — a heart, a pulse of everlasting mercy, a compassion infinite, exhaustless, almighty, and enduring. The gospel's answer to humanity's obsessive problems of anxiety, mortality and meaninglessness is short and simple: God is love.

(b) But that demands proof, and John offers it. "What God *is* is learned from what God *does*", says Neil Alexander; the divine nature has been manifested in human experience on the hard ground of the world's history. John "has nothing to say of that benevolent wisdom of God in Nature, of that ever-enduring mercy of God in History, that kindled the faith and adoration of Old Testament psalmists and prophets" (Law): "In this. . . . In this . . .", he says (9, 10), fearlessly affirming the incontrovertible facts about Jesus. In the incarnation, in the atonement, we *see* that God is love.

"In this the love of God was made manifest among us, that God sent his only Son into the world, so that we might live through him." All the wonder of the incarnation, of the divine-human life, of the Word made flesh, in perfect manhood enshrining total Godhead, and all the excitement and joy of its consequence, "that we might live", lie in that magnificent sentence. God has shown that He is love in Christ's life-quickening presence among us. . . .

And more: "In this is love, not that we loved God but that he loved us and sent his Son to be the expiation for our sins". So exactly Paul argues for the Father's love from the Son's death — commending God's love to us. The atonement, no less

than the incarnation, makes plain God's love, and again, as in the
incarnation, it is manifested for a purpose — the expiation of
sins. That we might have life — that we might be forgiven:
these are the objectives that motivate the divine self-revelation;
God seeks not His own glory but our salvation — and that is the
essence of divine love.

"Not that we loved God". John insists that the initiative is
God's. Love (again) originates in God, and the meaning of
love must therefore be deduced from divine action and not from
its pale imitation in human hearts — "God's love to us, the over-
arching sky", and ours to Him "merely its reflection on the still
surface of the lake" (Law). This is John's high theology —
"agapology" — the divine nature self-revealed in the divine intervention at Bethlehem and Calvary for lifeless, sinful men, and
communicated to those whose answering love is evidence of their
rebirth and knowledge of God; and it provides the premise for
John's great argument for loyalty among Christians.

For — and the significance of this cannot be exaggerated —
it is high evangelical *theology*, defining the nature of God, the
identity of will between Father and Son, the meaning of the incarnation, the purpose of the atonement, the ethical significance
of regeneration, the communication of life and forgiveness through
expiation, the presuppositions of the knowledge of God, and the
true relation of gospel and ethics, but it is all affirmed, interpreted, made experientially real, only in the life of love. All is
made to turn upon love seen and received, manifested and imi-
tated. Failing this, nothing at all is known of God, that is
distinctively Christian.

In fact: No love — no gospel.

(c) The evangelical imperative follows by such clear necessity
from this evangelical indicative, as scarcely to need stating.
"Beloved (recipients of love), if God so loved us, we also ought
to love one another." G. S. Barrett observes, "We should rather
have thought that he would have gone on to say 'we ought also to
love Him', but he does not". The claim to divine vision and advanced knowledge (as made by the Gnostics and all theosophists)
is spurious: the height of human attainment in spiritual life is to
know God dwelling in us; not "seeing God" — for none has seen
Him — but having God abiding in us. And since God is love,
God's indwelling means love abiding in us, the divine life and
nature finding expression in our love one for another.

When this is accomplished, all the purpose of the gospel is

achieved; God's love itself reaches its perfect and glorious goal.
For it is the nature of love to pour itself out for others, and it rests
not until it has reproduced itself in those it loves. When through
our love for one another within the Christian fellowship — and
beyond it — the divine love manifested in Christ (4:9, 10), defined
in Christ (3:16), and bestowed in Christ (3:1) is also communicated among Christians, the very heart of God is satisfied: "His
love is perfected", reaches its destined perfection, "in us".

17: *Christian Assurance*

> By this we know that we abide in him and he in us, because
> he has given us of his own Spirit. And we have seen and testify
> that the Father has sent his Son as the Saviour of the world.
> Whoever confesses that Jesus is the Son of God, God abides in
> him, and he in God. So we know and believe the love God has
> for us. God is love, and he who abides in love abides in God,
> and God abides in him. In this is love perfected with us, that we
> may have confidence for the day of judgement, because as he
> is so are we in this world. There is no fear in love, but per-
> fect love casts out fear. For fear has to do with punishment,
> and he who fears is not perfected in love. We love, because
> he first loved us.   4:13-19

Theological statement needs ever to be checked by spiritual experience:
the teaching may be cogent, but how do we know that it is *true?*
John therefore supplements the doctrinal presentation of love's
imperative — the revelation of the nature of God in the incarnation and atonement — with an experiential argument, to the effect
that all our life in God is one of love, assured and fearless; so we
know, as well as believe, that God is love; and so too we love —
because we are so truly loved.

LITTLE-FAITH DWELT IN THE TOWN OF SINCERE, and
his "mind was upon things divine", but he was brutally attacked
by three brothers, Faint-heart, Mistrust, and Guilt, and robbed
of all his spending-money, leaving him "scarce enough to bring

* Notes on 4:13-19, pp. 257-259.

111

him to his journey's end. . . . He was forced to beg . . . and scattered almost all the rest of the way nothing but doleful and bitter complaints." Yet Christian defends him kindly.

Mr. Fearing, too, "had the root of the matter in him", but, said gentle Great-heart, "he was one of the most troublesome pilgrims that ever I met with in all my days. . . . Why.he was always afraid that he might come short of whither he had a desire to go. Everything frightened him . . . he lay aroaring at the Slough of Despond about a month together . . . stumbled at every straw. He had, I think, a Slough of Despond in his mind . . ." — and much else. Bunyan has great fun with him. But the refrain of the story is significant: "he would not go back", and though "the water stood in his eyes" and he would "often sigh aloud", yet "my Lord carried it wonderfully lovingly to him. There were but few good bits at the table but some of it was laid upon his trencher. . . . The valley of the Shadow was as quiet while he went through it as ever I knew it before or since", and when Mr. Fearing came at last to the River, "the water of that river was lower at this time than I ever saw it in all my life. . . . He was well at the last".

Coming out of the heart of Puritan evangelicalism, that is choice. The evangelical faith has laid much emphasis upon a present assurance of salvation: it builds upon a conscious "gospel experience", a sense of redemption accomplished, a vivid confidence in the operation of the Holy Spirit within the heart. Doubt, misgiving, hesitation, tend to be condemned as want of faith, or shallowness of life. One ought to be sure — to *know* — not only that God is love, and that the incarnation and the cross prove His love, but also that one is, for a blessed certainty, safe within that love. One of the most penetrating criticisms that evangelicals offer of more "Catholic" interpretations of Christianity, with their emphasis upon asceticism, discipline, penance, and sacramental mediation of grace, is that such dependence upon human effort robs salvation of all present assurance, confidence, and joy. As in Judaism, indeed as with every religion of "works", none can know he is saved: the gospel ceases to be "good news" and descends instead to "great exhortations". And the enormous ethical, emotional, and enduring power of apostolic Christianity has then evaporated.

It is of course right that Little-faith and Mr. Fearing should be gently dealt with: but Christ offers assurance, and to that assurance John turns as proving subjectively — within the individual heart — the truth of the theology of love which he has been expounding.

(i) *The bases of assurance* are three: the experience of the Spirit, the experience of history, and the remembered (baptismal) confession. *By this we know* that we abide in Him and He in us, first because He has given us of His own Spirit; secondly because we have seen and testify that the Father sent the Son; thirdly because whoever confesses that Jesus is the Son of God, God abides in him and he in God.

As to the first basis of assurance it must be recalled (as at 4:1) that the evidence of the Spirit in the early Church was not purely emotional, but also visible and audible in signs and wonders, tongues and prophecy — as tested by loyalty to apostolic truth. This evidence may appear more cogent for John's readers than for us, but it is not so. Taught by the New Testament itself we value more the moral and spiritual evidence of the work of the Spirit within ourselves, in the new appetite for spiritual things, in the desire for prayer as much as in the answers to prayer, in the anxiety for assurance (which certainly no unbeliever suffers), in the consciousness of new standards of conduct, new promptings and obligations concerning things one ought to do or to avoid, a new conscientiousness, new hope, and new joy. These are not self-creating, nor illusory, any more than tongues or ecstasy: they are real factors comprising a new quality of life, and sure evidence that the Spirit of Jesus is dealing with us in love — that "the Spirit is given us".

As to the second basis of assurance — the experience of history, we must note that what we have called "the fingertip certainty of first-hand experience" of the historic Jesus — never far from John's mind — was not a matter of merely individual memories, but (as C. H. Dodd persuasively argues) of the corporate memory of the living Church. The historic foundation lies in that which *we* have seen and heard; *we* have seen and *we* testify — together, with all the saints stretching backwards to the beginning. Nor is this simply witness of record and recall: it is a sharing of *experienced* fact — not just that Jesus lived, but that He was the Saviour of the world. So we not only "have seen", we "testify", adding the confirmation of spiritual experience to the message we have heard from others.

This again offers assurance, for a man must know whether or not he stands within that saving tradition that springs from Bethlehem, Nazareth, and Calvary. If he does so, then all the accumulated certainty of unalterable historic events, and of the historic community of believers fashioned and sustained thereby, stands behind his individual faith. This argument, also, from personal experience of the historic Jesus, might again be thought to be more cogent for John's readers than for us. But it is not so. What the historic basis of assurance loses for us in vividness and immediacy through the distance of time, it gains immeasurably in force and authority by being so extended and multiplied in the experience of the world-wide Church.

As to the third basis of assurance, the remembered (baptismal) confession, we must again bear in mind that the decisive admission which made a man a Christian, from Caesarea onwards, was the admission that Jesus is the Son of God, Lord, Christ; that in days of persecution and personal loss, this confession was not lightly and insincerely made; that it was early regarded as evidence of the Spirit's dealing with the soul (1 Corinthians 12:3), and that the normal moment in spiritual development for it to be made was baptism. It is true that John's opponents also had been baptised, making the confession, but John would be content to say: if they still hold to what they then confessed, they too have Christian assurance; if however (as appears) they now deny what they once confessed, their assurance is dissipated; they are not of God, and may know that they are not by this betrayal of their baptismal vows.

It is told of Luther that in moments of extreme anguish of soul and tormenting doubt, he would scrawl across his writing table, as a kind of defiance of the devil, '*I was* baptised'. True or not, the story usefully illustrates the kind of exterior assurance to which sometimes a troubled soul may cling, the memory of a solemn spiritual hour when all heaven seemed near, when faith soared to certainty, when the soul registered its conviction about Christ in deliberate confession and vow, and friends shared our joy. Whatever inward shakings may later come to us, nothing can take away this fact of our experience — we have stood, ourselves, with Jesus in baptism and have known that we are His. And only Christ could have brought us to do that.

It is impossible to ask greater assurance than this threefold certainty. To possess evidence of the Spirit's dealing with one's own heart; to know that one stands within the shared, historic tradition that runs back unbroken to Jesus and Galilee; to know that one has been led, at some ineradicable point of personal experience, by the saving grace of God, to the open avowal of faith in Christ, in accordance with His example and command: this is to possess a confidence that makes no claim to spiritual attainment, no comparison with others, but is utterly sure of Christ — and of one's own inexplicable share in the grace that saves.

(ii) *The content of Christian assurance* must not be extended to cover all the range of personal religious opinions that seem to us important! "So we know and believe the love God has for us. God is love, and he who abides in love abides in God, and God abides in him." John has offered assurance on other points also — that we "know Him", are "in the light", and "have passed from death to life", for example: but all these follow directly from the pure essence of the gospel which John here distils, the love of God and our place within it.

The gospel cannot be reduced to greater brevity. Even so, John is compelled to elaborate once each element of this prime axiom of Christianity. "The love of God" includes both His attitude ("the love God has for us"), and His nature ("God is love"); our place within that love includes both God dwelling in us and our dwelling in God. Thus John admirably concludes (verse 16) his whole discussion (from 3:19 onwards), and defines the precise truths upon which history (the incarnation and atonement) and experience (our possession of the Spirit, our testimony, and our baptismal confession) converge with strong assurance. We both know theologically and believe experientially that God is love, and loves us. The area of absolute certainty is small, but the depth of that certainty beyond disturbance.

And it is sufficient. When the heart's anxiety is really in earnest, and not just argumentative, or self-pitying, or indulging in self-tribulation mistaken for deep "spirituality" — that "minute inquisition of the religious affections" by which sometimes we seek to assure ourselves that we are making progress — then to know God loves is enough. That God is for us, in all circumstances, against all enemies, in face of all needs, in answer to all accusations and despondency, is sufficient for courage, for hope, and for great endurance.

(iii) *The fruit of assurance* is that special kind of confidence to which John has already referred, the frank fearlessness which was a mark of Christian life in the first century. John has earlier mentioned our seeking such confidence before Christ at His coming (2:28) and before God's inward judgement (3:21); he will presently speak of similar boldness in prayer (5:14). Here, perhaps, this confident boldness faces its severest test, the day of the final judgement of God.

It is true that "John writes in accord with current Jewish thought regarding the last things, the return of Jesus to the world for the effective establishment of God's kingdom and the future judgement of men to determine who were fit to share in its glory"; and that he "spiritualises" existing ideas — eternal life is a present experience, Christ is already present in the world through the Spirit, there is a contemporaneous judgement in process as men respond to the gospel. But nothing John writes throws doubt upon Christ's future visible return and a final judgement. For John the advent is "not the arrival of one who is absent, but the self-revealing ('manifestation') of one who is present", and the judgement likewise is but the final culmination of a continuous process. Both are real and certain events for which the Christian heart is prepared by that fearless confidence which springs from Christian assurance.

"There are only two motives that rule men in regard to God", says Alexander Maclaren, "only two emotions, either love or fear. There is nothing between the two. Love, liberty and joy are on the one side; fear, . . . issuing in torment, on the other." That exactly expresses John's thought. Fear is the motive power of paganism, and for that matter of a decayed and superstitious Christianity; dread of divine displeasure is the secret of its influence, fearfulness its prevailing emotional tone, and awe, asceticism and heartbreaking penance — like that of the *Miserere* — its highest religious expression. This is hardly the joyous discovery to which men are invited in the Gospels.

No one will deny that fear is among the most powerful motive forces, and one of the constant factors in human progress. Fear is the mother of caution, and so warns, preserves, and protects; it is also a potent spur to preventive action. No religion is healthy that has not somewhere within it that sober and persistent fear of the Lord which is, in every realm, the beginning of wisdom. "Even the love of God has room in its heart for the fear of God," says G. S. Barrett: to which Barclay adds the fine defining phrase "the fear of grieving the love which so loved us". But a religion which possesses no other spring of action, or which makes fear its foundation, will never be enjoyed. Whatever the correct translation of John's phrase, it is certain that "fear hath torment" — it is ever overshadowed by the pain of deserved punishment. Nor will such a religion ever be creative: fear tends more to discipline

116

and paralysis than to inspiration and experiment. Most serious indictment of all, fear cannot generate love, or even sympathy, tenderness, compassion. One cannot scare men into tolerance, or terrify into kindliness! Distrust, suspicion, resentment are fear's natural offspring. And a religion essentially joyless, fruitless and loveless is at least sub-Christian!

Against the lovelessness of fear John sets the fearlessness of love, and in place of the anxious, self-tormenting endeavour to placate God, the response of loving, confident hearts to a love already shown and shared. We *love,* says John — we do not live by fear; and we love because He first loved us. Christianity has foundations utterly different from those of pagan religion; it makes a different appeal, lives in another key. The nerve of the gospel is love's initiative responded to by love. Where threat of punishment, fear of judgement, produces at best a docile and tense restraint, God's declaration of love through Christ produces love in us, and with it liberty of spirit, joy of heart, and all assurance.

So the Christian whose life remains shadowed and sombre because of some unresolved dread of God "is not made perfect in love". Again Christ's example is determinative. Jesus "dwelt in love": He walked in perfect understanding, confidence, and fearless love toward God, obeying and enjoying God in complete freedom of soul. And "as He is, so are we in the world". Jesus too faced judgement, the judgement of men, the awful judgement of the cross: yet His relationship with the Father was never less than the perfect confidence of love. To us also — amazingly — it is given to walk and work and wait with God in that Christlike freedom and fearlessness of perfect trust. We too live by love.

Only, we must really live by love, and that means loving the brethren. There is no assurance for the loveless heart! But that is John's next point.

18: *Love's Arguments*

> If any one says, "I love God", and hates his brother, he is a liar; for he who does not love his brother whom he has seen, cannot love God whom he has not seen. And this commandment we have from him, that he who loves God should love his brother also. Every one who believes that Jesus is the Christ is a child of God, and every one who loves the parent loves the child. By this we know that we love the children of God, when we love God and obey his commandments. For this is the love of God, that we keep his commandments.   4:20 — 5:3a*

John's insistence upon love as the distinguishing mark of apostolic Christianity, resting firstly upon theological and secondly upon experiential foundations, has underpinned the supreme imperative of 4:7 — "let us love one another" — and so has furthered the declared purpose of the open letter, to foster fellowship. But in all such discussions, terms easily become vague, and the logic academic. John therefore once more drags the whole argument down to earth: to talk about loving God while hating one's brother is sheer falsehood! The epistle's teaching about love is therefore brought to a close with several searching, unanswerable, single-sentence thrusts. (The connection of thought with both preceding and following ideas is so very close that isolation of this paragraph is almost indefensible, and at best a matter of simple convenience.)

"THERE IS NO ASSURANCE for the loveless heart": even in a passage designed expressly to stabilize faith and encourage waverers, John cannot pretend. It is good to say "We live by love",

---

* Notes on 4:20 — 5:3a, pp. 259-261.

but nothing is easier to talk sheer nonsense about than the love of God. Love for God is evidenced only by love for man. If we are to find confidence by living in love, we must scrupulously remember that Christian love has always been a *triangular* relationship, involving necessarily God, myself, and my brother.

So, to the man out of fellowship with his brethren; to the man who nurses revenge, or spite, or contempt, or simple indifference, towards other Christians; to the man whose assumption of intellectual superiority makes him careless of others' needs, opinions, feelings, and faith, John offers no encouragement. For such, spiritual reassurance is mere make-believe — sheer self-deception. "If any one says, 'I love God'" — as the seceders certainly would say; even if he adds, "I have the Spirit, I believe, I was baptised and made the great confession" — the grounds of Christian assurance which John has just recited — and at the same time he hates his brother, then he is "a liar". John has no patience with self-satisfied assurance of acceptance with God that has no confirmation in character and conduct. In the last resort, only the merciful are sure of mercy, only the forgiving show evidence of forgiveness, and only the loving heart may consistently live in the fearless love of God. So, for the last time, John urgently presses the utter necessity of a loving loyalty between Christian men.

(i) *We must love the brethren,* if we love God, from the very nature of things. God is invisible: man is within sight and within reach. "He who does not love his brother whom he has seen, cannot love God whom he has not seen." An eccentric argument may be developed — indeed, it has been pursued — whether it is easier to love someone whom we have never met, or someone we have met and have disliked! But the question is surely foreign to the meaning of Christian love, which has nothing to do with liking people, or the recognition of intrinsic merit. Nor is it very relevant to stress that the Christian has his brethren continually before his eyes (so Plummer), as though God were but an intermittent Visitor to the soul. It is true that "he who fails to see God as He is revealed in his brother will even more surely fail to love God" (G. S. Barrett), but that is not what John says. Neither is it John's point that "the only way to prove that we love God is to love the men whom God loves" (Barclay).

Law comments, "Your brother is in sight, and when you will you may do him good. But God is invisible; your beneficence, your sympathy, cannot reach unto Him who is the bearer of all burdens, the giver of all good gifts. In the nature of the case there is no other medium through which our love to God . . . can be realised than by loving our brother". In similar vein Milton:

> *God doth not need*
> *Either man's work or his own gifts. . . .*
>
> *His state*
> *Is kingly. . . .*

and though this gives an extended meaning to "invisible" it is close to John's intention. Whether his words be question ("How can he love God?") or statement ("he cannot love God") they concern the practical content of such love. Do we love God by sitting alone for forty years on the top of a pillar? or by shutting ourselves away from God's creatures and the needs of the world in solitary contemplation? or even by songs and prayers and acts of worship in themselves? John's rigorous impatience with abstractions would demand concerning love for God what he has already demanded concerning love for men — "Let us not love in words, or in mere talk!" But what *is* love for God?

Micah's definition of the Lord's requirements began with justice and mercy. Isaiah demanded the worship that is strong champion to the oppressed, and gentle to the weak. James begins his definition of true religion with the visiting of the fatherless and widow in their affliction. And Jesus explicitly defines love toward Himself in the words "inasmuch as ye visit . . . feed . . . befriend . . . clothe . . . the least of these my brethren". John stands therefore in august company, and speaks with highest authority, when he argues that there is no meaning in love for God apart from love of the brethren. *How* — in what precise ways — can a man love God, other than this?

(ii) *John's second argument* likewise gathers into itself the authority of Jesus, together with all the appeal which His words and memory exercise over Christian hearts: "This commandment we have from him, that he who loves God should love his brother also". An air of finality, even of impatience, is in John's phrase; this the Master said — what more can anyone want? What the Master coupled together, let no man put asunder! Westcott stresses that the Greek particle points to the purpose, the aim, of the commandment (and not simply to its content), as something Jesus especially desired to see in those who followed

Him. To this John adds no further reason — no explanation why Jesus so coupled together love for God and love for man — for him it is enough that Jesus did so. But since he places this all-sufficient argument second and not first, it is evident that to John's mind the command of Jesus somehow bears out the point about God's invisibility and man's obviousness. To love one's brother is necessary to make love for God intelligible: the "second" commandment is required to make the "first" comprehensible: Jesus Himself said so!

(iii) *Nevertheless John is prepared* to appeal to considerations wider than those of reverence for Christ. "Love me, love my child" is a universal principle, and so is "offend my child and you make an enemy of me!" Every birth is into a family circle — even where it is confined to mother and child — and so into a set of obligations, privileges and relationships. We begin life as members of a community, in the divine family no less than in the human: every Christian (that is, by John's trenchant definition, every one who believes that Jesus is the Christ) is at once child of God and brother to all God's other children. And the inescapable principle applies: "Love God, love His children"; when we love God and obey His commandments, we love all members of His family.

This is more than emphatic reiteration: John's implication is that the plainest common sense and natural feeling would realise this obligation if specious theorising and intellectual conceit had not clouded the conscience. To deny one's duty towards fellow Christians (as in practice the seceders did) was to deny also the relationship which created it. A common faith in Christ created the family of sons: the family bond is love: to sever the bond is to dissolve the relationship, contract out of the family, and forego all spiritual sonship. For men so proud of their spiritual standing before God, the argument could scarcely be more forceful.

(iv) *And love's fourth argument* is equally cogent and far-reaching. It returns upon the second — the Master's commanding of love towards God and towards one's brother-neighbour — but it generalises the underlying principle in the widest possible way. "This is the love of God, that we actively perform all that He commands."

There speaks the whole spirit of the Old Testament, in law, priesthood and prophets alike. Indeed, there speaks all ethical religion. Love *is* obedience.

"Has the Lord as great delight in burnt offerings
and sacrifices
as in obeying the voice of the Lord?
Behold, to obey is better than sacrifice,
and to hearken than the fat of rams. . ."

says a prophet to a king.

"To do righteousness and justice
is more acceptable to the Lord than sacrifice"

comments a wise man. To worship is to "bow down" before
authority having the right to command, and to give thanks to a
holy love that seeks only man's perfection, and is therefore a delight to obey. Devotion is the ardent will to please One infinitely
worth pleasing, and love to God is an empty religious emotion until
it is harnessed to deliberate dedication, so that heart and soul and
mind and strength are laid under tribute for its service. So Jesus
had said of love towards Himself, "If you love me, you will keep
my commandments" — love is obedience; "He who has my commandments and keeps them, he it is who loves me" — obedience
is love. Many and various are the things that have passed for
religious devotion in the long story of man's spiritual pilgrimage:
John's epigram is the final word, this is the love of God, that we
do His commandments.

But if, with the lawyer of the Gospels, we enquire what is the
greatest of all His commandments, we shall receive the same reply
— to love God and one's neighbour: which in the context of John's
immediate problems and purpose, means first (though not exclusively) to love God and your fellow Christian. There is no devotion without that obedience.

This is John's last word about love. He could hardly say more.
He who hates his brother is lost in darkness (2:7-11); he who does
not love his brother is not of God (3:10); he is of the breed of
Cain (3:11-12); and is abiding in death (3:14). Love is *known*
in the death of Christ, and its obligation flows from that event
(3:15-16); Christian theology (4:7-12) and Christian experience
(4:13-16) alike demonstrate that God Himself is love and the
origin of all love between Christian brethren. Love is divine
(4:7). Brotherly love alone gives meaning to the love of God;
love is what Jesus desired and commanded; our membership in
the divine family involves it, and all godliness implies it (4:20—
5:3).

Because God Himself is love.

OPEN LETTER TO EVANGELICALS

19: *Faith's Basis and Benefits*

And his commandments are not burdensome. For whatever is born of God overcomes the world; and this is the victory that overcomes the world, our faith. Who is it that overcomes the world but he who believes that Jesus is the Son of God? This is he who came by water and blood, Jesus Christ, not with the water only but with the water and the blood. And the Spirit is the witness, because the Spirit is the truth. There are three witnesses, the Spirit, the water, and the blood; and these three agree. If we receive the testimony of men, the testimony of God is greater; for this is the testimony of God that he has borne witness to his Son. He who believes in the Son of God has the testimony in himself. He who does not believe God, has made him a liar, because he has not believed in the testimony that God has borne to his Son. And this is the testimony, that God gave us eternal life, and this life is in his Son. He who has the Son has life; he who has not the Son has not life.

5:3b-12*

The oblique, unprovocative approach of the first chapters now gives place to entirely unambiguous directness and inescapable definition. Presenting love's arguments led John to define the Christian as believer, child of God, and set under divine commandments: he now adds the comment that the commandments are not burdensome when a true faith lifts us above all opposition and imparts a life essentially victorious. True faith is then again defined, its bases and its benefits expounded, and the final issue ruthlessly exposed: to possess the Son (as apostolic faith does) is to possess eternal life; to deny the Son (as the seceders do) is to call God a liar and forfeit the life God gives in Him.

* Notes on 5:3b-12, pp. 261-263.

FAITH, BELIEF ARE SCARCELY MENTIONED in John's epistle. Remembering the primacy of faith in the apostolic gospel (and the 94 references in the Fourth Gospel against the epistle's nine) it is impossible to doubt that up to this final paragraph of controversy John has been deliberately avoiding the words, while multiplying significant synonyms. John's opponents claimed a more mature faith, a deeper, more intelligent belief, than they ascribed to apostolic Christians. To use the words without definition would therefore have been confusing; to define them earlier would have been provocative; now for the last time the issues must be stated, meanings all cleared up, and the benefits, the content, and the foundations of apostolic faith bluntly asserted in the face of Gnostic denial.

(i) *The importance of true belief* is shown by the benefits attending it: every one who believes is born of God, overcomes the world, finds obedience no burden, and enjoys eternal life.

Nothing is here said of the precise relation between belief and divine birth except that they coincide. But the entire representation not only of Johannine Christianity but of the whole New Testament makes belief in Christ the crucial pre-condition of every salvation-gift and privilege. The call of Christ to repent and believe; the invitation of the apostolic Church to believe on the Lord, Jesus Christ, and so be saved; the whole basis of Pauline teaching, and of Hebrews, and 1 Peter, are equally insistent that faith in Jesus is the means of salvation. In Johannine thought, the power to become children of God, freedom from condemnation, and eternal life are all given to those who believe: the Fourth Gospel is written "that you may believe that Jesus is the Christ, the Son of God, and that believing you may have life through his name".

And this is the teaching of the epistle also. It is God's commandment that we believe in the name of His Son, and everyone who believes is born of God. The cruciality of faith is presupposed by the whole argument of the letter that in departing from apostolic belief the dissentient groups have forfeited (or proved they never really possessed) the blessings of the gospel. There is no question therefore that John means that by faith in Jesus as the Christ men become children of God.

This is the highest benefit John can conceive the gospel conferring upon men — that men should be called, and should be, children of God (3:1), possessing the divine nature (3:9), sharing the one divine life (5:11, 12) and set within the divine family and the pattern of loyalties which that family-life creates (5:1, 2). As

"Son" is the loftiest title John can apply to Jesus, so sonship is the supreme privilege he can affirm of *believers* — and it carries within itself every other gift of grace.

Among such gifts is victory. By faith we are delivered from the hostile world: "whatever is born of God overcomes the world", and John asks, "Who else ever does?". This victory is ours partly because by new birth we are raised to a level of experience beyond the world's enmity or reach (5:5). Partly, too, it follows from appropriation of the victory of Christ (John 16:33). "The world did its worst to Jesus. It hunted Him and hounded Him and slandered Him. It branded Him heretic and sinner and friend of sinners. It judged Him and tried Him and crucified Him and buried Him. It did everything possible to break Him and to eliminate Him — and it failed. . . . That is the Jesus who is with us. . . . One who saw life at its grimmest, One to whom life did its worst . . . and who offers us a share in that victory which was His" (Barclay).

But the Christian's victory follows also from the nature of faith itself: "this *is* the victory that overcomes the world, our faith". By its very meaning, as adherence to Christ, it defeats all attempts to detach the soul from Him: and if when the world has done its scornful, persecuting worst the soul is found still cleaving to its Saviour, that is *victory*. "Simply to believe in Christ is, in principle, complete victory over the world. This alone puts the world, with its false ideals and standards, under our feet" (Law). So, in a passage exactly parallel to this, Paul defines "overcoming", "more than conquering", by declaring that *nothing shall separate* the Christian from the love of God in Christ. That is triumph. To have come through all opposition, all tests, saddened, chastened, humbled, perhaps, but with faith clinging yet to Christ, unseparated from God's love by any evil heart of unbelief, is to have conquered. Faith is important, John says, because faith *is* the victory.

Faith's third benefit is silently implied. It is the opposition of the world, and its allurements of the flesh, of spectacle, and of pride (2:16), which make Christian obedience difficult: but faith finds that God's commandments are not burdensome; they make no impossible demand upon available strength. Had not Jesus graciously invited men, even those already labouring and heavy laden under Judaism, to take His yoke upon them and learn of Him, so finding refreshment and rest, a yoke easy and a burden light? To obey in faith is to find obedience delightful —

125

the statutes again become songs, and the commandments prove to be the stepping-stones to freedom.

Rebirth, victory, and free obedience are benefits that flow from possession of divine life. The life that was in God, that was made manifest, that was in God's Son, is imparted to all who "have" the Son; and to "have the Son" is to receive by faith and make one's own the life that is in Him. That life is divine, abundant, satisfying, and — to crown all other benefits of faith — it is imperishable. It is the life of eternity, which the Gnostics strove after in seeking release from the world of time and matter; it is the gift of immortality, which the Mysteries promised to all who sought initiation and perfection through their strange and secret rites; and it is given, here and now, to all who believe. He who has the Son *has* life.

All this faith confers — all this, and heaven too!

(ii) *But John's opponents* too made much of faith, though conceived in more intellectualist terms: everything turned, therefore, as between apostolic Christians and Gnostic dissenters, on the content of faith — on the definition of what was believed.

John's definition has been anticipated frequently throughout the epistle in the titles he has used for Jesus and the statements made concerning Him: now he focuses all that the epistle has contended for concerning Jesus: faith is believing "that Jesus is the Christ", that Jesus "is the Son of God".

This is the testimony of God (5:10); whatever else passes for faith is counterfeit. And the firm identification of the Son, the divine Christ, with Jesus, which has recurred through the epistle, is now asserted in the most unmistakable and uncompromising way. This is He who came by water and blood, by baptism and death. The baseless fancies of all the Gnostic evasions of the plain facts of the gospel are here set deliberately aside. He who was baptised, He who really died, is the Christ, the Son — not some temporary, human vehicle for a divine emanation which could neither become man nor die!

Here again John is ruthless. Nothing less than the full apostolic faith in the incarnate Christ is adequate to the experience of the apostles, or to the message heard from the beginning, or to the eternal issues of life and death bound up with the gospel. Only a truly incarnate Saviour can really save men in the flesh, or redeem the material world for God, or suffer for sins, or raise mortal humanity to resurrection life. A phantom Christ means a phantom salvation, a dualistic ethic, a mysticism of visions and

126

theories and emotional excitements unrelated to time, to history, or to everyday human life. But "the Word became flesh, and dwelt among us". *This* is faith, to believe that Jesus of Nazareth, of our flesh and of our bones, is the Christ, the eternal Son of the everlasting God.

(iii) *The foundations of that faith* are wide and strong. It rests upon *history*: for behind all that Christians believe concerning Jesus is the story that (so far as the public ministry is concerned) began with Christ's baptism and ended with His death. John's manner of expressing this is determined by the Gnostics' mishandling of the gospel narratives. As they declared that Jesus was not the Christ, the Son of God, but only somehow allied to the divine being from his baptism onwards, so John insists that Jesus the Son of God (5:5) "came by water", entering as "by a door" upon His saving work by baptism at the hands of John, — already one divine Person who in His perfect humanity had grown in secret preparation during the pre-baptismal years for this moment when the Father should attest, "Thou art my beloved Son, in whom I am well pleased". As they declared that the divine Christ had not died, but only the human Jesus who was deserted by the Christ in Gethsemane or at some similar moment before the crucifixion, so John insists that Jesus the Son of God "came by blood", closing His public life and entering upon His present universal ministry through the door of death, as the *one* divine Person who in His perfect humanity was the expiation for our sins and those of the whole world. This, says John, is what *happened*. The vital importance of the historical foundation of faith has never been far from the writer's mind, from his first "that which was from the beginning, which we have seen and heard", to the present final summary.

Faith rests upon *the witness of the Spirit* (5:7). John has already referred to the presence in the apostolic Church of inspired spokesmen of the faith, "prophets", "witnesses", whose testimony was to be checked by their confession of the real humanity of Christ. Historically, the continuing presence of the Spirit in the Church originated in the gospel events, in the baptism of Jesus, the miracles, the promise of the Upper Room, and the experience of Pentecost, which were the bases of the apostolic message. Evidentally, too, the descent of the Spirit was, to John the Baptist, the outward token that Jesus was the Messiah, and the presence of the Spirit in the apostolic communities was held to "confirm the word" of the apostles, "a sign . . . to them that believe not" (as Mark 16:20, Acts 14:3, 1 Corinthians 2:4-5, 14:22, Hebrews 2:3-4 sufficiently illustrate). In John's thought, witnessing to the things of Christ was the primary task of the Spirit within the Church. The testimony of the Spirit through His spokesmen confessed just the apostolic incarnation faith which John affirms. The inspiration and quality of enduring Church life, its variety, power, enterprise, and progress, both in understanding and in holiness, bear witness to the truth of the apostolic message that Jesus did indeed come in the flesh to save. And every spiritual revival of Christianity since has been associated exclusively with just that message and confession. Truly "the Spirit is the witness".

Faith rests upon *the fixed pattern of the Church's worship,* in the "ordinances" of Christ. Alongside the witness of the Spirit in the life of the Church John sets the witness of "the water and the blood", and declares that these three witnesses agree — "converge upon the same object" — which, even in human courts, leaves no room for argument (Matthew 18:16, etc.).

The meaning here is far from certain, for "the water and the blood" is not at all a usual New Testament way of speaking of baptism and the Lord's Supper — even when the references in John 6 to "eating bread" and "drinking blood" are borne in mind. But neither is there any very obvious value in an appeal to the record that from Christ's side at the moment of His death there flowed blood and water, for just how this testifies to apostolic faith, to a real incarnation, or to anything else, is very hard to see. John's opponents would certainly say that this proves nothing about who it was that died; and in fact so long after the event no evidential value could be attached to a detail so ambiguous, unprovable, and circumstantial.

On the other hand, the continuing practice of baptism and the memorial Supper stemmed (like the continuing ministry of the Spirit within the Church) directly from the whole story of Jesus. Jesus' baptism brought the witness to the forerunner that Jesus was the Christ, and John's Gospel especially gives to both Christian baptism (in chapters 3 and 4) and the Lord's Supper (in chapter 6) an enormous significance in Christian life. Further, the two ordained patterns of worship represent in a concrete, objective form the extension through time of the actual baptism and real death of Jesus. So, they bear testimony in all ages to the basic facts of the gospel story, the Supper "showing forth His death, till He come", and baptism providing a "likeness of His

128

death . . . of His resurrection" into which believers are "planted together with Him". "Their value as evidence lies precisely in their being concrete, overt, objective actions, directly recalling (or re-presenting) historical facts of the gospel" (Dodd).

As Law finely says, "Every successive generation of Christians has baptised and broken bread as the first company of believers did, and has received in these sacraments the same testimony to the foundation-facts upon which our salvation rests. Older than the oldest of New Testament scriptures, of an authenticity which no criticism can impugn, they lead us back to the birth-hour of Christianity, and perpetuate in the Church the historical basis of its faith". Thus equally with the ministry of the Spirit in the Churches' gatherings, the ordinances provided eloquent testimony to what the original faith had been, and by their stress on the physical death and resurrection of Jesus they emphasise especially that real incarnation which the Gnostics denied. If, as is probable, the seceders themselves retained the Christian pattern of worship, then John's argument gains immensely in weight, as he draws out the evidential implications of their own practice of the ordinances.

Faith rests upon *the inner witness of the Christian soul*: "He who believes in" (so as to rest upon) "the Son of God has the testimony in himself." It may well be that John is here thinking again of the anointing that believers possess by which they "know" the truth (2:20, 27) — of the inward conviction by which truth is its own best witness within the soul. But it seems probable that John would not be content with an emotional, or intuitional, "awareness" that could not be defended by reason and moral results. Rather, the witness to truth which the believer "possesses in himself" lies in the totality of the Christian life — in the soul's experiences in the gospel, in the change of character, of direction, of feeling-tone, of resources and appetites and standards in the answered prayers and guided decisions and empowered endeavours and all else wherein the gospel of the incarnate Lord proves self-authenticating in Christian life. In the last resort a man knows the gospel is true by his experience of its power within himself: and only the original apostolic message about Jesus has that saving efficacy.

And faith rests, finally, *upon God's testimony to His Son.* John's phrase carries an echo of events like the baptism of Jesus and the Transfiguration, and perhaps of the miracles and the resurrection; it probably includes also the testimony of the Spirit and the inward conviction of the believer's own life: for all this derives from God, and forms the divine seal upon Christ's ministry and claim. But in thus tracing back the various lines of testimony to their original and unimpeachable Source, John is emphasising, first, that the divine testimony is infinitely to be preferred to that of any human demagogue, however eloquent, philosophical, "advanced", or successful with the world; secondly, that objective divine testimony is — in the contention before the Churches — set over against mere speculation and the theosophical theories of fallible human wisdom; and, thirdly, that rejection of the God-given testimony is, in effect, to call God a liar, for to disbelieve the testimony is to impugn the One who gives it, "a blasphemy beyond which blasphemy can hardly go" (Barclay). Behind the shaken human faith lies divine evidence and divine conviction, "the strong testimony of God in history and in the experience of the Church" (Dodd). The apostolic message has more than apostolic authority, and more than apostolic effect: for to accept it, and so to possess the incarnate Son, is to accept eternal life; to reject it is to choose everlasting loss.

So the great argument of the whole epistle ends with the direct and simple choice. To "have" the Son — to accept Jesus of Nazareth as Christ, the Son of God, come in the flesh to live and die for men, is to have life, the life of God Himself within the soul; to deny the Son, rejecting real incarnation and real atonement on the cross, for the sake of some speculative theory pandering to intellectual pride, is to forfeit the great gift and abide in death. The epistle closes its controversial message as it began, with the assertion of life, inherent in the beginning in God, manifested, offered, and given in God's Son, to all who accept Him as the Christ come in the flesh. So to believe is to walk in the light, to fall into line with the ultimate, unanswerable truth, to bask in the divine love and receive the divine life. To deny is to abide in darkness, falsehood, lovelessness, and death.

20: *Praying for Bacltsliders*

I write this to you who believe in the name of the Son of God,
that you may know that you have eternal life. And this is
the confidence which we have in him, that if we ask anything
according to his will he hears us. And if we know that he
hears us in whatever we ask, we know that we have obtained the
requests made of him. If any one sees his brother committing
what is not a mortal sin, he will ask, and God will give him
life for those whose sin is not mortal. There is sin which is
mortal; I do not say that one is to pray for that. All wrongdoing is sin, but there is sin which is not mortal.   5:13-17*

The new, closing, definition of the letter's purpose (13) is not really
different from that with which the letter opened — "that you may
have fellowship with us . . . that our joy may be complete." What
endangered fellowship and mutual joy was the temptation to secede
to non-apostolic groups challenging the "name" of the Son of
God and offering "true, advanced" spiritual life. To write affirming that Name, and assuring that the readers already possessed
eternal life, therefore preserved fellowship and safeguarded joy.
But what shall be the readers' relation to those who have gone out?
Part of their confidence is related to prayer, especially that prayer
for others which fosters fellowship: but there is obvious difficulty
in praying for unbelievers and heretics. John finely urges prayerful
concern towards all who acknowledge Christ, but at the same time
he recognises that rejection of the truth is a barrier to grace, which
even God's great promises concerning prayer cannot ignore or
set aside.

* Notes on 5:13-17, pp. 263-264.

THE CHURCH'S ATTITUDE TOWARDS HERETICS is one of the darkest stains upon her history. The long deprivation and persecution of the Jew, the sadist cruelties of the Inquisition, the thinly-veiled aggression and plunder of the crusades, the massacre of the Huguenots, and on the other side the disfranchisement, harrying, and martyrdom of Roman Catholics in the bitter politico-religious struggles of both Britain and France, the exile of Puritans, the suppression of Anabaptists, the discipline of dissentients by Luther and Calvin, and some later sporadic outbursts of the same fratricidal frenzies make a sorry tale. All illustrate the painful paradox of trying to defend by violence the religion of peace, and to coerce a faith that can only be sincere if it is free. Anything less Christlike than a persecuting Church is impossible to imagine.

Yet the problem of heresy is not solved by protests against violence. Truth matters: even John, with all his insistence upon love, cannot ignore that for the sake of a sentimental preoccupation with "unity" or a concentration upon "the devotion that unites instead of the teaching that divides". Truth matters, and to Christians the truth of the gospel matters supremely; love itself must wither and die if gospel truth be distorted or obscured. Defence of the Master's honour may not justify calling down fire from heaven "as Elias did" upon those who slight Him; but neither does loyalty permit easy good fellowship with those who deny His unique, divine Saviour-hood. One who defies the spirit of forgiveness makes himself "as a heathen man and a publican" — to be treated with compassion as in need of conversion; and in similar light the Christian must look upon the heretic. Hearts that love Jesus can find no true comradeship with unbelief, nor "love the blaspheming world".

As, at Corinth, the excommunication of the immoral was but the Church's necessary defence of its own reputation, standards, and fellowship, so blunt opposition to those who endanger the faith of others by distorting the truth is but the Church's necessary defence of her message and her converts. It is an inescapable part of that contention for "the faith which was once for all delivered to the saints", to which others besides Jude's readers and Paul's Churches in Galàtia are called.

But what if the contention be against former friends and colleagues? The day-to-day problems of right conduct toward those ignorantly in error or wilfully guilty of heresy, within the closely-knit Christian communities of the ancient world, are plainly illustrated by the warnings that abound in the epistles to Colossae and

Galatia, to the Lycus Valley Churches (of Revelation), to Timothy and Titus, in the "second" and "third" letters of John, and in the handbook of apostolic doctrine called the *Didache*. The counsel given develops from appeals not to be carried away with specious arguments and vain philosophy, into a clear exposure of error and strong counter-arguments, and then to a deliberate withdrawal of fellowship and withholding of hospitality (2 John 10, *Didache*) and support. Later still, much sterner measures of solemn "anathema" became the weapons of faith against falsehood — until even Christian men lost confidence in the power of truth itself and turned to violence.

For John's readers, daily relationship with those once members of the apostolic Churches and now adherents of the dissenting groups was plainly a problem of everyday Christian ethics, which all that John had said about love only served to sharpen. How should one *feel* toward those who desert the truth of Christ for some disloyal "deviationist" speculation — whether Gnostic, Mormon, "Witnesses", Christadelphian, "Christian Scientist", Spiritualist, or any other?

John's whole argument forbids bitterness, or contemptuous separation and indifference. He is anxious above all to preserve the apostolic fellowship and he well understands how controversy breeds hard feelings. A brother in need must be fed, clothed, sheltered, given to share in this world's goods — whatever his opinions! Hatred is "murder" (3:15); not to love the erring brother is to share his darkness (2:11), and not to pray for him is to share responsibility for his error and his fall. All that John has written about brotherly love confirms that he would bid his readers continue to pray for all who have seceded, led away by the lying spirit of Antichrist. He would have them retain the link of intercession when all other links — of shared belief, shared worship, shared table-fellowship — have been broken by disagreement, and even a friendly hospitality might seem to imply disloyalty to Christ.

And all that John has urged about abiding in Christ confirms that such prayer would be effective. He has spoken repeatedly of the Christian's confidence — "freedom of speech" — in relation to the advent, the fear of God and the final judgement: now he asserts the same utterly confident freedom of prayer. This prayer-confidence is twofold. The Christian knows that he is *heard,* if his prayer is within God's will. God does not turn away, the request is never ignored; praying, itself, is no futile exercise addressed to the unlistening skies — "It is not the mere abject cry that pain, helplessness, or black despair sends up to an unknown God on the chance that He may hear and help" (Law). God is there, to share the experience of prayer with the believer, and prayer has an intrinsic value as the conversation of the born-child with the Father who is love, apart altogether from what prayer "obtains".

The condition, "if we ask anything according to his will", necessarily determines *Christian* prayer, which can never be selfish, revengeful, lustful, directed in any way against another, or toward any course of action outside the will of God, without automatically ceasing to be prayer. "Jesus teaches us to pray 'Thy will be done' not 'Thy will be changed'", remarks Barclay. Christian prayer is by definition the voice of Christian faith, and so is informed with the spirit of Him in whom faith rests and obedient to the will of Him whose name is appended to its petitions. Thus it is certain of being heard, even if in God's far-seeing wisdom and deep-seeing love precisely the thing asked for is not vouchsafed.

But John declares also that such prayer is *granted* — or more exactly, that we know in the asking that we have received the answers. This is high doctrine indeed, and marks the summit of New Testament teaching on prayer — the prayer that is so identified with the divine will as to perceive, by the intuition of the spirit, God's readiness to fulfil its longing. So the deep, compassionate plea of a soul living near to God, on behalf of some weak, immature, misled, or sinning Christian, must carry within itself the conviction that what is being asked is what God also desires. Such prayer can impart new life to the one so prayed for: Westcott well says, "The sight of sin in a brother . . . necessarily stirs to intercession", and the same spiritual necessity lends authority to the request. No less certain is it that such prayer can bind in fellowship those sundered by circumstances, by history, by differences of emphasis and background. Intercession remains the strongest sinew of the Body of Christ.

But what of those sundered by unbelief, or false belief? John's keen sense of truth will not allow him simply to urge the loyal apostolic groups to pray for those who deliberately deny the incarnation-gospel, for the exponents of Antichrist. Some attitudes cut the soul off from grace — however earnestly that soul is prayed for; "he who has not the Son has not life" — no matter who intercedes for him. The freedom of each human will to reject truth and refuse grace is one of the inescapable conditions of prayer. Though we ought to go on praying, it must be on the clear understanding that God will never, in answer to our pleading, violate the freedom of another soul. Even Christ, in the Upper Room, prayed "not for the world".

The best the apostolic Christians can do, in the face of schism, is to pray for those not yet beyond the reach of prayer; in this way they will withstand the final and complete alienation which would sever fellowship altogether. When love has no other argument left, no other vehicle of spiritual communion, no other opportunity of comradeship, it still can pray, and must do so. But realistically, recognising that such errors as John has been refuting may defeat the prayer at last, and leave the heretic without hope.

If that seems pessimistic, it is an attitude at least a long way from the torture-chamber and the rack, the drowning-post and the stake. And it is equally far from the sentimentality which pretends that loving prayer solves all problems. What is perhaps most significant is that John is so vague. The affirmation about prayer, and the curious distinction between mortal sin (that can put a man beyond the power of prayer) and other sins (which intercession may cure), appear to be digressions — a disjointed postscript to a letter elsewhere so closely argued and condensed. But the vagueness is deliberately, and pastorally, right. For while between truth and heresy the distinction is absolute, who shall say of the individual man at any moment that he has — or has not — passed the dividing line?

Certainly not John, who all through the letter has avoided ostracising any group or teacher or individual member, by name or implication. John defines the truth, states plainly the issues: but in dealing with the individual fellow-Christian, the once-revered teacher now leading a heretical group, the once-fellow-member now hesitant, shaken, uncertain, it is not for anyone to prejudge whether another is already over the line that separates truth from falsehood, life from death, or only confused, misled, and taking his time to find his faith again.

With all John's vigorous definition of the only truth that saves, he will not by word or implication break the bruised reed of an individual's faith or quench the smoking flax of a soul's hesitating loyalty. Nor will he have the faithful among his readers ostracise their former colleagues. The breach may come — must come, if heresy is persisted in: meanwhile he writes in order that

135

fellowship may be preserved. So they should pray for the seceders, embrace them in intercession. In the face of John's assertions of intercession's life-giving power, it is not enough to say (with Plummer and others) that John does not forbid such prayer: that makes the whole paragraph meaningless and irrelevant. If he does not ask prayer for the seceding group, why drag in the subject at all in this way or at this point? John desires that love shall bridge the differences by prayer, but he balances his first broad assertion of the efficacy of intercession with the realistic proviso that he cannot "make a duty of prayer to which the certain assurance of being granted is wanting" (Huther). Pray for them, then, remembering that the result must depend on their final attitude to truth: yet still pray, for only God can know if the infection of Gnostic misbelief is already fatal. Pray with love, with confidence, with hope — and shut not your erring brother out of your prayers, or out of your heart.

Remembering the feelings that can prevail between Protestant and Roman Catholic, evangelical and modernist, the dedicated, instructed Christian and the muddled member of heretical modern sects, John's penultimate paragraph has considerable point! It demands an ecumenicity of intercession not easy to sustain — yet quite impossible to argue against.

21: *Certainty — or Sham?*

> We know that any one born of God does not sin, but He who
> was born of God keeps him, and the evil one does not touch
> him. We know that we are of God, and the whole world is in the
> power of the evil one. And we know that the Son of God has
> come and has given us understanding, to know him who is
> true; and we are in him who is true, in his Son Jesus Christ. This
> is the true God and eternal life. Little children, keep your-
> selves from idols.   5:18-21*

The "open letter" closes on a note of resounding reassurance, a triple
affirmation of certainties that stand unshaken in the midst of controversy. Each effectively crystallises a leading theme of the epistle,
and together they form a fairly complete framework of apostolic
faith. A blunt antithesis — the true God and eternal life on the
one hand, and the sham gods of Gnostic speculation and the sham
spirituality of Gnostic "experiences" on the other — confronts the
readers with a final challenge to decide, and the letter ends very
abruptly, with implied sympathy and appeal but no salutation and
no signature.

ALL CONTROVERSY CORRODES the treasures it seeks to
conserve, and especially religious controversy. Convictions are
shaken, confidence is undermined, fellowship evaporates, personal
relations are embittered; the exaggeration of inessentials replaces
the balanced proportions of truth, and honest desire for agreement

* Notes on 5:18-21, pp. 264-267.

is soon replaced by delight in scoring debating points. Too often, concentration upon defining what we do not believe, and arguing against it, deflects attention from the great areas of common ground which offer opportunities of concord and concerted action. How very often in evangelical experience have these unwelcome lessons needed to be learned!

It is therefore of the utmost importance to notice how John rounds off his great argument for remaining within apostolic fellowship, sharing the apostolic faith in the incarnate Lord. There is no impatient challenge, no gloating over a dialectic victory. He summarises his main conclusions in three affirmations that are — significantly — positive, fundamental, reassuring, having to do with salvation — experience rather than with abstract theology, and phrased unprovocatively as possible bases of agreement. John has much to teach us on the methods of controversy!

The first summarising affirmation concerns the believer's experience of deliverance from sin. John has strenuously maintained that the Christian life is fundamentally ethical: now he repeats, as agreed common knowledge among Christians, that "we know that anyone born of God does not sin" — as Dodd has it, "they do not live in sin", the tense of the verb thus implying continuation. So John again repudiates the Gnostic moral indifferentism, effectively outfaces the sense of defeat that marked the pagan moralists, asserts afresh the Christian's freedom from sin's power, and reaffirms for the last time the innate, inescapable antagonism between Christian faith and sin.

It is unfortunately not clear how (in John's thought) this emancipation from sin's rule is sustained. Some manuscripts say "whoever is born of God keeps himself", and others that "He [Christ] who was born of God keeps him [the Christian]" — and the arguments balance indecisively. Both statements are true. The Christian must "keep himself" as he must "purify himself"; John will in a moment appeal "with affectionate sternness" that his readers "keep themselves" from idols. But no less certainly the Christian "is kept" by the only-begotten Son, the good Shepherd whose sheep never perish because none can snatch them from His hand. The evil one "lays not hold" (G. S. Barrett) of the Christian ("catches him not", Moffatt), even as the evil one had "no power over" the Master (John 14:30). These echoes of the Fourth Gospel (and compare 17:12, 15) make it likely that John refers to Christ's "keeping" the Christian here, though the Christian's self-keeping is assumed as its condition.

"The Christian has an active enemy, but he has also a watchful guardian" (Westcott). He is never again indifferent to evil, nor its unresisting victim: yet the secret both of his antagonism to it and his emancipation from it is the deliverance wrought by Christ. The unusual description of Jesus as "He that was born of God" emphasises yet another implication of a true incarnation faith: Christ's close kinship with all God's children as the Elder Brother of the divine family (compare Hebrews 2:10-18), added to His personal triumph over sin within a human life, enables Him to keep from the evil one all who are born of God.

This certainty of deliverance from sin John reasserts as common ground with those tempted to secede. The "modern" way of dealing with evil is still the Gnostic way — to pretend to "think it away"; but sophistries about sin's being unimportant to the welfare of the human spirit cannot tempt those who have found in Christ not an excuse for evil but emancipation from it, not some clever and persuasive explanation of it but glorious triumph over its fascination and power.

John's second summarising affirmation concerns the spiritual standing of those loyal to the apostolic communities: "We know that we are of God, and the whole world is in the power of the evil one". Spiritual status has been, inevitably, one of John's major themes, partly because of the great claims of the seceders, partly because of the readers' need of reassurance. The tests by which we may be sure that we truly know God, are in Him, are children of God, born of Him, having passed from death to life, have been reiterated in varied but consistent ways: obedience, righteousness, and Godlike love are certain evidence of our standing in God's sight, and of our life's true origin in Him. The world, on the other hand, including those (like the seceders) "of the world", lies "within the devil's embrace" (Plummer), wholly in his grasp, in "helpless passivity" (Law).

Barclay emphasises the much sharper cleavage, in the ancient world, between Christian and pagan, while Neil Alexander speaks of pagan society "driven by the devil and dwelling in death". To some modern writers this sounds extreme. Looking back through two thousand years of Christian influence in the west, they find it hard to imagine the idolatry, violence, and corruption which made the whole of unregenerate human society appear in Christian eyes an empire of satanic hordes dominated by a Prince of Darkness. But unquestionably, demonology, a belief in exclusive divine election, occasional state persecution, the sense of an impending "end of the world", and the prevalent licentiousness and cruelty, all contributed to a starkly black-and-white conception of "saved" and "doomed", Church and world, light and darkness, life and death, "in Christ" or "in sin", "of God" or "lying in the evil one". Nor does our fondness for toleration — without caring too much what it is we are tolerating — or our love of grey mists of indecision and indefiniteness alter the fact that in the last resort a man is either for Christ or against Him, saved or lost.

It mattered supremely to those engaged in conflict with heresy to know that they were indeed on God's side, and their spiritual standing assured. To others, of course, this attitude sounds merely arrogant and self-righteous — "the small handful of Christian believers are right and all the rest of the world wrong; we on the side of God, and all the rest in the power of the evil one!" But this misrepresents John's thesis, which is that all our standing and privilege and opportunity are due entirely to divine action, to God's first loving us, to the incarnation of God in Christ and the propitiation of Christ for sin, and not to any moral excellence, or superiority of knowledge, we might possess. John insists, too, that this divine act, this love, this incarnation and propitiation are addressed to the whole world — and if the saved are few it is because the majority spurn God's grace.

Here is no arrogance, but only humble and adoring wonder. "See what love the Father has given us, that we should be called children of God!" The refusal of many to accept, or even to acknowledge their need, does not lessen the security or the certainty of those who gratefully believe. We know that — no thanks to us! — we are of God. We seek no other standing ground but God's grace toward us, no other confidence but in Christ incarnate, the Saviour of the world.

John's third summarising affirmation concerns our Christian conviction — that Jesus has revealed once and for all, and has introduced us to, the ultimate and incontrovertible Reality. He who in the Gospel is the true Light, the genuine Bread from heaven, the ideal Shepherd, the real Vine, has *come,* abides with us, is here. And, in consequence, we have the final truth, the definitive, terminal reality for which the whole Greek intellectual world had groped.

"The attempt to escape from the illusions of this transitory world into communion with the world of eternal reality was the Greek quest under Plato's influence", says Dodd; and it was the chief motive of all forms of Gnostic speculation. That is why John has been so concerned with the confession or denial of the *Son of God,* with the sending of the Son to destroy the works of the devil, with the sending of the Son to manifest the divine love; for it is only in the incarnate Christ that we know and touch reality, where Gnostic theorising merely explores imagination. Now that the Son of God has come, the Christian has done with illusions, and with gropings after truth! This is John's final thrust against the self-appointed propagandists of a "deeper wisdom".

But reality, for John, is not merely intellectual: an idea to be grasped; it is personal, to be experienced, known, and loved. The Son has given us understanding, the capacity for receiving divine knowledge and perceiving divine truth, so that "we know Him who is true — the only true God". But more than this: we are also "in Him that is true, in His Son Jesus Christ". Amid all that is false, misleading, disappointing, transient, we make contact with that which is ultimately real, unchanging, and true, when we know God, and through Christ live in His companionship.

In a world of illusion and make-believe, feeding its soul upon "lying vanities" and romantic fictions, confused in mind, bewildered in purpose by the very cleverness of its theorising, we touch bedrock truth in Jesus, and on that truth we build for all eternity. Thus — runs John's conclusion — all this that I have expounded is the true God, becoming manifest in Christ as Life, as Light, and as Love, as the Father sending the Son, as the Source and Giver of eternal life, as everlasting Truth. No specious wisdom of the intellectuals will get you beyond Him! And to know Him, be in Him, through Christ Jesus, *is* eternal life. No pseudo-mystical experience or emotional ecstasy can add anything to its reality or power.

So keep yourselves from shams! Beware of all spurious religiosity, every specious argument that obscures the gospel's truth, every shallow spiritual claim that fails to pass the tests of loyalty to the original message, of righteousness, and love! Keep yourselves from every counterfeit gospel, from every imaginary "experience of the divine" that yields no fruit of obedience and charity. Keep yourselves from every misrepresentation and distortion, every exaggeration and substitute, that seeks to supplant the God and Father of our Lord, Jesus Christ, as the Object of your faith, devotion, and love. You *have* the true God, the true eternal life: keep yourselves — and let the truth keep you

141

— from every form of idol; intellectual, emotional, or material, that would hide reality from you, draw you away from fellowship with the true God in Christ, and rob you of everlasting life!

Little children, keep yourselves from *shams*.

Part Two:

CONTEMPORARY REFLECTIONS

1: *Evangelicals and Authority**

FOREMOST AMONG PERENNIAL QUESTIONS with which 1 John is concerned, is that of the seat of authority in religion. In any controversy, whether about doctrine or conduct or group-loyalties, the supreme question is not "Who is right?" but "Why?" — by appeal to what standard, what first principles, what final unchangeable authority, shall conflicting ideas be tested and differences resolved?

The problem of authority is the central one for modern theology, but the issue arises also from the widespread challenge to every inherited ideal and belief, from the prevailing mood of intellectual unease and wilful revolt, from the nagging uncertainties and cautiously qualified convictions that rob so much earnest Christian work of impact and power. The hunger for pulpit authority too often gives to dogmatists and demagogues their finest opportunity, but it testifies also to a growing realisation that nebulous, wistful platitudes are not enough. Firm definitions, clear-cut ideals, the sense of unassailable truth and unimpeachable authority behind the message must be regained if evangelism is to abandon its pathetic attempts to persuade and become again a life-or-death proclamation of what "thus saith the Lord".

All problems of Christian reunion focus at last upon the issue of authority: for where the very sources of truth are in dispute, discussion towards agreement can scarcely begin. Moreover,

* Notes on Essay 1, p. 268.

145

among all the experiments, restatements, retranslations, and "new approaches" that litter the modern Church, it is essential to find some stable, authoritative centre of reference by which genuine developments of Christian thought and practice can be distinguished from mere aberrations, simple foolishness, or deliberate heresy.

Some seriously doubt whether Protestants should concern themselves with this problem: "they cast their eyes upon the actions of the Roman Church, with its claim to infallible authority within itself, and feel thankful that they are free to do and believe as they think best" (Nelson). Yet Protestantism has never been content with an appeal to individual "taste" in matters of eternal moment. The very variety of answers given in Protestant circles to the question of ultimate authority well illustrates both the importance and the complexity of the whole question.

The Current Debate

The seventeenth-century Anglican divine, William Chillingworth, bears upon his tombstone the maxim of his later life: "The Bible, alone, is the religion of Protestants"; this is supported by Luther's description of the Book as "the cradle wherein Christ is laid". Regard for scripture as "the only sufficient, certain, and infallible rule of all saving knowledge, faith, and obedience" is basic to evangelical faith, and Professor J. H. Nichols explains why: "The fact that the true understanding of God should be found in a mere book . . . is a necessary consequence if God has revealed himself in history, since a history must be recorded". Hence Forsyth's epigram — the Bible is "history preaching".

There are obvious advantages in a fixed standard of reference for doctrine and practice, portable, translatable, and undenominational. Unfortunately, the appeal to scripture begs many awkward questions. The situation of the modern Church is not that of the apostolic Church; new occasions teach new duties: life in a democracy, under nuclear threat, within a divided Church, in an industrial and affluent society, in a scientific milieu, raises innumerable questions to which scripture offers few plain answers.

Moreover, the appeal to scripture is normally highly selective. "Scripture" means, in practice, (parts of) the New Testament, and even then evangelicals do not usually enforce fasting, veiling, the kiss of peace, or the complete silence of women at worship; nor do they concede that state-established episcopacy and infant baptism are wrong because unscriptural. Uncertainty of text, translation, and interpretation leads to increasing domination of Biblical study by experts and scholars; even so, a dangerous and foolish idea is widespread that the Bible can be made to prove anything. The exact limits of the New Testament are somewhat arbitrary: other apostolic letters were certainly written, and some non-canonical books possess high spiritual value; to claim sole authority for all time for those which became canonical involves some delicate explanation.

Then, too, assertions like, "Protestants regard the Church as the guardian and not the proprietor of scripture" (Gilmour), or, "Obviously the Church can have no authority over against the word that created it" (Micklem), must be tempered with the reflection that the Church was prior to the written word. It was she who first wrote, then selected the sacred writings, and finally closed the canon: to that extent the Bible *is* the voice of the Church. Yet the Church "was not thereby conferring authority on the books; rather, it was acknowledging the books to possess authority" (Ramsey); as Dodd well says, "The Church did not at first regard these writings as specially authoritative because they were canonical: they became canonical because they had already made good their authority" to the Christian conscience and in the Church's experience.

But that experience was no uninformed enthusiasm, but a rich, enduring, and creative quality of life, corporate, ethical, worship-ful, and redemptive, in which a clear tradition of historical truth and a clear vision of God in Christ were articulately ex-pressed. The Church possessed multitudinous memories of Jesus, a jealously guarded tradition of His words and deeds; she pos-sessed a determinative pattern of evangelistic preaching, and of later instruction for her converts; she treasured baptism and the Supper as eloquent embodiments of much of her gospel-faith; and she sustained a corporate life of prayer, propaganda, and love, which derived directly from her devotion to the person of her Lord. All this became distilled in the few precious writings that remain to us from that golden age of superlative Christianity, when the inspiration of Jesus was fresh and full. And by the same rich, common life of that ongoing Church the various claimants to a place in the scripture-canon were attested.

So Winward summarises: "We may not contrast scripture and tradition: the primary tradition is scripture, and scripture is the primary tradition". Because the New Testament crystallises the thought, faith, and life of the Church as she stood nearest in time and understanding to her Lord, it becomes the test for all subsequent Church tradition, distinguishing true from false "developments" of original Christianity. Thus it is that in all later centuries, the Church stands under the judgement of the scriptures, and by them is continually recalled to her origins to be reformed and re-inspired.

And this judgement has authority, because what scripture enshrines is, in the last analysis, not opinion but the apostolic testimony to Christ. Micklem holds that the Protestant doctrine of the *word* always implies the *Gospel;* Barth that the presupposition which makes proclamation to be proclamation, and therewith the Church to be the Church, is the word of God; and A. M. Ramsey that "sacraments, oral teaching, apostolic ministry, were all means whereby the word of the gospel ruled in the Church. . . . It was therefore within a Church already ruled by the divine word that the writings were made which were to become the Holy Scriptures". But the only sufficient definition of that "word of the Gospel" is — Christ, the Word made flesh.

"To say that Jesus Christ, in His earthly, human life, in His death, and in His risen life, is the divine Word, above all other forms of it, is simply to restate the primary proposition of the Christian faith" (Nelson); and when we thus identify Christ Himself with the final Word of God for Church and world, "we are on the bedrock of the Christian concept of authority". So Christ is "Lord and King of scripture", Himself its theme, its judge, its origin and consummation, its deepest ground of authority. By Him even the apostolic witness about Him must be tested; by Him even the Gospel-stories concerning Him must be evaluated — as for His sake they are reverenced and loved. If the Bible is to some extent the voice of the Church, it is nonetheless, through its embodiment of the apostolic witness to Jesus, the voice of the Lord *to* the Church in every generation.

Yet the story of Jesus belongs to the first century. It is the specific task of the Holy Spirit to take of the things of Christ and reveal them unto us. Winward's warning that "exclusive attention to the New Testament writings is a denial of the doctrine of the person and work of the Holy Spirit", since it confines the Spirit's revelation of truth to a strictly limited period, must weigh seriously with evangelicals. With his usual penetration, Dean Inge declared that "not the Bible, but belief in the inspiration of the individual, is the religion of Protestants". J. S. Whale refuses to pose this contrast: "The Bible is authoritative because of the witness of the Spirit to its truth, in the heart. God's word carries its credibility within itself because it is authenticated by the witness of the Holy Spirit within the believer . . . . In the Holy Spirit and Holy Scripture are the two inseparable aspects of one and the same testimony". This overstates the close relation of Spirit and scripture, but the emphasis is valuable: modern groups like Moral Rearmament, the Prophet Movement in Africa, and to a less extent the Society of Friends, illustrate an appeal direct to an experience of the Holy Spirit only partially (if at all) controlled by the historical revelation and the redemption story. As Dodd says, the appeal to the indwelling Spirit easily declines into the individual experience of "inspiration", and if such experience is made the criterion of faith or doctrine, persons with little grasp of the central truths of the gospel "may mistake their own 'inspiration' (or bright ideas) for the truth of God, and so the corporate, historical tradition of Christianity is imperilled. . . . If on the other hand we are referred to the gospel itself, which is a recital of what God did for us in the life, teaching, death, and resurrection of Jesus Christ . . . then there is an objective standard by which the faith of the Church is kept true. . . . The interior testimony of the Holy Spirit is confirmation of the datum in the gospel".

The scriptures were produced within a Church superintended by the Spirit. All attempts to test later developments of the faith by appealing to the scripture are simply appeals to the Spirit's self-consistency. It is the use of the written word as a mechanical and automatic code wherein all truth resides in final and fossilised rigidity, fixed forever in words divinely chosen and never again to be retranslated into living speech, that misses the eternal truth in idolatry of the print and paper. Unless the scripture brings to me the voice of Christ in the present power of the Spirit, I have not read *in faith*.

The necessity that truth should thus "come home" to the heart of the believer is the final stage in this debate about religious authority. "The ultimate authority is truth as it reveals itself in experience and compels assent", says Dodd; and Inge means the same: "The ultimate authority, which alone is infallible, is the eternal and living truth". This is at once unanswerable and perilous. Unanswerable, in the sense that, in the last resort, *all* knowledge of fundamental things — of truth, beauty, or goodness, of mathematics, of logic, or even of the external world — must be intuitive: we "see" that certain things are so, or we stand convicted of want of perception — blind, even insane. The final statement of spiritual authority lies in the words of the Samaritans: "It is no longer because of your words that we believe, for we have heard for ourselves and we know that this is indeed the Saviour of the world".

And yet this emphasis is perilous, if it be understood to make truth essentially subjective — a decision of individual "taste" and perceptiveness, so that until a man "sees" a thing it is not yet true, and when he does, it is still only true "for him". That way lies intellectual chaos, and total agnosticism, in which nothing is objectively, eternally true, and science no less than religion and philosophy dissolves in a welter of conflicting personal opinions.

Amid all this discussion of an obviously vital and complicated question, the characteristically evangelical view seizes upon scripture, the Spirit, and individual experience as sources of authority, rejecting Church, hierarchy, and tradition. Only on reflection would most modern evangelicals admit the limitations of the appeal to scripture, or the dangers of stressing too much the individual's private experience of the Spirit. Only upon second thoughts, too, and with reservations, would some evangelicals concede that none but Jesus Himself, supreme over Church, scripture, tradition, and experience, is our final authority on all matters of faith and life.

The Contribution of 1 John

Authority became a problem, inevitably, with the passing of the first generation, the undisputed eyewitnesses of Christ's majesty and the interpreters of His mind in the apostolic Church. But the problem was made more acute for John by controversy, and intensified by schism as new voices claimed allegiance. It was still further complicated as apostolic authority was challenged by a philosophy appealing to self-evident intellectual insights, the intuitions of the "wise" or "advanced" Gnostics, and to "experiences" of ecstasy or direct divine inspiration. For the gospel itself made similar appeals to the common moral intuition of ordinary folk (as Jesus did), to "every man's conscience" (as Paul did), to "the light that lighteth every man" (as John suggests), and to the self-authenticating power of truth in the Spirit-taught soul (1 John 2:20). John's opponents, moreover, by attacking the very source and citadel of apostolic authority in the life and teaching of Jesus Himself, in the denial of His divine sonship, might seem to make John's problem quite insoluble.

In seeking ground to reply, John makes no appeal to the Old Testament, or to any Christian scriptures (contrast 2 Peter 3:15-16). His use of the Cain story for illustration, whether an allusion to Gnostic interpretations or not, is hardly a claim to scriptural "proof". Whatever power of conviction Christian writings held for John himself, it is probable that his readers would challenge their validity.

Seven times John appeals explicitly to "that which was from the beginning", plainly meaning the original gospel message. The opening words of the letter set this keynote and it chimes again, with emphasis, in 2:7 — "the old commandment, the word which you have heard"; and in 2:24 (twice) — "Let what you heard from the beginning abide in you"; in 3:11 — "the message which you heard from the beginning"; with less emphasis, but still significantly in 2:13 — "I am writing to you, fathers, because you know him who is from the beginning"; and again in 2:14. These explicit references are strengthened by oblique reminders of the pool of common knowledge handed down in apostolic circles — the message we have heard from Him, the word which you have heard, what you heard, as you have heard that Antichrist is coming, the message you heard, as He commanded us, this commandment we have from Him, His word in us, the way in which He walked, what He promised us, the anointing we have received, as His anointing taught you, you know that He is righteous, you know that He appeared, the Spirit He has given us, the testimony God has borne. Interwoven with these are more veiled reminiscences of the Christ of Johannine tradition, as in 2:10, 11; 3:13, 16; 4:9, 10; 5:3, 6, 20. The appeal to Christ's appearing and walk, to His righteousness and His words, to the cross and to the imitation of Christ, "are almost automatic with John".

All that is thus shared, "handed down", including message, commandment and memories, is "the truth", "the word of God" (2:14, 21), which all possess already. It is expressed in, and supported by, the worship-patterns of the Church — the Lord's Supper, and baptism (5:6-8) as it is testified to also by the ministry of authentic, inspired prophets in the Church's gatherings (4:1-6). It is certainly no esoteric secret possessed only by the elect (or intellectual) few: "under the new covenant, knowledge is the common possession of all", as Brooke well observes, recalling Jeremiah 31:34. Gore sharpens the implied contrast with other conceptions of religious authority. "St John would not tolerate the Romanist division of the Church into 'the teaching Church'

151

(i.e., the priesthood) and 'the Church which learns' (i.e., the laity, which simply receives from its teachers what it is to believe)." John's own strong counsel sufficiently justifies the teacher's function within the Church; but the power to discern truth from error, and the ability to possess the truth itself, are repeatedly affirmed of the whole Church (2:20, 21, 27). The apostolic tradition was common knowledge in the apostolic Churches: in all, John refers some twenty-three times to the great verities of the faith which his readers already know.

Of this appeal to the common tradition circulating in the Churches, two features are especially important. One is that it rests upon eyewitness experience of the incarnate Lord, and not that of the writer only but that shared by the whole apostolic fellowship — *We* have heard — seen with our eyes, touched with our hands — we saw, we proclaimed. The "we have seen and proclaim" of 1:3 becomes "we have seen and testify" in 4:14, the assured announcement of unchallengeable fact being supplemented by the personal evaluation of the fact in spiritual experience. Winward acutely remarks that the testimony of eyewitnesses of unique and final events must itself be a unique testimony; therein lies the unique authority of the apostolic tradition.

C. H. Dodd explains the reason for this emphasis both on what was from the beginning and what was personally attested: "Faced with novel doctrines of a speculative cast, the author recalls his readers to the unchanging apostolic gospel, which is the word of God, and to its attestation by eyewitnesses of the historical facts about Jesus Christ". Gore, too, well expresses John's position: "The distinctive note of John's mysticism is an internal intuition of spiritual truth based upon and moulded by external experiences or facts. It can therefore be a corporate and not merely an individual conviction, because the facts are common to all".

The second, supremely important feature of this appeal to the common tradition follows from the first: it is essentially a direct appeal to Jesus Himself. The message is heard from Him; He it is whom the readers know; His are the decisive commandments and word; His appearing and sinlessness determine Christian attitudes; His coming and action disclose the meaning of love. It is the Son who has given us understanding and knowledge; He is the source of all faith, and of eternal life. The words, deeds, and character of Jesus lie behind John's whole argument as its sufficient and unanswerable foundation.

Hasler well argues that such adherence to the historic Christ does not mean necessarily a clinging to ancient terminology or opposition to progressive Christian thought: but "no interpretation of Christianity can be true which eliminates the fact of incarnation, obscures the marvel of the atonement, or omits the crowning message of the resurrection". Progress in Christian thought, to be real advance and not merely deviation, must be Christocentric; "advance is possible only when it is conjoined with abiding" — abiding in fellowship with God and in fidelity to the facts of the faith. It is here that John's analysis of spiritual authority proves so stimulating.

(i) The backward look, via the apostolic tradition, is not our only avenue to Christ: the Spirit of truth Himself is present within the Church and within the believer as the constant divine witness, in every generation, to Christ and to His meaning for men. The most probable explanation of the "anointing" in 2:20, 27 is the gift of the Spirit of truth to all who are Christ's as inward illumination and intellectual Guide. In 3:24 and 4:13 the Spirit is named as the source of knowledge; and in 4:1-6, and again in 5:7, it is the Spirit, speaking within the Church through prophets, who witnesses to the apostolic faith.

This is more than an appeal to average Christian experience as the ground of authority. The inner illumination experienced by the teachable soul brings its own conviction that it is "given", not self-originated; just as the voice of the Spirit acknowledged by the common Christian conscience in the assemblies of the Church (compare 1 Corinthians 14:29) is to that extent an objective confirmation of faith, independent of individual prejudices. Jesus had promised that the witness of the Spirit to the world and to the Church should be given as something additional to the disciples' own witness to Himself (John 15:26, 27), and John has no hesitation in appealing to the readers' personal knowledge that the promise had been faithfully fulfilled.

(ii) Nevertheless, immediate awareness of the Spirit's testimony to Christ is indistinguishable in fact (though not in thought) from the Christian's own inner experience. We shall see that John analyses that mystical experience with quite exceptional thoroughness. Here, we anticipate only to notice that such experience includes intellectual, emotional and moral elements: an inward conviction of the truth and efficacy of the gospel — a knowledge which (as John's choice of terms makes clear) includes both intuitive perception of the truth ("part of our consciousness as Christians"

153

— Plummer) and the kind of understanding slowly accumulated through varying and continuous experiences of grace; an emotional assurance of one's own spiritual standing before God; and the experienced ethical consequences of the apostolic faith.

So the divine origin of the gospel is evidenced by its outcome in a divine quality of life. This is not just to say that sound life and character prove sincerity of profession: behind that lies the fact that the truth with which Christians are concerned is truth of a moral depth and dimension, "living" truth, the truth about life, and for living by. The "lie" is a distortion of life's meaning and aim; life according to the lie must therefore be itself distorted from the Christian norm. The "practical reason" of an informed Christian moral sense is involved in the assessment of the truth and its authority; and in turn, a true experience of God and of godliness is part of the self-vindication of the truth in the lives of all who truly believe. John's whole epistle is on that theme.

(iii) And, finally, a sincere intellectual consistency also bears its witness to the truth's authority. For 1 John is, when all is said, a powerful *argument;* its appeal is constantly to a fundamental spiritual logic. The repeated "If you know . . . you know . . . by this we know" is unmistakable; 1:6-10 is a deliberate examination of logical alternatives in our attitude to sin; 2:8 explores the logical possibilities of an accepted metaphor; 2:15 pungently summarises a whole argument about the world, its nature, and its fate; the "logic of denial" (2:18-25), of sin (3:4-10), and of love (4:7-12), and again of "witness" (5:6-12) all illustrate John's method of severe analysis of claims and professed experience in the light of a spiritual consistency and common sense which more emotional and ecstatic Christians do not always appreciate.

All kinds of varied and inconsistent impulses, "leadings", and desires, contradictory attitudes and "principles", changes of plan, abandonment of responsibilities and neglect of promises are sometimes defended by "spiritual" people on the ground of some immediate emotional and mystical "conviction". John expects Christians to cherish the "thought-out" life, which looks for some regularity and consistency in divine leading, some reliability and steadfastness in the mood and direction of Christian living. For John, the way of the Spirit will stand examination, Christian teaching will sustain thorough intellectual analysis, and the logic of an intelligent and responsible faith will lend its testimony to the authority of spiritual truth.

Conclusion

The apostolic tradition has become crystallised for us in the pages of the New Testament. Supreme over all details in that tradition was — and is — the original message concerning Christ (the "kerygma"), and this itself rests upon eyewitness acquaintance with Jesus. Thus Christ Himself is the source of all spiritual authority as it is transmitted to us from the historical origins of our faith. Yet John does not rest upon that alone. The continual ministry of the Spirit within the Church and the developing spiritual experience of believers under His direction are equally important to John's argument: and that experience bears witness to the truth by its own quality, morality, and consistency.

This is the evangelical position. The authority is Christ. Neither scripture, nor Church, nor tradition, nor individual experience must be allowed to obscure or overshadow His place as God's last and satisfying word to man. But He is known both "horizontally" in the apostolic testimony preserved in scripture and in the ordinances of Christian worship, and "vertically" in the teaching-ministry of the Spirit within the ongoing life of the Church and the experience of the believer. What the Spirit saith to the Churches — this also is Christ.

It is here that evangelicals commonly hesitate, suspecting some device for setting scripture aside, and fearful of the risks if the absolute standard in the written word be once qualified or weakened. Yet, with the deepest possible reverence and love for the written word, the need for some further guidance, some continuing, contemporary, progressive spiritual authority, is inescapable. John's open letter provides the invaluable answer, within evangelicalism, to our misgivings. The Spirit within the Church is likewise the voice of Christ Himself, the Word of God: and the testimony of the Spirit may itself be known, with certainty and conviction, by its consistency with the teaching of the Spirit in other times — with the apostolic testimony (4:1-6), by its fruit in Christ-like living, and by its self-authentication to the conscientious Christian mind. The function of the scriptural tradition, under the illumination of the Spirit, is to form again in us the mind of Christ: in this way the message that was from the beginning comes to be the truth *in us,* His word *in us* (1:8, 10); we live *according to the truth* (1:6) and, as to the deepest sources of our life, we can be said to be *"of the truth"*. These strange phrases represent nothing less than a re-incarnation of the Truth that was in Christ afresh in every generation of those who are His.

Scripture is imperishable treasure: yet our authority is not in the words but in the Word. We — evangelicals — must have faith in the Spirit, while recognising the need to test the spirits by all we know of Christ and the Christlike life. Evangelical Christians are not likely to lose their love for the written word, but fearing to follow the guidance of the Spirit in the Church and in the soul, they are sometimes found unready for the new things the Spirit of Christ would say to a new age. As Winward well says, "We cannot go back. We must move on with the Lord the Spirit, who makes explicit that which from the beginning was implicit in Christ, and evermore causes new light and truth to break forth from God's word".

2: *Evangelicals and Spiritual Experience**

A FRIGHT IN THE DARK is a spiritual experience; so is learning one's ABC's, listening to Beethoven, or falling asleep. No more ill-used word circulates in religious discussion than the nebulous term "spiritual", and when to it is joined the almost equally vague "experience" we coin a phrase well-nigh meaningless — yet irreplaceable.

"Experience" comprises all that one observes, feels, knows, enjoys, suffers, or does; "spiritual experience" limits that wide field to the things that affect one's *spirit*; by common usage the phrase is confined to the specifically religious aspects of thought, morality, emotion, and will. For evangelical Christians, spiritual experience implies especially an experience of God, closely involved with worship, obedience, prayer, trust, peace, and consecration; echoing Paul's distinction between "flesh" and "spirit", it implies experience of the "higher" life, purged of sensuality and selfishness, the blessing enjoyed by the "spiritual" man; and it suggests some measure of emotional intensity — it is of the heart, and carries a *feeling* of earnestness, prayerfulness, conscientiousness, sometimes, too, of pride and self-assurance.

Throughout Christian history a varying tension has divided those for whom religion is essentially a discipline imposed by creed and Church from those who crave some more vivid experience in which the divine shall be immediately felt and known. The mystics no less than the Montanists, the non-conforming Revivalists no less than the ebullient and undisciplined Corinthians, have al-

* Notes on Essay 2, p. 268.

ways posed problems for Church order and organisation: yet without the spontaneity and immediacy of spiritual experience which they represent the best order and organisation would be useless because lifeless. A strong preference for inspiration, freedom, personal acquaintance with God in a "vital spiritual experience" has always been evangelicalism's strength — and weakness.

Two weaknesses are present to John's mind. On the one hand it is perilously easy to value spiritual experience for its own sake, as though it constituted the purpose of salvation. Neil Alexander well summarises this danger in Gnosticism, the spiritual snobbery that claims "we, of the deep experience, are specially privileged . . . (ours) the divine experience of initiation and knowledge . . . itself the supreme good, the goal of religious life . . . the mystical contemplation of the eternal is . . . beyond mere moral duties. . . . Spirit is all and we are spiritual!".

On the other hand it is perilously easy to mistake for genuine spiritual experience states of mind and soul that are in fact sub-Christian, even anti-Christian. As Dodd says, "If the history of the Church shows that appeal to tradition could work in the direction of a sterile institutionalism . . . it shows also that enthusiasm, mystical experience, assurance of special guidance and all the marks of inspiration may be associated with doctrines subversive of the gospel".

Illustrating the new importance attached in modern theology to individual religious experience, two eminent scholars quote F. H. Bradley's dictum: "There is nothing more real than what comes in religion. . . . The man who demands a reality more solid than that of the religious consciousness, seeks he does not know what". But they add, "No experience can be taken at its face value: it must be criticised and interpreted". This is precisely what 1 John does so thoroughly and so fruitfully. When it is remembered how wide a range of facts, attitudes, reactions, and beliefs is comprised in the religious experience of Roman Catholic, Buddhist, Pentecostalist, Quaker, and Spiritualist, the need for clarification, definition, and interpretation becomes very plain!

John's Analysis

The New Testament does not contain a richer or more varied analysis of the inner life of the Christian than is offered in 1 John. It is remarkable that the epistle which lays so great stress upon historicity and the apostolic tradition, and which at the same time presents so rigorous an ethical challenge, should also find large place in the Christian life for mystical experience. Yet John contrives to emphasise all three, and to strengthen each in counterpoint to the others. So penetrating, and balanced, is his representation of Christian life.

John's description of spiritual experience is many-sided; almost the entire vocabulary of mysticism appears in his brief letter. Some classification of his expressions, however arbitrary, is therefore inescapable. We may attempt first to group the more "elementary" aspects of spiritual life, then those of somewhat "deeper" or more analytic significance, and then those in which language itself falters in trying to express the inner life of the soul.

On what we may call (begging many questions) the lower levels of mysticism, John speaks of believing and of hope, of forgiveness and of victory, of fearlessness and of joy, of prayer and of fellowship with God, and — as explaining these — of rebirth into the divine family. This is his pattern of "first-stage" mystical experience, so to speak.

The readers are assumed to be "those who believe", and "belief in the name of God's Son, Jesus Christ" is divinely commanded; "we believe the love of God" is the mature response of Christian hearts to the gospel story. It is belief that Jesus is the Christ which sets a man within the divine family and constitutes his victory over the world. Such belief is essentially the acceptance of God's testimony to His Son, the resting of mind and heart upon what God has said and promised in Jesus. This representation of the beginning of spiritual experience in *faith* is wholly in harmony with the primitive Christian gospel — the *kerygma* — while the definition of faith's content as "in the name of God's Son" and the basis of faith's confidence as "the testimony of God" to His Son are direct and clear echoes of the confession of Peter and the comment of Jesus at Caesarea Philippi. That more is implied than intellectual assent to propositions about Jesus is clear not only from John's whole exposition of faith's effects but from his insistence upon "confessing Christ" (not certain things about Him); and also from the illuminating cognate idea of "having one's hope built on Christ" — that total orientation of life and character which centres life's highest expectation and confidence upon Jesus Himself. Here spiritual life awakes.

The immediate consequences of this faith, within the soul, are moral, emotional, and spiritual. The moral consequence of believing — so believing in Christ the Saviour that you confess sin and trust His sacrifice and advocacy — is *forgiveness,* as to sins already committed, and *victory,* as to sins that still beset the soul. Forgiveness (mentioned twice) rests upon God's faithfulness, Christ's atoning work, and interceding prayer: its sole condition is acknowledgement of need and faith in divine willingness to pardon. Victory (mentioned six times) is the fruit of strength, the indwelling of the word of God, and is over the evil one (twice) and over the world (four times). Thus the Christian is delivered from sin and kept by Him who is Himself God's Son, but the victory is not alone over subjective influences within the soul (the lust of the flesh, of the eyes, the pride of life) but over the prince of evil and his realm, within which even delivered Christians must still live out their discipleship. Faith liberates from the guilt and power of evil: John's message is the basic Christian evangel.

The emotional consequences of faith are fearlessness and joy. John's "fearlessness" is very close to what Paul would call "peace with God", and John's "confidence" in the face of judgement corresponds to Paul's "no condemnation to them that are in Christ Jesus". It is a fearlessness that rests undisturbed in the perfect love of God. Joy is mentioned only once, and then in the context of fellowship with God and comradeship with other Christians. We might suspect that in the circumstances of the epistle joy was not prominent in the spiritual life of the readers' circles. Yet (as in the Gospel of John) joy is present, in the background, as the necessary evidence within the soul of acceptance with God. Faith sets the heart free from gloomy doubt and fear of punishment — and brings a deep inward happiness nothing else can impart.

The "spiritual" consequences of faith are prayer and fellowship with God: fellowship with God is mentioned twice, somewhat as a background assumption of everything Christian; prayer is mentioned three times, first as an example of the fearless heart, set on doing God's will and pleasing Him, and so obtaining its disciplined requests with confidence; secondly as the conviction that God listens attentively to all His children, ever hearing with patience and answering with love — whatever the answer be; and thirdly as the foundation of very careful counsel on intercession for erring brethren. This sharing of life with God, revealed as Father in Christ, which is the essence of fellowship and merely becomes articulate in prayer, is hardly distinguishable from faith itself: it is belief laying hold in practice of Him in whom it believes, and living in consequence in divine company.

Such things are commonplace to elementary Christian experience: there could be little practical Christianity without them. Yet their possibility is a glorious privilege, and a miracle. Forgiveness and victory, fearlessness and joy, prayer and divine fellowship are all possible because we are God's children, and that through the wonder of rebirth into the divine family (mentioned six times). This spiritual birth is wonderfully expounded: it is a rebirth of character (everyone who does right is born of Him); of nature (God's nature abides in him who is born of God); of relationship (everyone who believes is a children of God); of victory (whatever is born of God overcomes the world); and of security (anyone born of God does not sin, but He who was born of God keeps him). It would be difficult to elaborate or further explain that presentation of the gospel's initial miracle: John has pondered deeply on Jesus' words to Nicodemus — and not in vain!

With such evangelical experiences the gospel fulfils its promise, spiritual life begins, and the soul tastes salvation. What we may call the second level of mystical experience merely explores the first more deeply. Belief becomes knowledge of God, involving illumination and a closer personal relationship with the truth believed; the emotional consequences of belief deepen into love for God and the indwelling of God's love; and rebirth yields a life that is "of God" and of the Spirit.

John shares with the Gnostics a very high valuation of "the knowledge of God". The idea of revelation is native to Hebrew faith, and John's thought closely agrees with that of the prophets (for example, Jeremiah 9:3, 22:16, Isaiah 1:12-20) that the knowledge of God consists in knowledge of His will and obedience to it — more a moral appreciation of the character of God than a merely intellectual grasp of His existence. It is the sure knowledge of "Him who is true".

All who are children thus know the Father (2:13); no others do (3:1). The seniors possess also a knowledge accumulated "from the beginning" (2:13-14). Such knowledge is made evident by moral conformity to what is known: no one who sins has known Him; he who loves knows God. And this moral understanding is as near as man can get to the vision of God — never wholly granted, but approached as man approaches sinlessness and love (3:6, 4:12). Such moral understanding is also the nearest thing to the "illumination" claimed by pagan (and later Christian) mystics. To have fellowship with God means to walk within the irradiating holiness of the divine purity, so that sin is exposed and cleansed, and life progressively illumined, by the light that came in Christ (1:5-7, 2:10). Thirdly, this inner knowledge of God is the Christian reality corresponding to the symbolic and ritual "anointing" of which the Gnostics made so much. The immediate instruction of the Spirit through the word of the gospel qualifies all to "know" — with inner certainty of perception and conviction — where truth lies (2:20, 21, 27). So belief brings a man to possess "the testimony in himself" (5:10), and "we know . . . by the Spirit" (3:24, 4:13).

Finally, as we have seen, this manifold inward knowledge constitutes a special relationship to the truth itself, as not merely something to be comprehended and assented to, but itself an indwelling principle, an illumination of the whole life from within (1:6, 8, 10; 2:14, 24; 3:19).

All this "intellectualist" emphasis in John's mysticism (despite the moralist conditions and overtone) is wholly in accord with the Fourth Gospel's conception of Jesus as the Light of the world and as the Word who is the Truth. To John, the Christian lives constantly in a realm of light and knowledge: "the Son of God has come and given . . . understanding." So the open letter ends with threefold insistence upon the Christian's knowledge, because for John these intellectual certainties are the foundation of all spiritual experience and the natural flowering in the Christian soul of the faith by which Christian life begins.

Nevertheless, John will not confine his description of the Christian's inward experience to intellectualist terms: he shows that the emotional consequences of belief — fearlessness and joy — deepen in the same way into a mutual bond between the Christian and God, for which he freely uses the name "love". John explains this love by seizing upon the deepest implications of the story which faith accepts — that God is love: firmly and wholeheartedly believed, this naturally creates the typically *Christian* mystical relationship, in which man's love responds to and reflects the love man has received (4:16, 19). In two passages John hints at more. God's love is not only seen and responded to: it is "given us" (3:1), and so man's love for his fellow is in fact God's love abiding in him (3:17). This exactly parallels what John said about the truth — first believed, then indwelling. Mystical experience is thus more than "contemplation" (either of truth or of love): it is the active reception of what is believed into the soul's inner life as a permanent element of experience and a ruling principle of conduct.

Human love toward God reaches its perfection and end in obedience to God's word (2:5); it cannot be reconciled with love for the world (2:15); it is not to be too sharply distinguished from love for men, since as the Master showed it is never present where love for men is wanting (4:20, 21). Love for the Father God can only be evident when we love God's children in obedience to His command (5:2, 3). So once again the term "emotional" has to be qualified, like the term "intellectual", by clear moral overtones: the distinctions are tenuous — and that is very much John's point! Yet it is important to note that John does use the more emotional language of love. He cannot, like the Gnostics, reduce religion to philosophy, or spiritual life to knowledge. The whole man — heart, mind, and moral will — is in this inner relationship to God. To know, and be mastered by, the truth, to be loved and be mastered by love, are equal parts of a total experience in which God is met as Truth and Love — and totally surrendered to.

To this second level of mystical experience it is tempting to add the conception of "withdrawal" — again a notion familiar in later mystical literature, especially of ascetic and monastic type. But this would be to misrepresent John's many references to "the world", which have to do more with ethical disengagement from the world's ways and judgements than with psychological withdrawal from the material realm into some "realm of pure spirit" where abstract thought, mystical contemplation, and the negation of all desire attempt to achieve the vision of the eternal. On one side, John's exposition of spiritual experience approaches this idea, in that he exhorts his readers not to love the world, or the things of the world, nor to live as those "of the world", but as those "of God" — which once more means "belonging to God and deriving life from Him".

Repeatedly, the Christian is described as "of God" (4:4-6, 2:16, 5:19); "of the world" or "of antichrist" or "of the evil one" is the nearest antithesis in each case. The source of the motives and pressures, the energies and aims, the assumptions and actions, that fill each hour of existence, is obviously of immeasurable importance in making us the sort of people we really are. We easily assume that the source is within ourselves, that we provide our own inner resources and govern our own springs of action and feeling. In truth, we are pressed upon and prompted by innumerable influences scarcely conscious to ourselves, and are directed, far more than we realise, by the environment in which our lives are set. John means us to *choose* that environment, to live "of God", "of the Spirit", by the inward focusing of life upon Him — rather than let the world provide the hinterland, the watershed, of our daily conduct. To some extent, every Christian does this. For a few saintly souls it is the constant determinative factor of their lives — but that brings us to what we have described as the third level of spiritual experience.

For again this is but the earlier experience intensified and analysed more deeply. Faith and love remain the substance of mystical life: but faith and love can be shallow and fitful moods of the religiously inclined soul, or they can rise to the immeasurable potency of an abiding union in God, such as John urges his readers to seek.

One of the oldest phrases of Christian teaching is that which fastens upon the "interpenetration" of spirit with spirit, and speaks familiarly of God, Christ, the Spirit "indwelling" man, and of man "indwelling" God, dwelling "in Christ". The ancient divine promise to put the Spirit within men, replacing the stony heart with one "alive and quick to God", finds repeated echo in the New Testament doctrine of the Spirit; while "Christ in you", "Christ dwelling in the heart by faith", finds its complement in the constant phrase "in Christ" which belongs alike to Peter, Luke, Paul (innumerable times), Matthew, and John (Gospel, epistles, and Revelation). Matthew 18:20 or John 15:2 may well record its origin. What between men, under physical conditions, is "fellowship" or "comradeship" is described, as between man and God (where of course physical nearness means nothing), in the still more intimate and immediate language of closeness to the point of "mutual indwelling". This is John's most frequent term (thirteen times) for the highest relationship of the Christian with his God.

Four times the meaning is (apparently) that the believer is "in Christ" (2:5, 6, 28; 3:6) — the commonest New Testament form of the conception; four times the meaning is more probably "in God (the Father)", (3:24, 4:13-16); twice it is plainly "in the Son and in the Father" (2:24, 5:20); in several of these cases only the context determines the meaning, and that doubtfully. The interchange of expressions arises from the distinctive feature of *Christian* mysticism: it is an experience of God, but essentially of the God revealed in Christ; it is an experience of Christ, but that necessarily presupposes His divinity. To say we are "in God" is to say we are in God as Christ reveals Him; to say "in Christ" means "in Christ as Christ is God". Three times (4:12-16) the emphasis falls wholly the other way, upon God's dwelling in us. Here the knowledge of God, love for God, possessing the life of God pass into an identification with God; the personality of the believer is never submerged in God (else the dual expressions, we in God, God in us, would become impossible), yet fellowship is complete. A community of interests, of life, and of blessedness is experienced, in which God is immediately confronted within the soul and the soul is wholly possessed by the God it adores.

Rare moments? Yet John repeatedly uses of this relationship the word "abiding". It is true that he uses the term also of the anointing abiding in us and we in it, of God's nature abiding in us, of the word of God and the love of God abiding in us, and of life abiding in us; and this usage serves to remind us that the word means simply "remaining", "going on indwelling". Nevertheless, from its use in the Upper Room discourse the idea has come to possess for us, and probably possessed for John, nuances of affection and warning closely associated with the parting words of Jesus. There, the whole weight of the closing exhortations of Jesus falls on the need to perpetuate unbroken the experience begun in Galilee and Judea — "remain in Me . . . as a branch. . .".

This is John's thought also. We must not be content with rare moments of ecstasy or illumination or special ritual excitement. Our fellowship with God, our mutual indwelling, is to be the constant background of Christian life. Though rising at certain times into exceptional power and joy, it should remain at all times the true light of all our seeing, the deep spring of all our day-to-day existence. We *remain, steadfast, unseparated, in Him,* going forth refreshed and armed from Him to the tasks of the kingdom in the world, returning with rest and infinite peace to Him, the Source which is also our Home.

And so, finally, John can insist that the spiritual experience of the believer is — embracing all its elements — eternal life (nine times). The adjective carries the clear implication of immortality: we have passed from death to life, have eternal life abiding in us, and he who does the will of God abides for ever; God sent His Son that we might live through Him, and so we have confidence in the day of judgement. John's mysticism shares the confidence of Psalm 139, that a fellowship so deep on earth cannot be broken by death: a life so "spiritual" must be eternal.

But that does not exhaust John's meaning. This, that He has promised us, eternal life, *is* abiding in the Son and in the Father

(2:24, 25). It is possessed now, by those who have the Son, and we may know now that we have it (5:12, 13). The total spiritual experience which the letter so fully expounds "is eternal life" (5: 20), and when the last truth is uttered about it, eternal life is seen to be the gift of God in His Son (5:11), the very life that was in the beginning of all things with the Father and was made manifest to us (1:2). It is the life of God Himself.

So the epistle rounds again upon the Gospel, and the conception of the living Father who gives to the Son to have life in Himself, so that all who believe may live by Him. Spiritual experience turns out to be the divine life within the soul, imparted in birth, nourished through faith and love, and expressed in the life "of God" that lives now and forever "in God". So to abide, in the Father and in the Son, is the highest John can conceive for all who — in any age — read his appeal.

John's Comments

To this searching analysis of the meaning of "spiritual experience", John adds two telling comments. It is plain that he is with the evangelicals in laying great emphasis upon the soul's immediate experience of God, but it is equally plain, from the way in which he chooses to do this, that he is alive to its dangers.

First, John is keenly aware of the peril besetting all evangelicalism — of mistaking the mere jargon of religious profession for the reality of spiritual experience. His "If we say . . . if any one says . . ." and his "let us not love in word or in speech" reveal this; and so does his quoting of others' high-sounding claims, in warnings like, "No one who 'abides in him' sins. . . . No one 'born of God' commits sin. . .". Where open profession of faith "with the mouth" is highly valued, and even required (as it is not only in 1 John but in the New Testament generally and in all evangelical circles), profession may easily be taken for conversion, knowledge of the right words to use being accepted as evidence of a true experience, and the well-phrased confession of belief being equated with deep faith. This is the "confessional fallacy" of evangelicalism. John is prepared to go so far as to contemplate a "saying" by the leadership within the Churches, and still to deny that (in certain circumstances) such "professors" were ever truly "of us".

John's antidote to this confessional peril is his apparatus of tests for keeping mysticism healthy, and lofty professions of profound experience safely "down to earth".

(i) A true spiritual experience will be manifest in the open confession of Christ, the Son of God (4:15), but also in the contrite confession of sin, without evasion or self-deceiving excuse (1:6f.). In consequence, mysticism can never pretend to sinless perfection: the rarer the atmosphere the clearer the sight; the nearer to God the fiercer is the self-exposure.

(ii) A true spiritual experience will be manifest in obedience (2:3, 3:23, 5:2, 3), in utter antagonism to sin (3:6, 9; 5:18), in unworldliness (2:15, 3:1, 4:5, 5:19), and in positive acts of righteousness (2:29, 3:10). What is significant, again, about this collection of Johannine "platitudes" is that each idea in all twelve verses cited is directly linked to the great phrases of mysticism — knowing God, abiding in Him, loving God, being born of God, being children of God, being "of God". The consequence here is that mysticism can never claim independence of morality. "The heretics' claim to 'remain in Christ' — that is, to be in mystical union with Him — can be allowed only if they imitate His example", says Dodd in summary of John's argument; and emphasising that "to walk" describes not only inward disposition but consequent outward action, Huther remarks, "In the fact that John brings this out . . . it is evident how far his mysticism is removed from mere fanaticism".

(iii) A true spiritual experience will be sharable. John desires throughout to preserve and promote fellowship between brethren and in the Father and the Son. The privileges belong to everyone who believes, who has hope built on Christ, who is born of God; and Christ is the Saviour of the world, the expiation not for our sins only but also for the sins of the whole world. So, very emphatically, the great mystical expressions — born of God, knowing God, abiding in God, God in us, loving God — are explicitly and directly linked to the command to love the brethren (4:7, 8, 16, 20). The consequence is that mysticism can never become the private experience of the crank, of the "alone and superior expert" in spiritual things. "You all know", John insists; "you have been anointed . . . you have no need that any one should teach you." The deepest spiritual experiences are not for the few but for all in Christ.

A mysticism contrite, ethical, and sharable is psychologically and religiously sound and socially valuable. It is common Christian experience raised in temperature and intensity to the level of enjoyment and power. But not all high-sounding talk about "deep spiritual experience" is as earthly as John's, or as loyal to the example of Jesus.

John's second telling comment upon the importance of immediate spiritual experience is the complement of the first: it follows searching tests with comforting assurance. We have seen that pastoral encouragement in the face of controversy and challenge is one of the purposes of the "open letter", in spite of its ruthless quality and unrelenting analysis. The writer, deeply understanding the effect of his words, continually reasserts his confidence in the readers, and would have them reaffirm that confidence also for themselves.

Intellectually, John has insisted upon the certainties revealed within spiritual experience as individual faith puts to the test of personal life the great verities of the gospel: illumination by the self-authenticating truth is in the end the most steadying of all forms of assurance. But John offers also an emotional assurance that concerns the individual's standing with God. "Nine times at least the writer offers his readers tests by which they may assure themselves about the truth of their Christian position", says Brooke, referring to 2:35; 3:14, 16, 19, 24; 4:2, 6, 13, and 5:2. The verses assure us that we are in God, know God, have passed from death to life, are of the truth, and abide in God — on certain conditions. John returns continually to the greatness, the purpose, and the love of God, His faithfulness and fairness, as the ultimate foundation of all encouragement. He insists also on the fearless confidence with which Christians may approach God in prayer (5:14), silence their misgivings (3:21), await the advent (2:28) and contemplate judgement (4:17). He writes so that they who believe might *know* that they have eternal life; they already know the truth, have known it from the beginning, and may be sure they know "Him who is true". He would have Christians live in love, and not in fear. "God is greater" is his watchword against all doubt and all timidity. Law sums up by declaring the epistle "written to establish the genuine Christian in the certainty of his salvation".

We may be deeply grateful that a letter so rigorous and searching in its tests of all Christian profession and emotion does contain these reminders that Christian life can be enjoyed and a humble Christian confidence maintained in spite of all John's warnings and self-examination. Many may feel that his encouragements do not balance his criticisms, that the total impression of his letter is more disturbing than reassuring, and that John leaves one questioning with the disciples "Who then can be saved?", sighing wistfully with Paul, "Who is sufficient for these things?".

John would probably reply that the answer must rest not in any words of his but in our own experience; that no pronouncement by any authority can tell a man where he stands with God. If you do righteousness, if you love your brother, if your heart is set on the commandments, if you overcome the world, if you walk in the light, then you may be sure God has been dealing with you, that you have eternal life, that you live in His love, within His family. There is no easier assurance than that, and there could be no greater.

3: *Evangelicals and Ethics**

"EVANGELICALISM IS WEAK IN ETHICS" is a charge containing just enough truth to make it plausible. True, evangelical Christianity kindles profound zeal for Christian work, evokes great generosity, endurance, and consecration, inspires much social service, and is associated both historically and popularly with "Puritan" standards of thought and behaviour. Its emphasis upon conversion and regeneration tends to sharpen the distinction between Christians and the unconverted world until "separation" and witness become important features of evangelical conduct.

Nevertheless, ethical weaknesses are apparent. Serious moral breakdown is sometimes excused in casual and irresponsible ways by specious distinctions between status and character. Emotionalism makes for instability, and the thrill of decision, the relief of forgiveness, the joy of assurance may be so stressed that the deep changes in life's direction and attitude wrought by conversion seem unimportant — or are assumed to follow automatically. "A true and vital experience of Christ does all that is needful": instruction in righteousness is the devil's substitute for a true faith!

Where ethical teaching is given it is sometimes negative, world-denying, and trivial; towards anything more thorough evangelicals tend to be suspicious, fearing lest the free gospel of divine grace be overshadowed by "works of the law". Evangelicals of an earlier day preached law as preparation for the gospel. "It is a

* Notes on Essay 3, p. 268.

170

glass to show us our sins, that, seeing our pollution and misery, we may be forced to flee to Christ . . ." (Thomas Watson). George Whitefield said with approval, of certain evangelists, "They wound deeply before they heal", and C. H. Spurgeon echoes the thought: "I believe in instantaneous conversions . . . but I am still more glad when I see a thorough work of grace, a deep sense of sin and an effectual wounding of the law". This corresponds to Paul's "By the law is the knowledge of sin", but to Paul the law remained nevertheless holy and just and good — and what the law of itself, through the weakness of the flesh, could not do, God set about doing by the rule of the Spirit, that the works of the law might still be fulfilled in us (Romans 8:3, 4).

To all evangelical suspicions of "moralism" John's answer is copious and cogent. It is easy to summarise his entire letter in purely ethical terms. The axiom of his message is "God is light"; the substance of his warning that spiritual illumination devoid of righteousness and love is mere illusion; the assumption of all his exhortation is the absoluteness of the ethical test — "You know that no murderer has eternal life . . .". There cannot remain the least lingering doubt that evangelicalism of Johannine quality is inescapably ethical, nct only in implication but in its essential nature and meaning.

In this of course John is at one with the whole New Testament, but his presentation is marked by a profound inwardness, and a "downright concreteness, almost crudity" in stating the moral requirements of faith. On the one hand, ethical life and obligation are but the outward evidence of spiritual experience: being precedes doing. On the other hand, emotional experience, or the profession of faith — however eloquent — are worthless without appropriate behaviour: *doing* righteousness and *doing* love alone avail; all else is mere talk. Inwardness and concreteness are not often combined: in John's thought they belong together.

If for convenience we summarise John's teaching first negatively and then positively, any impression that John makes more of the avoidance of sin than of seeking good would be entirely misleading: warnings and prohibitions are simply the necessary preludes to a positive ethic of considerable inspiration and power.

Negative Counsels

John's exhortations — to avoid sin, to love not the world, to overcome the evil one — are provoked directly by Gnosticism, which made light of sin, cultivated the favour of the world, and represented the doctrine of Antichrist himself.

(i) John insists that though none may claim to be sinless, yet sin cannot be tolerated in Christian living; God has made full provision for the resultant problem. To disclaim sin is to deceive oneself and make God a liar. *Sin* consists in the denial of moral obligation — "lawlessness" — the repudiation of the rule of right; *sins* include all acts which express that attitude, every form of unrighteousness. This essentially *moral* concept of sin is important. Too often sin is conceived in a "spiritual" or "mystical" way which somehow decreases its ethical and social seriousness, making it a private and emotional concern of the individual Christian. To John, sin is the wilful rejection of the discipline of right, a moral rebellion against the constitution of the universe.

Because sin is defiance of the divine rule, because Christ appeared to take away sins, and was sinless, because "religious righteousness" cannot be divorced from moral rectitude, because all sin is of the devil, and because a divine life abides in the Christian, it is inconceivable that the Christian can tolerate sin. We walk in such companionship with the divine Light that sin is progressively exposed: confessed, sin is forgiven and cleansed — and the *double* cleansing, the present tense, are alike important for John's view: he knows no forgiveness that leaves the sinner just as sinful. Pardon is the beginning of purity, and salvation is incipient sanctification — or it is just a sham!

So the Christian whose hope is built on Christ purifies himself. No less earnestly, he prays for others who sin. And he knows that the sinless Christ keeps guard over His own that the evil one touch him not. John could hardly make more plain the ethical position of a child of God. Unable to claim sinlessness, he is yet fixed in a relentless antagonism to sin — sinless in desire and intention and hope, if not yet so in fact. He is meanwhile forgiven through the cross, cleansed through grace, and kept through Christ's everlasting strength. In that evangelical situation there is simply no room for moral compromise, for indifference, or carelessness towards the plain obligations of righteousness and love.

(ii) John's equally uncompromising attitude towards "the world" raises questions about the adequacy of John's social ethic. The world, in its moral blindness, did not know Christ and does not know the Christian; it hates the children of God, being more hospitable towards the spirit of Antichrist and the false prophets. Despite its power for evil, the world is overcome by whoever is begotten of God, conquered by faith, because He who is in the Christian is greater than he who is in the world. Lust and pride being the controlling factors of its life, and to pass away being its sure destiny, both loyalty and common sense demand that the Christian shall not love the world, but being once delivered from it shall "stay delivered". The world is not "of the Father" but in the power of the evil one, and so identification with the world and its ways is gross failure in love towards the Father. .

From all this it is clear that "world" has acquired for John "a moral sense" (Barclay). It no longer signifies the whole creation, or the totality of mankind, but human society as organised under the power of evil, alien from and in opposition to God. It stands contrasted with that part of mankind which has received eternal life through Christ; its "way" is opposed to the "way" of the Christian, its lusts to the will of God, its pride to the child's humble love towards the Father.

This hostile attitude towards organised pagan society is found also in James and 2 Peter. Dodd points out that at this time the greater danger was not the world's persecution but its sensuality, avarice, materialism, cruelty, and pride — a perpetual temptation to compromise. Neil Alexander notes also, in explanation of John's antipathy, the harm the world had done to the Church by enticing away some of its leaders. Alexander refers to an article by Barclay which turns out to be an astonishing catena of passages from Tacitus, Suetonius, Juvenal, Seneca, Dio Chrysostom, Petronius, Pliny and others, which add up to the severest imaginable indictment of Graeco-Roman society in New Testament times, for vicious immorality, fantastic extravagance, luxury, and love of pleasure, appalling cruelty, domestic infidelity, homosexuality, contempt for child-life, and confessed moral helplessness. When to these considerations is added the deliberate appeal of Gnosticism to popular opinion, John's cautions and condemnation towards society are sufficiently explained.

At the same time, Hasler rightly remarks that John makes no attempt to *escape* the world, either by holding it to be illusion (as Hinduism does) or by retreating into isolation and renunciation (as the Christian ascetics would do). Instead John offers victory over the world, by a new life implanted and faith in Him who overcame: he would agree with Paul that the world "belongs" to him who belongs to Christ. Nor is John's attitude *dualistic*: he who so insists upon "Christ come in the flesh" could not think of flesh or world as entirely evil. Nor, thirdly, is there anything in 1 John of *exclusiveness*. God sent His Son into *the world;* Christ's work has universal efficacy — "for the whole world"; and whoever believes, whoever confesses, whoever has the Son, has eternal life. If John says nothing about Christian witness to the outside world, his epistle has furnished some of the most telling arguments and some of the most glowing texts for evangelistic enterprise.

Nevertheless we miss from John's letter much of the Christian social obligation expounded by Paul (as in Romans 12-15), by Peter, and in the teaching of Jesus. It is obvious that if Christian witness is successful, society must become permeated, to some degree, by Christian truth and idealism; thus the Christian's situation changes from that which John describes — not by the evolution of any inherent forces for good, but by the efficacy of the gospel itself. Moreover, evangelism requires that we remain in the world with positive Christian purpose, to make a saving impact upon society, and every advance will call for sympathetic response from Christian hearts. Finally, responsibility must grow with privilege, obligation with opportunity: the Christian in a democracy, with two thousand years of Christian experience behind him and a world Church about him, cannot claim to stand precisely in the situation of John's readers. He must face new horizons of Christian witness as new doors are opened to him by the Lord of history.

John says nothing of this because his immediate purpose did not require it: he concentrates upon the present emergency — for him at the moment the world is that sphere which has produced the heresy and eagerly welcomes its exponents (5:5). Yet nothing he says tells against a wider view of social responsibility, and all he does say about the universal love of God and the saving purposes of Christ carry this corollary: while not loving, or compromising with, a godless order of society, the Christian shall yet so serve the kingdom of Christ within that order as to redeem it for God — until "the whole world" is saved.

(iii) Behind the believer's own sinning, and the hostility of a pagan society, stands the evil one. In common with almost all New Testament writers, John finds it no more surprising that human evil and ruin should have its background and explanation in the spiritual world, than that human goodness and salvation should do so. Whereas Paul, on the only occasion he mentions the matter, traces the origin of evil to the sin of Adam, John six times names "the evil one".

In 2:13 the "young men" *have* overcome the evil one, presumably by becoming Christians at all; in 2:14 their victory is again mentioned, as evidence of their strength; in 3:8 he who practises sin is said to draw his life from the devil, the devil is said to sin "from the start", and the Son of God appeared in order to undo the devil's work; in 3:10 the devil's children are to be distinguished by their not doing right; in 3:12 Cain the murderer is held to be plainly among those drawing their life from the devil; in 5:19 the whole world is seen to be in the power of the evil one. "He who is in the world" in 4:4 may be identified with the spirit of Antichrist (3) or the spirit of error (6), but some relation to the evil one is implied, as setting the world against the Christian.

It is idle to speculate what answers John would give to all the questions we would like to ask on this subject. That "the prince of this world", whom Christ confronted, overcame, and judged at Calvary (John 12:31, 14:30, 16:33) is a real figure of Johannine theology cannot be questioned, and not many will be wholly satisfied with Law's summary of "the three great truths . . . of permanent validity" contained in the New Testament conception of diabolic agency — that sin is the manifestation of an essentially evil will in enmity against God, that the moral conflict of which history is the theatre is one of personal agencies and not of abstract ideas, and that Christ will triumph. These things are true, but there is more in John's conception that we would like explained. From the point of view of ethics, however, the important truths are two.

First, that the moral life is one of conflict, and on a suprahumanistic level. The issues at stake reach beyond the individual's happiness, or growth in character, or experience of blessing: the Christian is engaged in a confrontation of good with evil, of God with the devil, in which he personally and his private overcoming gain immeasurable significance. "Overcoming" is, in Johannine thought, a badge of the greatest success in Christian life, and to the "overcomers" are promised all the highest awards in the gift of Christ, but always because the warfare is no private fight, but an engagement in the eternal war which God wages for truth, for righteousness, and for love. The language is perhaps melodramatic and militaristic to modern minds, but the implication of contending issues that reach far beyond the individual's measurement or comprehension is a necessary element in a truly Christian concept of the moral life.

175

Secondly, correlative to this is the assurance of supra-humanistic resources. The word and strength of God abiding within the Christian soul; the superior greatness of "Him who is in you" to him who is in the world; the guarantee of ultimate security within the keeping of the Son of God, so that the evil one does not touch us: these together form such reinforcement of human idealism and will-power as to make the whole conception of supra-mundane conflict credible and tolerable. To say that, in New Testament language, the human soul is the battlefield for contending super-human powers, is not quite enough: rather, human society, within time, is the battlefield for principles, forces, and persons that are ultimately beyond time, and men enlist for one or the other side of their own free choice — to be "possessed" by the devil, or endued with the word and the Spirit, and so to become vehicles and agents of forces outside themselves in a warfare of eternal significance.

Such a representation may be dismissed as "mythological", an abuse of metaphor, old-fashioned, or just incredible. The one criticism which cannot be made of it is that it reduces the significance of moral striving. In answer to Gnostic moral neutral-ism, John sets the individual Christian and his struggle with evil in the context of a supra-mundane conflict with eternal issues! He would make no weaker retort to modern evangelicals who be-little the place of ethics in spiritual life.

Sin, the world, and the devil constitute the perils that demand vigilant and resolute opposition: yet to deal with them adequately is not the whole duty of the Christian, but only leaves the field clear for the real and positive tasks of Christian discipleship.

Positive Ideals

John represents these tasks as three: keeping the command-ments, living by love, and imitating Christ.

(i) To John's fourteen references to the "commandments" must be added what he says about "lawlessness" and about the word or message received from Christ as controlling factor in Christian life and thought. This sufficiently surprising emphasis is underlined still further by the prominence John assigns to what in many minds is the contradiction of "commandment" — namely love.

Keeping His commandments is the evidence that we know God; disobedience of the commandments disposes of all spiritual claims; to keep God's word is to show love perfected. This moral principle is itself no new commandment, but an essential part of Christianity from the beginning, as the readers well know. But there is a new commandment, too: to love one another. All sin is lawlessness, the repudiation of the divine right to command. Prayer offered in the light of the commandments, from a desire to please God, is assured of answer. In view of Gnostic denials, it is well to remember that God's first commandment is that we should believe in the name of His Son Jesus Christ, and love one another as Jesus required. All who keep God's commandments abide in Him, and He abides in them. The commandment we received from Jesus is that he who loves God should love his brother also: to love God and keep His commandments therefore necessarily involves loving God's children — and this is what loving God *means,* obedience to the commandments. Nor, for loving hearts, are His commands any burden, for love delights to please. Such a summary constitutes a fairly complete exposition of the Christian moral law. It is needful to add only three remarks.

John assigns moral obligation to the great requirements of faith and love; but there is no attempt at casuistry, the multiplication of detailed rules for discipleship, as though men could be made saints by regulations. John presents the commandments always within the context of love, as guiding our devotion to Him through whom they come, and as the "ethos" of the divine family — the sense of obligation is never divorced from the sense of privilege, nor obedience from the love that alone makes it spontaneous and glad.

For all that, John is not afraid of the idea of obligation. He is no sentimentalist, assuming that high ideals work by their own unconscious fascination. He would not even say with Augustine, "Love God, then do as you please": he says rather, "Love God, and you will do what He pleases" — delighting to do it, but not free not to do it, and still doing it when obligation rather than delight impels you. For while God's service is perfect freedom, the Christian is not free to choose whether he will serve. God's commandments are still commandments — and God's. A Johannine sense of moral obligation would add considerable strength to modern evangelicalism, and not a little needed stability to some modern Christian lives.

(ii) Exposition of the epistle has repeatedly brought before us John's second positive ideal, love for the brethren. To illustrate properly its place in John's ethical thinking would be to rewrite

the letter. Love is his purpose; love the message from Christ, and
the commandment; love shows we are in light, and have life; love
is the meaning of the cross and the nature of God. Human love
is the reflex of divine love in human hearts: they who have been
so loved cannot help so loving. Man's love toward man is God's
love overflowing the heart on which it is "bestowed", and flooding
unconfined into a love-starved world. That is probably the high-
point of all New Testament teaching about love.

Nevertheless it has been criticised on two grounds. It is said
that "as an exponent of the practical implications of love John
does not come into competition with St. Paul. There is nothing in
the epistle that is comparable to the thirteenth chapter of 1
Corinthians, with its delicate analysis, or to the twelfth chapter of
Romans with its masterly exposition of the manifold applications of
the new commandment to the actual relations of life" (Law). The
critic goes on to show, nevertheless, to what depths John's own
analysis is pressed, as more to his purpose than practical details.

But John writes of basic attitudes, countering Gnostic lovelessness. It is of the essence of love that prescribed rules for detailed situations can never be drawn up: love must find its flexible
and various way in multitudinous circumstances that change with
every need and every person. Valuable as are the illustrative
parables of Jesus and the practical counsels of Paul, in the end
love must find its detailed duty by its own intuition at the moment
of opportunity: its tasks just cannot be catalogued. Moreover,
it is well not to be misled by John's terseness. Few things in Paul
(if we must make the comparison) could rival for practical application of great principles John's sharp warning about mere talk
of loving, his relentless translation of love into *seeing* the brother's
need and *sharing* this world's goods — or shutting up about it!
Or his immediate application of Christlike love as "laying down
our lives for the brethren"; or his searching counsel about prayer
for the erring brother, despite all the difficulties. John may not
grow lyrical, or didactic, but he is anything but impractical.

The second criticism is that John limits the scope of love entirely to "the brethren" — fellow-Christians (Brooke, Law).
He narrows the "neighbour" of the Great Commandment to the
"brother" (4:21), and Law remarks that "in point of Christian
insight the epistle lags far behind the parable of the Good Samaritan". Brooke emphasises that John does not say that brotherly
love completes the law of Christ: John confronts failure of
fellowship within the Churches and there is nothing inconsistent in

stressing that Christian charity should begin at home! Law also appeals to the immediate purpose of the letter, finding inadequate Westcott's view that "only through recognition of the relation to Christ is the larger relation at last apprehended", and Plummer's: "Other members of the human race are not excluded, they are not under consideration". John speaks specifically against the Gnostics' "arrogant and loveless intellectualism", resisting separatist tendencies by declaring that "Christian love must be extended to the whole Body of Christ, must comprehend without distinction all the children of God".

It should, however, be added that in deriving human love from experience of the divine love, and emphasising that divine love is *universal,* John plainly implies that ours should be universal also. His extension of love, in prayer, to the erring brother, carries the same implication. In the masterly analysis of the growth of the Christian soul in 2 Peter 1:5-7, brotherly kindness is shown as the final step on the road from self-absorption to Christian charity — the love of fellow-Christians the gateway to the love of men as men. If this is the process by which all Christians learn love, how much more necessary is it for those who treat fellow-Christians with intellectualist contempt? Our wish that John had made clear that love of the brethren is not the ultimate requirement of Christian ethics probably arises from our love of system and completeness. John has no such academic interest in mind: he says what his divided readers urgently need to hear, without for a moment suggesting that when they have grasped that, there is not more yet which in due time will also need to be said.

For John, as for all New Testament writers, and for Jesus Himself, love is the very last word in Christian morality.

(iii) But for definition, standard, and motive of that ultimate obligation, John turns (as also does the whole New Testament) to the example of Jesus. The imitation of Christ is everywhere in apostolic teaching, but it may be doubted if anywhere there is a more complete exposition than John's of what the "imitation" means. The whole epistle is a comment upon the crucial words of John 13:15, in which gospel and ethic combine: "I have given you an example that you also should do as I have done to you".

When we enquire how the divine life given to those who believe will manifest itself in day-to-day experience, John replies: "The life was made manifest, and we saw it"; — we know its quality by watching Him. If it be asked what is meant by "walking in the light", John reminds us how He once walked, and now

179

is "in", the light — all His inward and outward life self-exposed to the divine holiness. So, the claim to enjoy fellowship with Him must be proved by "walking as He walked", an expression which (because "walk" connotes in Hebrew ethical teaching the most down-to-earth, everyday behaviour) states the principle of imitation in far less mystical and more practical terms than is often the case.

Again, the example of Jesus is, for the Christian conscience, the touchstone of righteousness, both as to the obligation itself and as to the meaning of "right". He is the Righteous One: "If you know that He is righteous, you may be sure that every one who does righteousness is born of Him"; and by "righteous" is meant this: "He who does right is righteous, as He is righteous". In the same way, Jesus is the standard of purity of heart: "Every one who thus hopes in Him purifies himself as He is pure". And Jesus is the standard of love, also: "By this we know love, that He laid down His life for us; and we ought to lay down our lives for the brethren".

Moreover, the example of Jesus illumines not only our obligation but our experience. We can expect no better treatment from the world than He received: "The reason why the world does not know us is that it did not know Him". On the other hand, as Jesus dwelt in love, walking in perfect understanding, fearlessness, and delight in God, in perfect freedom of soul despite the antagonistic judgements of men and the awful judgement of the cross, so we (in spite of judgement) may walk in the love that casts out fear. "As He is, so are we in the world" — on which Dodd comments: "The context shows that John is appealing to the example of Christ as the One of whom it can be said, without qualification, that He 'remains in love and love is complete' in Him. . . . Christ is in perfect union with the Father . . . and this union with God by mutual indwelling is held up as the archetype, or ideal, of the communion of the Christian with God".

So close is the parallel between the Christian's experience and Christ's that John can even say, somewhat unexpectedly, that Christ also is "born of God" (5:18), and so able to keep from the evil one all who are one with Him in the divine family. Beyond this moral identification and imitation of Jesus, John can see no higher destiny or glory for the Christian: "It does not yet appear what we shall be, but we know that when He shall appear we shall be like Him, for we shall see Him as He is".

180

To some minds, "imitation of Christ" suggests an external and automatic "copying" of Christ's life, ignoring the many features that make our situation and task and personal status so vastly different from His. John's exposition of the great New Testament ideal should settle that misunderstanding. To be "conformed to the image of God's Son", to be "changed into His likeness from one degree of glory to another", means more than copyist-imitation of His acts and words and gestures. It means an inward approximation to Christ, possessing and being possessed by His Spirit, "having the mind of Christ", being "transformed by the renewal of your mind" to be like Him, and so — in our very different world and age — expressing His outstanding qualities, His prevailing attitudes, His ruling thoughts, in whatever ways our need and opportunity direct. Christ *is* the Christian way, as He is the Christian truth and the Christian life; He *is* the ethic, as He is the gospel. In the last resort, every Christian moral obligation is summed up in the first of all gospel invitations — "Follow Me".

Commandment, love, the imitation of Christ: these constitute for John the foci of all positive Christian ethics. And by concentrating on these three principles, John successfully demonstrates the identity of evangel and ethic, of salvation and sanctification, of spiritual experience and moral transformation. Paul did this by making saving faith *mean* that union with Christ in which believers die with Christ to sin and rise with Christ to newness of life. John does it by making the Christian ethic *mean* keeping Christ's commandments — which is only the active confessing of Christ as Lord and Son; by making love central — and showing that Christian love is divine love bestowed; and by making imitation of Christ the controlling consideration — for to believe in Him, know Him, abide in Him, is to be like Him, since "like is only known by like".

So, to call Jesus Lord, to have received the divine love, to know Him and abide in Him, is to be *necessarily,* by the same token, set upon the way of Christian morality. The evangelical experience is the threshold of ethics, and saving faith proves itself the faith that saves — from sinning.

181

4: *Evangelicals and Ecumenicity**

MODERN ECUMENICITY HAD EVANGELICAL ORIGINS,
not only in the sense that it arose out of the World Missionary
Conference at Edinburgh in 1910 and its predecessors, but also in
the sense that evangelical leaders and motives had long prepared
for that beginning. At the rise of the modern missionary movement stands William Carey, proposing in the famous "Enquiry"
a denominational Missionary Society with the comment: "I do
not mean by this in any wise to confine it to one denomination of
Christians. I wish with all my heart that every one who loves
our Lord Jesus Christ in sincerity would in some way or other
engage in it. But in the present divided state of Christendom, it
would be more likely for good to be done by each denomination
engaging separately in the work, than if they were to embark in it
conjointly. There is room enough for us all, without interfering with
each other; and if no unfriendly interference took place each denomination would bear good will to the other, and wish and pray
for its success . . . but if all were intermingled, it is likely that their
private discords might throw a damp upon their spirits and much
retard their public usefulness".

Earlier Carey had said that prayer is perhaps the only thing
in which Christians of all denominations can cordially and un-
reservedly unite, but in this we may all be one; and when the great
college at Serampore was instituted, open to every Christian de-

* Notes on Essay 4, p. 268.

nomination in Asia, the wry comment occurred: "It will be time enough a hundred years hence, when the country is filled with knowledge and truth has triumphed over error, to think of sects and parties".

The illustrious Henry Martyn confessed to being "very much struck by the grandeur of Carey's proposal of decennial World Missionary Conferences at the Cape" — to begin in 1810! Within three years, "ancient bigotries were carried to blest burial" at the founding of the interdenominational London Missionary Society. "I am more than ever anxious to know no man after his sect, as an independent, episcopalian, presbyterian, methodist or baptist. . . . Let us love him exceedingly in whom we see much of Christ though his opinions are contrary to our own. So shall we know we are passed from death unto life, and sectarian quarrels will cease." That sounds like an exhortation from Amsterdam or Evanston in the mid-twentieth century: it hails from India in the eighteenth.

To take only a second example of early evangelical concern for ecumenicity: "The unity of the Church is one of the most clearly revealed doctrines of the Bible. There is one fold, and one shepherd; one king, and one kingdom; one temple, an habitation of God through the Spirit; one vine, of which all believers are the branches; one body, of which all are members. The very expression 'the Church', so familiar to the ears of the readers of the Scriptures, implies that there can be but one Church which Christ loved and for which He died". So runs the opening sentence of a sermon by the great evangelical divine Charles Hodge, preached almost a century ago — in April 1866 — setting forth the principles of Christian unity as held by the "great body of evangelicals".

"The want of brotherhood, the isolations of Christians, so that every one seems to be seeking his own, and not the welfare of others, is perhaps the most glaring defect of Christianity. It was not so at the beginning, and it will not be so at the end", declares Hodge. The true Church has one faith, taught by one Spirit; the creeds and the fellowship witness to the Church's inward and spiritual unity — the spiritual or mystical union of believers scattered over the earth and in Churches separated but by the law of the Spirit striving to remain one. External unity "is a goal as distant now as it was centuries ago. Still it should be recognised as the goal to which the Church tends, for which she should strive, and the failure to attain which should be recognised as an imperfection and a sin". So, with very modern realism, Hodge pleads for mutual recognition of each Church's assemblies, sacraments, orders, for intercommunion, for non-interference, and for co-operation in common tasks.

The missionary impulse to ecumenicity remains one of its strongest motives. The oft-cited possibility that Hindu brothers sent to different mission schools and brought to Christ might well find themselves, returning home, unable to share the Lord's Supper together merely focuses a situation that for too long has made nonsense — in non-Christian eyes — of the gospel of reconciliation. "That the world might believe" is a challenge to unity which no evangelical can ignore. Nor will evangelicals deny that spiritual experience is enriched as fellowship widens; only "with all the saints" can we truly know the length, breadth, height, and depth of the love of Christ. "What the individual receives in Christ is fully realised", says J. S. Whale, "only in and through community", adding that the paradox — every believer has the whole of Christ, no one believer has Christ wholly — is resolved in the communion of saints, wherein all have all things common.

The Right Reverend Marcus Loane of Sydney names a third evangelical reason for concern with Church unity. "The eyes of the world are on the World Council of Churches as they have seldom been on any one Christian communion. It has rendered splendid service in the post-war age in certain spheres of social welfare work which no one denominational group could emulate. The work of Inter-Church Aid, for example, on behalf of refugees and migrants has been of the highest value. The World Council itself is well placed to act as a clearing-house for ideas, or to provide for effective intervention on such issues as segregation or persecution. Yet evangelicals continue to feel misgivings . . ." — although evangelicalism at its best has ever been deeply moved by social need and human suffering.

Yet the deepest impulse to unity comes, for evangelicals as for all others, from the New Testament: from the great High-Priestly prayer of Jesus that "they all may be one", from the glorious metaphors of the Church as Body, Vine, Temple, Bride, one Bread. The implications of one gospel, one cross, one table, one Bible, one family prayer, one law of love, all lend irresistible force to Paul's contention that unity is given, already, and our duty is to be "eager to maintain the unity of the Spirit in the bond of peace".

Evangelism, spiritual experience, social compassion, scripture — all the key notes of evangelicalism urge towards unity: yet there are misgivings.

The Evangelicals' Dilemma

It is easy to be impatient with evangelical hesitations about unity, but the impatience would be more impressive if it sprang from greater knowledge and understanding. Evangelical difficulties are varied and cumulative, and although — as a representative voice of the World Council of Churches has said — contact and conversation with the conservative evangelical Churches is in some ways more difficult than with the Roman Catholics, the reason lies as much in the shallowness, ambiguity, and provocation of ecumenical statements as in the prejudices and suspicions of some evangelicals.

It is *shallow,* for example, to pretend that all distinctions between Christians are trivial and stupid, matters of historical accident, tradition, hero-worship, or aesthetics, perpetuated by obstinacy and self-righteousness, so that divisions are "branded as sin" (Amsterdam, 1948). Episcopal government, liturgical worship, claims to priesthood, infant baptism, lay ministry, the meaning of the Supper are issues of principle and of scriptural loyalty for many hearts: "There are such conscientious differences of opinion on questions of doctrine and order as render harmonious action in one and the same externally united body impossible; it is better to separate than to quarrel or oppress" (Hodge).

When an Anglo-Catholic declares "schism is the greatest sin of all . . . there is always an element of petulance and immaturity in the schismatic mind", many must reply with Dr. Lovell Cocks: "We can never admit that schism is the worst evil that can befall Christ's Church: witness must be borne to gospel truth even at the cost of unity", or with Leith Samuel: "There are limits imposed by the teaching of Christ in Holy Scripture beyond which evangelicals are not prepared to go in search of unity. . . . Loyalty to Christ matters more than unity with professing Christians. . .". To confess the "sins" of John Huss and the Wesleys, of Calvin, Luther, and the Pilgrim Fathers, may be more comfortable than to confess our own, but evangelicals cannot forget that divisions have often arisen around those who *resisted* sin and protested against error, with deep reluctance and at immense sacrifice.

The *ambiguity* which makes some evangelicals hesitate affects both the basis and the purpose of the ecumenical movement. The statement of Stockholm, 1925, that "it is not 'credo' that they wish to hear us say, it is 'amo'; there have been times when it was

185

dogma that was needed, today it is action in charity and union" sounds a little thin this side of Nazism and the ideological cold war. The declaration at Delhi (1962) that "the World Council of Churches is a fellowship of Churches which confess the Lord Jesus Christ as God and Saviour according to the scriptures to the glory of the one God, Father, Son and Holy Spirit" should (in the words of a leading British evangelical, A. T. Houghton) "go far to meet the criticisms of those outside the World Council, who have objected to the nebulous basis of its membership", especially as the Central Committee has declared (Toronto, 1950) that "no Church by virtue of its membership . . . is under an obligation to suppress, truncate or alter its full confession of truth".

But when it is maintained that the World Council is the meeting ground for men of all schools of thought, and each Church must interpret the basis for itself, who can cite the confession as proof that the ecumenical movement is orthodox? "What can one think of that kind of self-delusion which asks those who do not agree to join hands and to act as though they were one, on the ground of a formula which each may interpret in his own way?" It is of course totally unfair to criticise the whole movement for the variant opinions of individual delegates appointed by the member-Churches; but so is it unfair to dismiss as bigotry the conviction that "a least-common-denominator unity", that blurs legitimate doctrinal considerations for the sake of harmony, will prove spiritually valueless.

The ecumenical goal is as ambiguous as its basis. Reunion is often represented in terms of a "mammoth super-denominational structure", "churchly unity", "the coming Great Church"; and Dr. Visser 't Hooft has said that "the only goal worthy of a Council of Churches is to manifest the one undivided Church. Our Council therefore represents the emergency solution — a stage on the road — a body between the time of the complete isolation of the Churches from each other and the time — on earth or in heaven — when it will be visibly true that there is one shepherd and one flock". One reads that "ecumenical thought is utterly impatient with the Reformed doctrine of the invisible Church . . . an opiate for a divided Christendom", and Nelson speaks of those who "subordinate empirical unity to a vague and chimeric spiritual unity".

Yet at the same time appeal is frequently made to the example of the New Testament Church — which was patently *not* uniform in organisation, worship, or discipline. The synagogue-type Church in Judea, and presupposed in the letter to the Hebrews, differed as substantially from the Church life of Corinth, or that presupposed by the letter to the Galatians, as does that of the modern Anglo-Catholic from Pentecostalism; and Romans 12-15, 1 Corinthians 12-14 reveal similar differences of office, outlook, ethos and emphasis prevailing between groups within the same Church. The unity of the New Testament Church was emphatically a unity in diversity, and so long as human nature is various and conscience is free, the potent new wine of the kingdom will need new and flexible wineskins to preserve it. If fragmentation is costly, merely external uniformity of organisation, without the inward unity that shall make machinery subserve spiritual ends, is perilous: the Inquisition may suffice to prove the point.

In the same way it is less than candid to use our Lord's prayer in John 17 — "that they may all be one" — as though this required of the Churches some unifying structure like the World Council. As Leith Samuel says, the unity the Lord prayed for was quite clearly characterised by the following words — "even as We are one . . . even as Thou, Father, art in Me and I in Thee" — which scarcely refers to a unity of ecumenical pattern!

Evangelical apprehensions are *provoked* by the much publicised determination to work towards eventual inclusion of the Roman Church within the World Council. The trumpeted admission of the Russian Orthodox Church, with the adaptation of certain credal statements to meet Orthodox opinion, the omission from the Basis of any soteriological definition, and the ready confession of the "sins" of the Reformers only strengthen the suspicion that "Protestant influence would appear to be receding".

Without questioning that "there are individuals within the Roman Church who have a saving knowledge of the Lord Jesus Christ and with whom one can have fellowship" (Houghton), we can say with Samuel "quite categorically that evangelicals do not desire to be part of any union with an unreformed Church; there are so many points on which we are bound to part company". Nevertheless, evangelicals must remember that to stand aloof from a movement for fear of what that movement *might* do, when standing aloof may make more likely the thing you fear, involves some responsibility for the thing you foresaw but did nothing to prevent!

Other, more practical, difficulties arise where the ecumenical doctrine of non-interference requires "recognition" of sacraments, orders, and status belonging to other Churches in defiance of one's own theological beliefs. Is one always to refrain from seeking to persuade a Roman Catholic that the Mass misinterprets the Supper — for fear of "proselytism"? Is it "interference" to suggest to paedobaptists that their rite is unscriptural? Are we, in fact, to bear witness to our convictions only to those who already agree with us?

In established Christian communities this might reduce to ecumenical good manners, but on mission fields the problem is more serious. The "comity of missions" has long guided the Churches' co-operation and choice of fields, but comity can become exclusion, if — for example — Roman, Orthodox, or Coptic Churches already "in possession" in European, South American or North African areas are to be held sole representatives of Christianity in those regions. Non-interference then amounts to a veto on evangelical witness; and unity means the loss of the right of individual Christians to change their denominational affiliation — or to change their minds!

In the light of so many and so various difficulties, hesitation is surely not surprising. Doubtless some patience and experience in growing together will dissipate many fears and discover fellowship where once only problems existed. Doubtless, too, evangelical witness presents a tragic history of secessions and often trivial separations, appearing sometimes to produce the schismatic as the price and punishment of freedom. It is the judgement of J. R. Nelson that the numerical strength and vigour of those sectarian bodies which will have no part in ecumenical conversations are on the increase; one estimate says there are twenty-four million Protestants in North America remaining outside the World Council of Churches — "more missions and missionaries . . . outside . . . than inside". It would be hard to choose which does the greater harm to the Christian cause: a wholly uncritical ecumenism, or a fragmenting independency, wilful, or merely ignorant. To exalt "Where two or three . . ." as Christ's last word about the Church, to the tune of "Lord keep us little and obscure" is to court spiritual impoverishment and invite fanaticism. An aphorism of Hodge's still finds its mark among evangelicals: "A solitary Christian is but half a Christian!"

But what to do? It is easy to say, "At all costs we must avoid divisions on lesser things", so long as the lesser things remain unspecified. Some evangelicals say with Professor Knox, "I simply cannot conceive of the union of Christendom except on the ground of . . . the full acceptance of the historic episcopate"; others with I. H. Marshall, "Where there is agreement on the basic tenets of the evangelical faith, problems of Church order and government . . . do not stand in the way"; others that no fellowship is possible, or moral, without entire agreement. Paul Rees thinks that ecumenists are often more zealous than evangelicals to interpret and to implement the meaning of the Church, and says it is clear there is need for a "vastly more serious coming to grips with the whole concept of the Church" by evangelicals. Houghton thinks, "All that the evangelical asks is that within the united Church he may have complete freedom of expression in teaching and worship" — which seems to ignore the real problems.

The situation does not stand still, and some conscientious response, in which all evangelicals can join, to the ecumenical challenge, becomes increasingly imperative. The dilemma appears inexorable. Loyalty to truth seems to preclude the unity that truth should promote; the pursuit of unity seems to endanger that truth without which unity would be worthless.

Meanwhile either compromise or exclusion appears inevitable. A great number of active and well-organised bodies, the World Evangelical Fellowship, the National Association of Evangelicals, the Evangelical Alliance, the Scripture Union, the Inter-Varsity Fellowship, and many large or small missionary societies, in addition to groupings like the International Council of Christian Churches, may find themselves forced into growing isolation as the ecumenical movement develops, and the Christian alignment at the close of the century may very well find the multifarious divisions of the last three centuries reduced to two main groups: a "catholic" world Council, marked by unity of organisation, political power, and a measure of uniformity, in worship and ethos, in line with the tradition of the "older" Churches, alongside a loose association of evangelicals marked by diversity of organisation, spiritual fervour, and a large variety of worship and ethos of a mainly biblicist and conservative type. Outwardly an improvement on the present situation, such a polarisation of Christian faith and feeling might in fact produce a division as deep, intractable, persistent, and embittered as any in Christian history — an ideological cold war within the reconciling society!

The Insights of 1 John

It is interesting how often in ecumenical discussion the Johannine literature is appealed to, and not least the open letter of John. It would be foolish to suggest that this short first-century tract contains the answers to the modern evangelical's problems, but it is no exaggeration to say that 1 John is the one New Testament book which deals explicitly with questions of Church unity in the modern sense. In Romans and 1 Corinthians the disunity dealt with is domestic to the local fellowship; in Galatia factors of history, race, theology, and liturgy produced a division nearer to that between Roman and Protestant, but even here the attempt was to impose a particular view upon the whole Church. 1 John, however, faces a situation of deliberate schism, a voluntary and formal withdrawal into secession. In John 10 and 17 something like this may be hinted at, in 1 John it is the focal problem. The word "Church" does not occur, and yet the "Church problem" arises for John with quite exceptional urgency just because he writes with the purpose of retaining fellowship — of preventing further schism. All that he has to say about Christian relationships with disagreeing brethren gains immense force from the fact that he is not at all concerned with the Church as an institution, or with questions of organisation, orders, or ritual.

Nothing in the New Testament is more eloquent of concern for Christian unity than John's interpretation of the breach of fellowship by heretical teachers as sufficient sign of the coming end of the age — the last hour — and evidence of the presence and power of Antichrist. It is difficult to summarise John's teaching on unity without once again reviewing the whole epistle. He is acutely aware of the *Church's* existence, life, and corporate worship, with her inspired prophetic leadership, her teaching ministry, and her witnessing sacraments; and twice he sets the Church-community as one body in sharp contrast to the "outside" world. The apostolic fellowship is "of God", and indestructible, since those who do the will of God abide for ever.

(i) John holds that communal Christian experience — which is the value ecumenicity safeguards — is inseparable from the enjoyment of eternal life as children of God. New birth may be — in a restricted sense — an individual experience, but it is not, for John, an individualist conception: it connotes membership, and loving membership (5:1), in the divine family. The divine life, inherent first in God and manifest in Christ overflows to all who believe, and the imparted life is indivisible in Father, Son and family.

Thus only by right relationship with our brethren do we know that we have passed from death to life. To secede from the unity of the fellowship is to reveal long-standing alienation (2:19); to fail in love of the brethren is to prove oneself no child of God, but of the devil. To deny the spiritual life of another, by hating him, is to "murder" him — and as we have seen, the whole point of the sudden reference to Cain and Abel lies in the parallel between the ancient family tragedy and the hatred that had arisen between Christian brethren on religious grounds — almost a miniature of divided Christendom. Similarly, to love the Father is to love the Father's other children (5:1); to claim to love the Father and not love the brethren is to lie (4:20). Christian life is essentially a family affair: community is *necessary* to its enjoyment and its rightful expression.

(ii) John holds that communal Christian experience is inseparable from fellowship with God; *our* fellowship is with the Father and with His Son, walking in the light is a fellowship with God which immediately establishes fellowship with one another (1:7). Only in such mutual comradeship is Christian joy complete: division brings impoverishment to all. With the same implication John adds to the Christian's prayer-life the "dimension of ecumenicity" in his counsel concerning prayer for the seceding brethren. In prayer, the will to unity can be sustained even where nothing more is possible.

(iii) John holds too that (of course) communal Christian experience is inseparable from the Christian ethic, since the highest Christian good — love — simply cannot be realised without ecumenicity. The whole weight of all that John has to say about love of the brethren moves irresistibly in the direction of Christian unity. Bad ecumenical relationships — hatred of the brother Christian — are darkness itself (2:9); he whose heart is closed against his brother lives and walks in darkness; he knows not where he is going — he is spiritually blind. The whole gospel of divine love manifest in incarnation and atonement makes the loving unity of Christians obligatory — it becomes a *commandment,* with all the solemn authority of the Master's remembered words behind it.

John's overwhelming emphasis upon the absolute necessity of love towards one's Christian brethren, even across the gulfs of disagreement, is John's main contribution to the ecumenical debate.

191

But it is almost balanced by his emphasis upon truth. This, too, is conceived communally. It is the apostolic community which testifies through the letter (1:1; 4:14) and the effect of such collective testimony is to promote still wider fellowship (1:3). "False teaching and bitter antagonisms threaten a dissolution of partnership in the common faith and a breach of the common bond of charity. To counter the menace he would recall his readers to the word of life, to the gospel . . . a return to the gospel and commandment will restore and confirm the threatened fellowship of the Church. *Nothing else will . . .*" (C. H. Dodd).

"Truth", says Law, "is the medium of Christian fellowship . . . 'as every stream of water makes for the sea, every rill of truth makes for fellowship of souls'". And Augustine makes an exceptionally suggestive comment upon the denial that Jesus has come in the flesh (4:3), with which 1 John is so concerned: he finds a close link between the love that brought Christ into the flesh, the lack of love which cannot believe in such self-denying incarnation, and the "dissolving" of Christ — of the one Body — by disrupting the Church with the consequent heresy. The implied exegesis (and text) may be doubtful, but the spiritual perceptiveness is unchallengeable.

When Law says that "the writer reveals himself as one whose mind is dominated, in an exceptional degree, by the idea of *truth",* one knows that he might just as fittingly have said "by the idea of love". All that John says about unity between brethren is made more provocative by his contention for truth — for in the present ecumenical debate truth and love seem, to many earnest minds, to present irreconcilable imperatives. Unity in falsehood, or at least in deliberate ambiguity, is the very real peril of uncritical ecumenicity. If 1 John leaves no shred of doubt that the attitude which glories in division, in the exclusive self-preserving separation, the self-congratulatory isolation which sets us apart from our brethren, is wholly deplorable and condemned, it leaves as little doubt that the sacrifice of Christian truth for the sake of conformity or compromise is equally deplorable, and as sharply condemned.

In this way John poses the ultimate and painful question that confronts evangelicals in Church relationships, and the only issue that really matters. The tension between truth and love is inescapable. When theological consistency seems to oppose ecumenical charity — who shall choose? Dr. Visser 't Hooft trenchantly opposes a conception of tolerance which owes its origins not to the Bible but to modern humanitarianism. "Its weakness is that it isolates the question of unity from the question of truth." And that is precisely what 1 John forbids. For John there is no unity without truth, and the truth itself requires unity in love; yet it is so often varying conceptions of truth, and varying loyalties to it, that constitute the obstacles to unity.

Genuinely to forego a shallow Christian unity for the sake of conviction and loyalty to truth is painful, but it sacrifices only an appearance of good. To forego truth for the sake of unity is in the end to surrender unity also — for all Christian unity is grounded in the Gospel and created in Christ: if that goes, if He be misunderstood or misrepresented, the foundation of all ecumenicity is destroyed.

So long, therefore, as evangelicals are convinced of the truth of their interpretation of the gospel, so long they must acknowledge two inescapable duties. First, to witness to that truth, fearlessly and plainly and with love, in ecumenical circles. Houghton describes the difficulties of doing this, where the evangelical group finds itself a patronised minority, too obviously tolerated as intellectually "weaker brethren". But he adds unanswerably, "Surely the place where such testimony is most urgently needed is not among convinced supporters but among those who at least will give a ready hearing to views which differ from their own if put forward with Christian courtesy".

But the second duty may nevertheless arise, and if it does, it will be even more difficult to fulfil properly. It is to withdraw, at the point where the price of unity becomes too high, and to do so *only* for the truth's sake — regretfully, humbly, with no trace or appearance of self-righteousness, well able to conceive that we might be wrong, yet until error is proved upon us, unable to compromise conviction for the sake of comradeship. If the choice has to be made, John's rigorous clarity leaves no alternative: the first obligation is to love the brethren, but the brethren are those who share the truth.

So the truth must stand. Yet even in the painful divisions that loyalty to truth demands, there can be no abating the imperative of unity. We must pray for the erring brother, share our goods with him, and humbly seek to witness to him, never isolating ourselves in pride, in contempt, or in despair of him. We may only differ from him because — in immortal words of spiritual anguish born of severance from a Church long loved and diligently served, "Unless I am convicted of error by the testimony of scripture . . .

or . . . by manifest reasoning I stand convicted by the scriptures
. . . and my conscience is taken captive by God's word, I cannot
and will not recant. . . . On this I take my stand. I can do no
other — God help me!"

5: *Evangelicals and the Cross**

"THE CENTRE OF DOCTRINAL INTEREST in the epistle is *the incarnation"*, declares Law; "in presenting so fully *the work of Christ* . . . John has bequeathed to the Church a treasure she cannot measure and dare not lose," replies Vincent Taylor. The truth is that for John the primary purpose of the incarnation is to accomplish man's salvation: "the Father sent the Son to be the Saviour . . . God sent His Son to be the expiation for our sin". As Law himself says, "The apostle's wholehearted denunciation of the Docetic Christology was due to the fact that it not only 'dissolved' Christ but took away from men their Redeemer".

John refers to the redeeming work of Christ in no less than seventeen verses of his short epistle, and reproduces nine separate ideas which were associated with atonement in primitive Christian teaching. Nevertheless it is in John's clarification and development of that earliest teaching that chief interest lies, for such clarification is one of our deepest needs. It is perilously easy, on the subject of the cross, to sound impeccably orthodox and mean nothing. "Once a blurred and indistinct view of the atonement is accepted in the Church, it is more than likely that the next generation will come to the ultimate obscurity of a man like F. W. Robertson of Brighton, of whom it was said, 'Robertson believed that Christ did something or other, which, somehow or other, had some connection or other with salvation'." Unfortunately Robertson's position — if that is a true judgement — was not unique.

* Notes on Essay 5, p. 268.

The Common Gospel

John's most comprehensive statement of the doctrine of salvation is, "The Father sent the Son to be the Saviour of the world". To this may be added the general statement that Christ was manifested to take away sins, to destroy the work of the devil. When we seek further analysis of the *means* of salvation, 1 John directs our thought to salvation by divine life made known and imparted (1:1, 5:11, 12); to salvation by divine love manifested and bestowed (4:9, 3:1); and to salvation by revelation received (1:1, 4:14, 5:8, 20). But the life, the love, the revelation, are all conveyed in a sacrifice offered on our behalf, an expiation made concerning our sin (1:7, 2:2; life — 4:9, 10; love — 3:16, 4:10; revelation — 4:9, 14).

The *effect* of Christ's work in relation to sin is to "cleanse" it, analysed as "forgiveness" (a cleansing in God's sight, the stain of sin no longer hindering fellowship with Him), and "cleansing from all unrighteousness" (actual moral purification). The general *nature* of Christ's work in relation to sin is also clear: He laid down His life (soul) for us (3:16). Plummer cites for the translation "paid down" examples of paying ransom, interest, taxes, on another's behalf, but he still prefers "laid down" (as John 10:17, 18 and elsewhere). The emphasis, as both Denney and Brooke remark, falls on the contrast between Him and us — such as He for such as we! But substitution is here (3:16) excluded by the way in which what Christ did is affirmed to be the pattern for what we must do for the brethren.

John, however, offers more than a general description of the nature of Christ's work: he defines that work in a term which lexically means "propitiation", but which by usage and context may represent rather "expiation". With this John conjoins the theological shorthand phrase "the blood of His Son" (1:7, 5:6, 8). And this already rich conception of Christ's work for sinful men is further supplemented by the affirmation of Christ's advocacy with the Father (2:2). It is upon the meaning of this language that discussion mainly turns.

(i) "Propitiation" derives ultimately from the idea of someone made propitious or merciful toward a suppliant. Psalm 130:4, "There is forgiveness with Thee", is literally "There is propitiation before Thee". To propitiate, in classical thought, means to appease, conciliate; in Luke 18:13 it becomes "God be merciful [propitious, kindly disposed] toward me", but in Hebrews 12:17

it is translated "to make expiation". John's statement is that Christ is the means of appeasing, of making propitiation — a thought closely paralleled by Paul, who says (Romans 3:25) that God "put forward" Christ "as an expiation by His blood".

Dodd likens the means of propitiation, in Old Testament thought, to "a powerful disinfectant" by which the taint of sin is removed; "by what Christ had done and suffered, the sin that had brought Him down was so to speak neutralised, and its corruption sterilised, by the love and power of God". If our guilt needs an Advocate with God, it might be said we need also to placate God's anger: but John rests our forgiveness not on placating but on God's own faithfulness and justice.

Barclay too recalls that the aim of religion is perfect personal relationship with God, that sin interrupts that relationship, and sacrifice is designed to restore the relationship when it is interrupted; and taking up the metaphor of "disinfecting", he declares: "The great basic truth behind this word is, that it is through Jesus Christ that man's fellowship with God is first restored, then manifested. . . . Through what He did the penalty is remitted, the guilt is removed, the defilement is taken away". So Westcott: "The propitiation, so to speak, neutralises the sin".

Brooke contends that the object of propitiation, in Jewish thought, is not God but man — estranged man — or the sins which have intervened between him and his God. These must be "covered" before right relations can be restored. Vincent Taylor prefers to say sins are "annulled" by Christ's propitiation, so that they no longer stand between ourselves and God. Denney, commenting that "the characteristic words of religion cannot be applied in new ways at will", says that propitiation is related to sin and its removal, to sacrifice and blood, to the divine order that sin has violated, and which is acknowledged in its inviolable rights by the propitiation. "All that is divine, all the moral order of the world, all that we mean by the law of God, has right done by it in the death of Christ. Sin is . . . neutralised . . . no more a barrier to fellowship with God."

And this is the substance of Law's exposition. Propitiation "expiates the guilt of sin, restores sinful offenders to God by rendering their sin null and inoperative as a barrier to fellowship with Him". Thus, whether expressed in ancient terms — expiation, propitation, covering, removal of sin — or in modern expressions like annulment, sterilisation, disinfecting, neutralising, or rendering sin inoperative, the nature of Christ's work in relation to sin is plain: through Him sin, a just barrier to man's fellowship with God, is got out of the way.

(ii) As to the *method* by which Christ's propitiation is achieved, Dodd can say: "Jesus went willingly to death at the hands of His enemies having a few hours earlier plainly declared by solemn acts and words that He dedicated Himself to death as a sacrifice on behalf of men"; Vincent Taylor, in an exhaustive examination of the sayings of Jesus about His death, leaves no doubt that Jesus thought in terms of sacrifice; and Law points out that when the work of Christ was described as a propitiatory sacrifice, and was seen to embody the full truth which the sacrificial system of the Old Testament faintly and imperfectly expressed, no need of further elucidation suggested itself, the necessity and the efficacy of sacrifice being "simply axiomatic". According to the analogy of the Old Testament, and in consonance with every type of New Testament teaching, "the propitiatory virtue of all Christ is and has done and does is here regarded as concentrated in His blood; and what this term connotes is the life offered to God in His death".

This raises the whole question of the interpretation of sacrifice, expiation, and the term "blood". The last occurs thirty times in the New Testament, three times as often as the "cross" of Christ, five times as often as the "death" of Christ.

C. H. Dodd makes a strong attempt to reduce the New Testament's sacrificial language to modern non-sacrificial terms: Christ, left at the last utterly alone to bear the consequences of rejection and desertion, of concentrated human wickedness against Himself, yet returns to the disciples in a manifest act of forgiveness, and sends them forth preaching forgiveness — "a signal exhibition of divine forgiveness". This makes the cross not necessary to forgiveness but necessary to its effective demonstration; it does not explain at all convincingly how the "blood of His Son" *cleanses* us from all sin.

Westcott elaborated a theory by which "blood shed" in sacrifice means the death of the victim, and the "blood offered" represents the victim's life made available as the source of life to the worshippers. The blood is conceived as still living when shed, as Abel's blood cried to God for vengeance: "the life of the flesh is in the blood" (Leviticus 17:11). So "the blood of Christ is, as shed, the life of Christ given *for* men, and, as applied, the life of Christ now given *to* men — the life which is the spring of their life". Brooke restated this: "The power of

Christ's life . . . set free by death for wider service . . . is effective for the gradual removal of sin"; and Law: "The warm fluid blood was considered as the life of the animal, not a symbol of life but the life itself, and the essence, ritually, of the sacrificial act consisted in the offering of the life-blood to God". Says Vincent Taylor: "The victim is slain in order that the life, in the form of blood, may be released . . . the bestowal of life is the fundamental idea in sacrificial worship . . . the use of the term 'blood' . . . suggests the thought of life, dedicated, offered, transformed, and open to our spiritual appropriation".

But John does not say that the blood communicates the life of Christ to us, congenial as that idea would be to his opening sentence, but that it achieves our *cleansing*. Moreover, on this interpretation no assurance based upon a finished, perfect work of Christ is ever possible: His death makes His life available, but our salvation rests upon our appropriation of that life — our own personal and moral effort to be saved. That is not the apostolic gospel.

Denney wrote long ago of the "strange caprice which fascinated Westcott", adding that "no more groundless fancy ever haunted and troubled the interpretation of any part of scripture than that which is introduced by this distinction" between blood shed and blood offered. "There is no meaning in saying that by His death, His life — as something other than His death — is 'liberated' and 'made available' for men: on the contrary, what makes His risen life significant and a saving power for sinners is neither more nor less than this, that His death is in it; it is the life of One who by dying has dealt with the fatal necessities of man's situation and in doing so has given a supreme demonstration of His love."

The most painstaking examination of the whole subject of "the blood of Christ", however, has been made by A. M. Stibbs. He has no difficulty at all in showing that the crying of Abel's blood does not indicate continuing life but only a vivid metaphor; that appropriating life through sacrificial blood would lend itself most readily to ritual blood-drinking — but this was most strictly forbidden; that the blood is not "life" but "the life of the flesh" — that is, only so long as it is in the flesh; once shed, the life of the flesh is gone. Hence the innumerable examples of "blood" as signifying violent death, with overtones of responsibility or blame, of someone's blood upon one's head. In none of these instances is the liberation or making available of life part of the meaning.

This is equally clear in the passages where the overtones are of sacrifice and atonement. In Jewish thought, life belonged to God who gave it, and not to men, and "God will require blood of any man that sheds it". So in Numbers 35:33 — "Blood pollutes the land, and no expiation can be made for the land, for the blood that is shed in it, except by the blood of him who shed it". Yet the blood of animals, forbidden as drink or for any other use, was expressly provided for the purpose of expiation: "I have given it for you upon the altar to make atonement for your souls: for it is the blood that makes atonement" (Leviticus 17:11).

Thus, expiation by the blood of the guilty is in sacrifice replaced by expiation by the blood of a guiltless substitute, a lamb without spot or blemish. Given by divine appointment, such guiltless blood could be used, in sprinkling, to purify things and persons for God's presence and use. Blood wrongly shed could remain upon a person, crying out for vengeance, marking guilt, and involving danger of penalty: blood sacrificially shed could likewise remain upon a person, or between him and God, for expiation, cleansing from guilt, releasing from penalty, and securing access to God.

The expiation which covers, annuls, or makes inoperative the sin that bars man's access to God is therefore a sacrificial self-offering by which the death of the guiltless atones for the guilty. That is the method of Christ's work at Calvary.

(iii) This is not all John's meaning, in 1:7-2:2, as we shall see; but it is certainly part of his intention when he names Christ the propitiation and speaks of His blood as cleansing from all sin. To this divine provision for man's sinful situation, John then adds the assertion that we have also an advocate with the Father. The "advocate", it has already been said, is a friend of the accused called in to aid his cause and speak to his character. The term, or the idea implied, is used both of Christ (here, Romans 8:34, and throughout Hebrews) and of the Spirit (John 14:16, 26; 15:26, 16:7, Romans 8:26-27). The immediate proximity of blood and propitiation suggests that in John's mind the advocacy belonged within the same circle of ideas as the sacrifice — as in Hebrews — and Law interprets John's meaning in straightforward priestly terms, assuming that John avoided the word as not familiar, or familiar but debased, in Asian pagan circles.

Brooke cites a striking Jewish aphorism, "The sin offering is like the paraclete before God, it intercedes for man . . ." and Plummer to the same effect paraphrases John's words as "Jesus

Christ, as being righteous, is ever present before the Lord as the propitiation". Huther relates the propitiation and the intercession by saying the latter presupposes the former. To say as does Brooke that Christ's advocacy is valid because He can Himself bear witness that the only condition on which fellowship between God and man can be restored has actually been fulfilled, almost suggests that God might not otherwise know! The essential truth is probably best stated by Dodd: "How if there be within the divine Being Itself that which sympathises with us and pleads our cause? The Christian gospel declares that this is so; and . . . that this everlasting mercy was incarnate for us in Christ, who as Man had personal acquaintance with our moral conflict, and now represents us within the eternal Godhead". It is an unforgettable conviction of the evangelical faith that He who died to atone for the sins of the world is "able for all time to save those who draw near to God through Him, since He always lives to make intercession for them".

John's gospel for the sinner, then, comprises forgiveness and cleansing, affording access again to the fellowship of Him who is light, granted through the expiatory sacrifice offered through the violent death of Christ, in bearing responsibility for our blood-guiltiness — an expiatory sacrifice whose virtue is commensurate with Him who offers Himself, God's own Son. And with forgiveness and cleansing, the personal advocacy of One who though He came in the flesh to live our life yet remained the righteous One, and so pleads not for Himself but for us, before the Father's throne.

The Special Emphases

Faithful to the original gospel of the death of Christ, John yet contributes his own especial emphases to that gospel, for which his brief epistle is especially precious to evangelical hearts.

(i) Consonant with all he has to say of God's love for the world, and the assurance offered to *whoever* confesses that Jesus is the Son of God, John explicitly *universalises the atonement* of Christ. He lays unmistakable stress upon the fact not only that Jesus is the Saviour of the world, but that He is the expiation "not for our sins only but also for the sins of the whole world". The cross is not for the elect only, certainly not for any exclusive Gnostic coterie of mystics or intellectuals: nor is it only for believers, though faith is necessary to make its saving energies

201

operative in any individual life. But the atonement offered for sin was for *all* sin: and the forgiveness and fellowship made possible thereby were for all men.

Paul deduces from this fact — that God was in Christ reconciling the *world* to Himself — the unlimited missionary obligation to preach the reconciliation to all men. John deduces the social obligation to keep the new commandment of love, adding thus to Paul's evangelistic zeal the universal compassion of Christian hearts towards a whole world embraced within the arms of Christ's cross.

It is a curious misinterpretation of Christ's death that supposes the atonement comes to apply to my sin at the moment when I believe. The glorious, subduing, reassuring truth is that the atonement has been made, Christ has already died for *my* sake, long before I believe, or understand, or know of it. But just because it does not wait for my acceptance to be acceptable to God, so it does not belong *in any sense* just to me: it belongs "also" to the unbeliever, and avails for his sin. If he does not know it, that may be my fault. If he knows and does not believe, he is condemned not for his sins but because he does not believe (John 3:18), because he chooses not to "have the Son" (1 John 5:12). Yet still the cross stands, alone, unique, sufficient, the finished work of atonement for the sins of the whole world — a fact not always remembered in more exclusive evangelical circles.

(ii) John likewise *personalises the atonement* in a way not always familiar in Christian thought. This is the further truth (beyond that simply of expiatory sacrifice) in the crucial passage 1:6f. For John's climax is an epigram which "gives the word [propitiation] an application which it bears nowhere else in the Greek Bible" (Taylor): "He is the propitiation", He Himself is the cancelling and annulling of sins. Law remarks that this is John's "most notable point" but without pursuing the point at all. Yet not this phrase only, but the whole exposition of the work of Christ implies this truth: His is the blood — God's own Son; He is the propitiation; and He — the righteous One — is the Advocate. All the work centres in the person of Jesus.

It must not be supposed that this is an unparalleled conception of the cross: all the New Testament writers, "though they speak often of Christ's death, never think of a dead Christ", and though they speak of His death, His blood, His cross, they never signify by these expressions some abstract, mental image, or sacrifice generically, but Jesus dying, and rising with the marks of death upon Him (Luke 24:39, John 20:27, Revelation 5:6). This is the truth in Dodd's remark that the expression in 2:2 does not in itself connote a blood-sacrifice but is "wide enough to cover the whole work of Christ, His death especially, no doubt, but not to the exclusion of His incarnation, His earthly ministry, and His resurrection and ascension; the entire work of Christ is an expiation. . .".

Not the cross, but the Christ, is the propitiation. Not believing in a thing, or an event, or even in an attitude of self-sacrificing love for men, saves the soul: but believing in Him who mounted the cruel thing, who endured the horrible event, for the sake of the redemptive attitude — believing in Him because He did these things, but still remembering that *it is relationship to Him which saves, and not merely knowing what He did.* The life is in Him: to relinquish (by denying) the Son is to relinquish eternal life, even though you cling, in some intellectual dogmatism or emotional sentiment, to "the cross" but fail to abide in Him who died and rose again.

This emphasis accords with the view of the Fourth Gospel that the cross was the glorifying of Jesus. For the Evangelist, the cross was a command laid upon Jesus from eternity, and had eternal relevance. The historic event is absolutely necessary to the timeless message, and the Fourth Gospel describes that event with quite exceptional vividness and detail: but still the thought "is always steadily moving towards a spiritualised expression of the sacrificial principles of life through death and access to God through a mediatorial ministry, in a characteristic manner in which all the emphasis falls upon the person of Christ as Himself the Word of God, the Giver of life, and the Way to the Father" (Vincent Taylor).

(iii) In a certain sense, the effect of this emphasis is to *"contemporise"* the atonement. The relation of Christ's "finished work" at Calvary to His yet unfinished work in the life of each generation of believers is a very large question, but the personalising of the atonement in the timeless figure of the Master Himself, and the use of the present tense — the blood cleanses, He is the propitiation, we have an Advocate, His work of destroying sin goes on, the Father still witnesses through baptism and the Supper to His Son — help us to see that for John there is a continuous and contemporary aspect of the cross. All was not finally done at Calvary.

Certainly something was finished: the past tense recurs — the blood was once shed, the Father sent the Son, He came by blood,

He laid down His life for us, the love of God was made manifest (aorists, compare John 10:11, 15, 17; 13:27); the atonement was complete. John's thought fastens, not generally upon the self-sacrificing spirit of Christ's earthly life, but upon the final surrender of that life through death. Nor does John "spiritualise" the cross into some timeless atonement — the perpetual offering of the sacrifice of Christ upon the altar of the Church — or into the abstract principle of vicarious love. In Denny's firm words, "There is no sublimation of the historical into 'ethical' or 'spiritual principles' or into 'eternal facts' which absolve us from all obligation to a Saviour who came in blood. Except through the historical there is no Christianity at all, but neither is there a Christianity until the historical has been spiritually comprehended".

John is perfectly clear about the historical foundation of faith (1:1f.), but equally clear that the spiritual comprehension and response which make the historical fact a timeless, saving power in generations of Christian lives, belong to no one age but extend through time, renewed in each new Christian's experience, bringing the cross to new effectiveness as a "contemporary" fact for every age. The paradox has to be accepted that the crucifixion of Jesus under Pontius Pilate in Palestine in the first century is both a fragment of the world's history and a timeless, undateable reality, a continuing factor in man's religious experience. It is so, not only in the sense that, as with the achievements of Moses or Isaiah, the historical figure and event has abiding significance, but in the deeper, existential sense that the historical Figure and event of Calvary abides as the determining fact upon which contemporary understanding of God's nature and love, contemporary experience of God's grace, and contemporary access to God's presence perpetually depend.

Yet this is but to emphasise from another side that the living and ascended Christ in the presence of the Father is the abiding propitiation. It would preserve evangelicalism from a number of crude, transactional images of the atonement to remember, in this light, that it is not the intellectual apprehension of a historical record — even an inspired record — which saves, but a living, penitent, and grateful relationship with Him who is the timeless expiation for our sin.

(iv) But John's greatest contribution to our understanding of the cross is in the thorough way in which he *moralises* the doctrine of the atonement. On all sides it is held to be the most distinctive element in John's teaching that he roots the expiation made for sin in the love of God the Father. So Vincent Taylor: comparing John 3:16 with 1 John 4:9, he says the latter is the greater utterance in that it presents the *startling* thought that the expiation in the Son is the expression of the love of the Father. "In the light of both passages, any opposition between the Father and the Son in the ministry of redemption is seen to be entirely false to the spirit and teaching of the New Testament."

Law speaks of "one intensely illuminating ray which John sheds upon the idea of propitiation: the sacrifice of Christ is the sacrifice of God. This was the epistle's great contribution to Christian thought, the vision of the cross in the heart of the eternal love". And Denney suggests that "perhaps the most striking thing . . . is the manner in which the propitiation of Christ is related to the love of God". Such surprise suggests that the prevalent impression left by evangelical doctrine concerning the cross is that the work of Christ and the love of God are set over against each other — that Christ died to make God love us, or to persuade Him to let His love be known!

Of course this is caricature. Paul insists that God put forward Christ as an expiation, and showed His love for us in that Christ died for us; that God is for us, not sparing His Son but giving Him up for us all. And John 3:16 states the source of salvation unforgettably. But — as Denney says — 1 John rises to an absolute point of view: it defines propitiation as the act of love (4:10) and love as that which makes propitiation (3:16). Neil Alexander rightly finds the same emphasis in 1:7, where cleansing and forgiveness are ascribed to the justice of God: "the cleansing work of Christ is not only offered to God but is of God, God's purpose, God's work".

Evangelicals unquestionably need this reminder, not only to correct superficial statements of the purpose of the cross, but to illumine the meaning of the love of God. It was *paganism* which conceived propitiation as a means of changing the disposition of the Deity, mollifying His displeasure, rendering Him propitious. The gospel's declaration is that propitiation has its *source* in God. So far from being designed to induce a reluctant Father to forgive, it is His own plan for bringing His estranged children back to Himself.

"It is said that God is love and needs no propitiation: what John teaches is that God is love and therefore provides the propitiation. We never reach the teaching of the New Testament concerning sin until we realise that sin affects God as well as man, that God has to deal with it" (G. S. Barrett); equally, we never reach the teaching of the New Testament concerning divine love until we realise that it is not an infinite sentimentality, a disposition to forgive "with a weak, injurious mercy", but the will to forgive in such manner and on such costly conditions that sin is recognised and dealt with for what it is, with no wrong done, no truth obscured, no responsibility evaded.

This is the strength of John's exposition. When he points to Calvary as the definition of love he is explicitly giving to love its *Christian* quality and depth, such that it no longer appears to make propitiation unnecessary, but imperative. When it is said that a doctrine of propitiation has no logical place in John's characteristic thinking, but is retained from the primitive teaching only at cost of inner contradiction, the moral quality of the love of God is being overlooked. If the propitiatory death of Jesus is eliminated from the love of God, "it might be unfair to say that the love of God is robbed of all meaning, but it is certainly robbed of its apostolic meaning" (Denney).

What is perhaps insufficiently realised is that the message of God's *love* first came to a people nurtured through experience, prophetism, and the law to think of God as supremely King, the moral Governor of the race, the final Judge of men, the Lord of conscience, of history, of human destiny. To say the *King* is Father, that the Lawgiver loves the law-breaker, was at once news and paradox, sufficiently safeguarded against sentimentality and emotionalism in conceiving God's mercy towards sinners. We need, on the other hand, to remember that the loving Father is still the King, Lawgiver, and Judge, and the divine law must be satisfied because it is right: otherwise man's forgiveness is no everlasting mercy but the shoddiest of moral fictions and the undermining of the moral universe. John's definition of love by propitiation forcibly reminds us of just that.

(v) Finally John moralises the doctrine of the atonement also by emphasising, at least as strongly as Paul or Peter, that the gospel of forgiveness through the cross exerts a moral energy that power-fully transforms all who believe. Paul had said this in his doctrine of faith in the Crucified as a dying with Christ. Peter holds to the example of the cross as part of those "steps" in which we are to walk, following Jesus. By declaring that the cleansing of Christ's blood is a present and continuous experience as we walk in the light; by defining Christ's work as a direct and unrelenting opposition to sin; by arguing immediately from Christ's laying down His life for us to our laying down our lives — and our goods — for the brethren; and by insisting that Christian love, the supreme moral imperative for the believer, is but the divine love shown on Calvary reflected back from hearts redeemed by love — John makes the gospel of the cross the most powerful force in all man's religious experience.

Moreover, the double cleansing — from guilt and from all unrighteousness — through Christ's blood presupposes that we walk continually in the light of the divine holiness, frankly confessing the sin there exposed, denying no fact and evading no responsibility, but casting ourselves upon the faithfulness and justice of God: such an experience *cannot* leave us as we were. However it may appear, superficially, that Christ's taking our sin's responsibility relieves us of moral obligation, "it is when that awful experience of Jesus is revealed as a propitiation for sin, an assumption of our responsibility by one who does right by the eternal law which we have wronged, and does it at this tremendous cost for us — it is then that the soul of man is reached by the divine love and through penitence and faith drawn away from evil and born again of God. It is then that the blood of Jesus, God's Son, cleanses from all sin".

It is therefore entirely misleading to suggest that our understanding of the death of Jesus must follow *either* the line of expiatory sacrifice through substituted responsibility for sin, *or* the line of the "moral influence" theories, which find all the effect of the cross in Christ's example of patience, fortitude, and love. The antithesis — a commonplace assumption of most "histories of the doctrine of the atonement" — is wholly false: the view which sees the death of Jesus as an expiatory sacrifice for the sins of the world exerts the most effective moral influence of all.

Such a doctrine of the cross, universalist and not exclusive, rooted in personal relationship to the living Christ as Himself both expiation and Advocate, continuing in power in contemporary experience and not left behind on the shores of the first century, expressing and defining the divine love but never set over against it, and working the moral regeneration of believing hearts, is not one that needs to be apologised for, or exchanged for some attenuated modern theory that enervates love, belittles sin, and appeals simply to the feelings of sympathy which suffering evokes in cultivated hearts. It may be admitted that evangelicals have not always so spoken or sung about Calvary, but such is John's powerful exposition of the work of Christ, and such is the faith we still must hold if Christ is to be set forth as still, in the twentieth century, the Saviour of the world.

6: *Evangelicals and Jesus**

IT CANNOT ESCAPE NOTICE that these contemporary reflections on the message of 1 John keep drawing our gaze back to the lonely, glorious, challenging Figure who stands "in the beginning" of all Christian things, and from whom all Christian thought, experience and hope derive.

The reassertion in the Church of apostolic authority is, in the last analysis, a recall to Christ, Source and Centre of all truth from the beginning. The validity of Christian mystical experience, as John meticulously analyses it, depends upon a tested relation to Christ Himself as Christ mediates God to the soul in transforming ways. The evangelical ethic builds upon the commandment, the love, and the imitation, of Christ: without Him it has nothing distinctive to say.

The problem of ecumenicity appears in 1 John as that of reconciling loyalty to our given unity in Christ with loyalty to the sure truth about Him when other brethren deny it. The high point of John's doctrine of the cross is that in Christ Himself the love of God has found a Way, and a Bearer, of expiation for the sins of the world. And every statement, argument, and allusion which the letter contains is evoked by the Gnostic denial of Christ's unique divinity.

Thus the First Epistle of John is as Christ-centred as the Gospel of John; if in the Gospel we behold His glory, full of

* Notes on Essay 6, pp. 268-269.

grace and truth, in the epistle we are taught the importance of His glory, if grace and truth are ever to be ours.

John and Jesus

Our contemporary assessments apart, it is impossible to read 1 John attentively and miss the supreme place which the person of Jesus held in the mind and heart of John. All begins, for John, with the historic, touchable, visible Jesus — no phantom, no idealised figure, but one remembered by the senses with vividness, conviction, and great love. All the evasive re-interpretations by which Gnosticism sought to get around the scandal of a real incarnation are solidly met by John's assertion of the historic reality of Christ. The great Christological thesis of the epistle is — in Law's words — "the complete, permanent, and personal identification of the historical Jesus with the divine Being who is the Word of life, the Christ, the Son of God" — and the Expiation, the Advocate, the Saviour of the world, in whom is life eternal.

For John, the confession of Christ is all-important. He who confesses the Son has the Father; every spirit that confesses Jesus Christ come in the flesh is of God; whosoever confesses that Jesus is the Son of God, God abideth in Him. Jesus is the object of faith (5:13), of hope (3:3), and of obedience (3:23); our fellowship is with the Father and the Son, and in His name we are forgiven. This is to say that Jesus has for us the full religious value of God.

Yet beside all these explicit assertions, two silent assumptions of 1 John remain impressive. One is that the enemies of the apostolic gospel are not, in John's mind, anti-God, anti-morality, anti-cleric, or anti-Church, nor is it important that they are antagonistic to the apostles: the crux of their position, and the consummate condemnation of their attitude, is that they are anti-*Christ*. The other silent assumption is revealed in the fact that John uses the pronouns "He" (seven times), "that One" (six times) almost as a name yet frequently leaving it doubtful whether the Father or the Son is meant — "an ambiguity which would be reckless except on the presumption of their religious equivalence". This usage blends "a certain idealising of reverence with the allusiveness of familiar affection. . . . Although the mists of time have gathered round the image of the historical Jesus, He is still the ever-present living Personality" (Law).

Yet the mists have not gathered all that thickly. A convincing illustration of the place which the Master held in the faith and feeling of John is the quite astonishing extent to which reminiscences of the gospel story enrich the open letter. Truly, for John "the record of His life is the message of the gospel" (Westcott).

At least a dozen times the "coming" of Jesus is appealed to as the root from which all things Christian stem. His human birth ("came in flesh") is assumed, and the sense-experience of hands, eyes, ears, is emphasised as in Luke 24:39 (compare John 20:27); yet Jesus is also "He that was born of God" as the Lukan account especially declares. He is "the only Son", (the "beloved") as in Mark 12:6, and He is "sent" (a constant Johannine phrase, but found also in the Synoptic tradition, as Mark 15:24, 12:6).

Jesus is "He that should come" of Messianic prophecy (1 John 5:6) and the "Holy One" — also a Messianic title (so in Mark 1:24); "Christ" is now so familiar as to become a "surname", though its meaning is remembered (1 John 2:20 "anointed"). "The righteous One" may recall "My righteous Servant" (of the Synoptic Christology), or simply underline His perfect obedience, as the assertion of His sinlessness certainly does. Neil Alexander notes that the present tense is used in the three expressions, "even as He is pure", "in Him is no sin", and "even as He is righteous", where the past tense, referring to the days of His flesh, might seem more natural: "Doubtless the earthly phase of Christ's life was most in John's mind, but the statement is made of the whole human life of the Christ, and not confined to the earthly part of it". The more important point, however, is that neither of the three statements would possess any clear meaning except as summarising the Master's earthly life, even though each asserts the perfection then revealed to be an inherent and timeless quality of Christ's character. The human perfection of Jesus is plainly of great importance to John, and "the way He walked" becomes our perfect example, including His abiding, even in this world, in the free confidence of perfectly loving the Father (4:17), and His constant living within the searching light of the divine holiness, as we must strive to do (1:7).

Jesus came by water of baptism, God and the Spirit bearing witness to the Son there as elsewhere (5:6, 7, 9). The evil one, in whom the whole world lies (compare Luke 4:6) cannot touch the children of God because He keeps them — He in whom the evil one could find no hold (compare Luke 4:1-13, John 14:30) — even in temptation.

211

That Christ became a Teacher, the Bearer of a "message" of holiness (1:6), proclaiming a gospel with moral conditions (2:7), and bringing especially a message of love (3:11), is assumed as common ground. One echo of the Sermon on the Mount occurs in the statement that hatred of one's brother is equal to murder, and one near-quotation of Christ's reply to the enquiring lawyer concerning the "great commandment" (4:21); the "new commandment" of 2:8 rests directly upon John 13:34, but also upon the Good Samaritan and related themes. The over-riding metaphor of the divine family — Father, Son, birth, children, brethren — derives directly from the preaching of Jesus, and clear echoes are found in the principle that only those who have the Son know the Father (2:23 = Matthew 11:27), in the phrase about men being "called" the children of God (3:1 = Matthew 5:9) and in the precept that sonship implies likeness (4:7, 5:2 = Matthew 5: 43-48). In a famous parable Jesus argues from the divine mercy to the necessity for human mercy (Matthew 18:33), which John reproduces as "If God so loved us we ought also to love one another". True love "sees" the brother's need (3:17 = Matthew 25:37, etc.) and is not content with mere words without deeds (compare 3:18 with Matthew 7:21-23). The divine love should cast out fear — a reminiscence not only of Luke 12:32 but of the characteristic "Fear not" of Jesus. Because of His graciousness, the yoke of His commandments is never burdensome (5:3 = Matthew 11:29, 30).

The confidence that if we ask we shall receive (3:22 = Matthew 21:22), and indeed have already received (5:15 = Mark 11: 24) sustains prayer. We receive forgiveness through His "name" (2:12 = Luke 24:47), though there is sin which places beyond reach of forgiveness (5:16 = Matthew 12:31, 32, Mark 3:29). The call is to confession of Christ, the Son of God (2:22 = Mark 8:29, Matthew 16:16); to refuse to confess is to be lost (4:3 = Matthew 10:33, Mark 8:38).

There are many deceivers abroad (4:1 = Matthew 24:4, Luke 21:8), and false Christs, false prophets (4:1-3 = Matthew 24: 24). The work of Christ is to oppose the devil (compare 2:8 with Satan's falling from heaven, Luke 10:18); the "weeds" in God's field are "children of the devil" (compare 3:8, 10 with Matthew 13:38). The love of Mammon, god of riches such as the "Gentiles" (= the "world") seek, positively excludes love of the Father (2:15 = Matthew 5:24). The day of judgement (4:17 = Matthew 16:27, 19:28, 25:31) is sure as the hope of the advent

(3:2 = Matthew 24:30-37), and some will be "ashamed" at His coming (2:28 = Luke 9:26 inverted, Matthew 24:48-51).

So it is true of the teaching, as of the life, that the Son of God has given us "understanding" (compare 5:20 with Luke 24:45). Yet He was rejected, the world failing to recognise Him (3:1, compare Luke 23:21, 34), and He died by violence as a sacrifice (1:7, Matthew 26:28). Nevertheless He ascended to the Father's side (2:1) and lives in the power of eternal life (5:11).

Here are *fifty-one* echoes of the general synoptic tradition concerning the life, message, and death of Jesus. They are not, certainly, literal quotations, or borrowings from the written reminiscences, but they are clear indications of a mind and heart soaked with and nourished by the general outline of information about Jesus now preserved for us in the first three Gospels. To these may be added the many reproductions of thought and phrase borrowed from the special Johannine tradition, as represented in the Fourth Gospel, either as details of the Johannine story of Jesus (for example 5:6 seems a distant and muffled echo of John 19:34, though with new application); or as sayings of Jesus recorded in the Johannine "idiom" (for example 2:28 = "abide in me", John 15:4, and 3:11 = John 15:12); or as details of the Fourth Gospel's way of telling the story (1:1, "we have looked upon", reminds vividly of John 1:14, "we beheld His glory", and so with many turns of expression). There are four such allusions to details of the Johannine record, forty to "Johannine" sayings of Jesus, and seventeen reminders of John's way of telling the gospel story, adding another sixty-one references to Jesus as the Johannine circle remembered Him, to the fifty-one already mentioned. Thus, in 105 verses 1 John manages to betray knowledge of the Four-Gospel tradition no less than 112 times!

It is scarcely exaggeration, then, to say that "the epistle is *full* of Christ" — even more so than Hebrews or Colossians. And in what varied lights of faith and love John saw Him may be suggested by listing briefly the titles he accords the Master. "Jesus" (4:3, 5:5) is the endearing human name; Jesus Christ (4:2, 5:6) has become almost a formal name, though still reminding of One both man and Messiah, as "the Christ" (5:1) and "He that comes" (5:6, 7) explicitly affirm. "Jesus Christ the Righteous", "the Holy One", as we have seen, are both Messianic titles and tributes to His character. "Jesus His Son" (1:7) unites the humanity that made death possible with the divinity that made His death immeasurably significant for atonement; "His Son Jesus Christ" (1:3,

3:23, 5:20) adds the divine nature and relationship to the official designation as Messiah; while "the Son of God" (3:8, 4:15, 5:5, 13, 20), and even more "the Son", or "His Son", (5:9-12, 2:23-24) by isolating that divine dignity emphasize the uniqueness of the "only Son" (4:9) of the ever-living God.

Appellations can only enrich such titles with tribute and testimony. Christ is the life of God manifested in time within humanity (1:2). He is the Advocate and Expiation on whom sinners' hopes depend. He is described, with a marvelous implication of encouragement, as the Elder Brother in the divine family, Himself "born of God" (5:18). He is — perhaps the loveliest description of all — "the Saviour of the world" (4:14). Could love and faith possibly say more? It is remarkable, as Westcott notes, that the title "Lord" is not found in 1 John, although it occurs in the Gospel narratives, in Acts, in every other epistle except Titus, and in Revelation. Possibly the word had dangerous associations in the Gnostic mysteries. Christ's right to command is explicitly enforced (3:23, 24; 4:21), and in any case among the wealth of names and epithets John uses for his Master there is certainly nothing lacking which "Lord" would contribute to the glory and worship John adoringly ascribes to Jesus.

It is not necessary to elaborate again the theological significance of all that John says of Jesus, or its appositeness to the immediate purposes of the epistle. "The denial of the incarnation is in fact the denial of that which is characteristic of the Christian faith, the true union of God and man" (Westcott). Cerinthianism, "with its Redeemer-Christ untouched by birth, suffering, and death", was inadequate either to the facts of the gospel story or to the needs of sinful men.

Law shows well the higher theological consequences of denying a *real* incarnation of the divine in the human. It destroys the Christian revelation of God: the Gnostic's God was "a being so absolutely transcendent as to be incapable of actual relation to humanity, and the gulf between absolute Deity and finite being remained unbridged by all its intricate hierarchy of semi-divine intermediaries". Nor is that danger yet outgrown; "theism does not ultimately survive the rejection of Christ as the personal incarnation of God; the process of thought that necessitates the denial of the supernatural in Him has agnosticism as its inevitable goal". Moreover, denial of the incarnation removes "the one unambiguous proof" that God is love, and with it the foundation of the essentially Christian ethic. And in the third place, the incarnation faith is necessary to all hope of redemption: "the history of theology offers no instance in which the truth of the incarnation has been rejected and a doctrine of atonement or regeneration, in anything approaching to the Johannine sense, has been retained".

That is well said. And when Barclay adds that to deny that Jesus is the Messiah is to deny that He is the centre of history, the fulfilment of God's promises, the King, while to deny that He is the Son of God truly incarnate in the flesh is to deny that He is our pattern, or able to be our High Priest, or our Saviour — especially the Saviour of the body — and to reject any real union of God with man, he is only spelling out the further consequences of Law's great argument.

The fact is that 1 John defines the divine dignity and religious significance of the incarnate Son of God with incontrovertible force and clarity. "Always the truly human yet never the merely human Jesus", as Neil Alexander says, "without ceasing to be what He is, the Son of God has become the human Jesus, and Jesus without ceasing to be truly human is the Son of God. . . ." "The full impersonation of the divine life, the perfect effulgence of the divine light, the supreme gift of the divine love, is this: Jesus Christ come in the flesh" (Law).

Evangelicals and Jesus

Thus to expound the place Jesus holds in the evangelical faith of John is no mere concession to exegetical discipline: it underlines a theme native to true — but not to all — evangelicalism: the recall to the Jesus of the Gospels, the incarnate Son of God.

With all John writes about the Master most evangelicals would have no difficulty, but would rather rejoice in its forceful and eloquent assertion. Yet John's goal is not orthodoxy of belief, merely; he "proclaims the truth of the incarnation. . . solely from a sense of its supreme necessity to the spiritual life of the Church and the salvation of men". It is the experiential consequences of the place of Jesus in 1 John which make its message still sharply relevant to evangelical need. Barclay acutely remarks that the great and grave danger of the Cerinthian heresy is that it arises from what can only be called a mistaken reverence; it is afraid to ascribe to Jesus full and true humanity, regarding it as irreverent to think that Jesus had a really human, truly physical body as all men have. And Barclay adds that it is a heresy which to this day is held, usually quite unconsciously, by not a few devout Christians.

215

Certainly, the incarnation is not always taken seriously enough in evangelical theology. The storm aroused by the early "kenotic" attempts to define the difference which incarnation made to the Son of God may have been justified by unguarded and over-confident presentation, but the intention was sound and the attempt to make "incarnation" mean something clear and credible was a service to biblical theology. Popular Christology, says one modern authority, has always been incurably docetic: "the commonest vision of Jesus was not as a human being *at all*. He was a god in human form, full of supernatural knowledge and miraculous power, very much like what the Olympian gods were supposed to be when they visited the earth in disguise". Even treasured phrases like "taking our nature upon Him" or "Veiled in flesh the Godhead see" may hide from some the astonishing miracle of actual (not *apparent*) incarnation — the complete identification of the divine Son with man in a full, unsheltered human life. Jesus possessed no especial privileges, no immunity or insulation from the world; He "emptied Himself", He "was made flesh", He hungered, thirsted, was weary, prayed, asked questions, confessed ignorance (Mark 13:32), was tempted in all points, needed long communion with God before strenuous days and great decisions, sweat with agony and many tears, longed not to die, fainted with exhaustion, and "was crucified in weakness".

It is faithless and unscriptural to abate one jot of all the measureless cost of His identification with men; it is presumptuous dogmatism to suppose we know what incarnation "must have meant" without accepting frankly and studying closely the only example of it in human experience. Nor is it more reverent to imagine an elaborate masquerade of actual, illimitable divinity within a simulated human weakness and humility than it is to accept the gospel declaration "the Word became flesh". For *this is His glory*, His supreme uniqueness as Son of God and Saviour of men, voluntarily to submit to what is inevitable for us but not for Him — except at love's compulsion. This is divinity — by Christian standards; this is God — as Christ revealed Him.

But if the meaning of incarnation is sometimes obscured in evangelical theology by a timid fear of losing the deity of Christ in too frank an admission of His complete humanity, it is even more true that the Jesus of the Gospels has sometimes small place in evangelical piety. Devotion to "Christ" is unquestionably the great strength of evangelicalism: yet the danger is ever present of losing Him in the principles, the abstract ideals, the doctrines about Him, which evangelicals hold precious.

It is not impossible for evangelicals of one school to disclaim all responsibility towards "the Christ of the Gospels" as One whose words and deeds belong to the dispensation before the cross and the resurrection. "You attach far more importance to the words of Jesus than I do", said a "fundamentalist" critic in theological debate, unconsciously accepting the dangerous practical consequence of Brunner's dictum: "Faith presupposes, as a matter of course, *a priori*, that the Jesus of history is not the same as the Christ of faith". To those who think thus, the "Christ of history" means as little as to the demythologisers who either deny His historicity altogether or count it merely irrelevant.

For this type of evangelical faith, the risen Christ is only the summary of certain saving doctrines, the focus of vague yet powerful emotional experiences, the name we give to the personalised Christian conscience, the "projection" into heaven of traditional evangelical standards of piety, the ground of saving faith. "Christ", then, is the transcendent title which we give to One "in the glory", concerning whom we know essentially nothing but feel much. We then believe in atonement, in resurrection, in justification by faith, but not in *Jesus*. We are saved by faith, even by "faith in Christ", but not by the Christ of Galilee. This is the essence of Gnosticism — salvation by ideas, by teaching, and knowledge, divorced from the historic person of the Saviour; and it remains the greatest evangelical peril — to be Christians without Christ as He really was, to be followers of a Christ of our own devising, to prefer (as we falsely say) Paul's "risen Lord" to the too human, too vigorous and forthright Figure of the synoptic Gospels, to treat the parables as elementary, the epigrams as unimportant, the Sermon on the Mount as "not applying to the saved", and all the illumination and discipline of the superb story of Christ's ministry as but the "spiritually insignificant" prelude to Calvary.

This is what John condemns. For him, let it be said for the last time, all Christianity turns upon the historic revelation of God in Christ, the historic communication of divine life in Christ, the historic expiation for sin offered by the Man, Christ Jesus, the Son of God. That is why he recalls us so vigorously, in faith and feeling, to the Jesus of the Gospels, and sets Him centrally in every verse he writes. The "Christ-idea", distinct from the Figure of Jesus, to which some moderns attach supreme

217

religious value, is a mere catalogue of traditional Christian insights and ideals, much diluted and compromised by cultural, patriotic, temporal, economic and other influences, until "the teaching of Christ" comes to mean very much what we want it to mean, and the example, the words, and the searching gaze of the Master are left safely far behind. Against the whole perilous, self-deluding process of thus perpetually re-creating Christ in our own image, John resolutely sets his face and issues his challenging recall to that which was "from the beginning".

Belief in Christ is the beginning of life and sonship: and it is belief that Christ came in the flesh, that Jesus of Nazareth is the Son of God. To "accept" Jesus, the Jesus of the synoptic tradition, the Jesus of the Sermon and the parables, of the miracles and the ethic, of the manger and the cross, as well as the Jesus of the resurrection and the heavenly places, is to begin to live: to reject *Him* is to refuse eternal life.

Confession of Christ is the outward admission of that belief, and it is confession of the faith of Peter at Caesarea Philippi, that Jesus is the Son of God. Confession is closely linked to the rite of baptism, continuing in the Church as the perpetual witness of the Father to Christ, and recalling the Church ever and again to the Galilean origins of the gospel in the baptism of Christ (Mark 1:1).

Imitation of Christ is the ruling principle of Christian character, as keeping His commandments gives it direction and love of Him provides its motive power. But again it is imitation of His purity, of His righteousness, of His whole "walk", of His fearless confidence in God. Imitation is meaningless except as it fastens upon the treasured story of that gracious and powerful character in whose every word and deed the life of God was manifested.

Abiding in Christ is the inward resource of such Christian living, striving, and growing, and once more the abiding has to do with "what we heard from the beginning" (2:24f.), and with the anointing which has taught us all things (2:27). The echo here of the Fourth Gospel's Upper Room discourse shows that "abiding" has to do with the word and the joy of Christ remaining in the believer, and with the believer remaining in living relationship with the Lord, then there amongst them and soon — the same Lord — to be "in them" (John 14:17). "Abiding in Christ" must not be sublimated into some undefined mystical or emotional mood of the soul, construed as "fellowship" with the heavenly Christ. Jesus lives, and is with us always: but He is "this same Jesus", yesterday, today and forever — the divine Master whom we know in present faith as that faith takes its rise and direction and content and goal from the story of His manifestation among men. In both Gospel and epistle this is the meaning of "abiding" — remaining steadfastly in Him whom we met "in the beginning".

Expectation of Christ is, finally, the sustaining hope of the Christian life: the parousia is imminent, it is the last hour (2:11). And yet once more the expectation is that He who was pure, whom we shall see as He is (3:3), who is "coming" (2:28), is the same Christ who came. John's characteristic expression for the coming, as Brooke points out, is the same as for the earthly life of Christ — "manifestation". "The Presence (parousia) is no sudden unveiling of a man from heaven, it is the consummation of a process. . . . It is the final manifestation of the things that are . . . , the complete manifestation of that which is already at work. The true light is already shining" — has been since the Light of the world first appeared — "the darkness is already passing away, but He who is coming will come, and we shall see Him as He is". Law makes the same point, for it is John's point: emphasis on the continual presence of Christ with the believer replaces emphasis on the coming of Christ on the clouds, yet the coming remains sure: "the Coming is only the manifestation of Him who is here, a different mode of self-revelation on the part of Christ". We shall see Him, and be like Him, and can already purify ourselves in the way that He is pure, because we have known Him already: for the life was manifested, and we have seen it in the face of Jesus of Nazareth.

So the five great elements of Johannine Christian living take us back, relentlessly, to the foundation of all John's thinking, the Christ of the incarnation, the Jesus of the Gospel history. Evangelical Christianity has much to gain from a re-introduction to "the Stranger of Galilee". A faith and experience centred wholly upon Him will demand a diligent, and endless, rereading — with every spiritual and historical faculty awake — of the Gospel stories; it will demand a totally new appreciation of His immense intellectual and moral strength — with consequent adjustments of our too sentimental "image" of the Christian; it will certainly demand, if we return to the Gospels, a fresh assessment and understanding of the social concern, the immersion in the suffering, poverty, and sin of men, that Jesus makes the mark of the kingdom He preached and the ruling pattern of His own ministry. A truly Christ-centred evangelicalism will involve a new ethical urgency and a searching self-examination, as saying after saying, example after saying, example after example, stab awake the complacent conscience, so cheaply comforted by its "spiritual experiences" yet so often devoid of the Spirit of Jesus. It will mean a new examination of the whole gospel of the kingdom, and submission to many challenging insights and imperatives that might drive us out to the service of a sinful world. For many it would imply a return to much simpler churchmanship, to a lay-religion nearer to the simplicities of Galilee: and for all, a new vision of the Jesus of the manger, of the home, of the Jordan, of the wilderness, of the streets and hillsides and shores of Palestine, of the rich man's home and the sick man's bedside; the Friend of sinners, the Scourge of hypocrites, and the Saviour of the world.

This, in turn, would anchor our evangelical faith more firmly to God's good earth and to God's great purpose for *this* world. The gospel of a real incarnation of God in Christ Jesus carries far-reaching consequences for the meaning of redemption — as the Gnostics well knew. It involves salvation of the human scene and the human frame, the redemption of home and work, of sex and marriage, of childhood and womanhood, of money and friendship, of society and the State; redemption from sin and from sickness, from selfishness and from the isolation of the individual within society; and at the end the redemption of the body. Separation from the world's sin will be excuse no longer for contempt of the world's just claims, nor for insulation from the world's despair. We shall know ourselves called to follow Jesus along the rough pathways of a truly human life, our feet firmly on the ground of common human experience — and that has not always been the mark of evangelical Christianity.

But if we consent, letting John recall us to the historic Jesus, until our fingers too have touched His nailprints, and we have shared to the full His wounded humanity, we shall lose nothing of wonder, of supernatural grace and revelation and love. Instead, we shall find the human Christ transfigured, the cross radiant with more compelling meaning, the empty tomb ablaze with hope for mortal men, and ourselves gazing into the eyes of "the Man, Christ Jesus", constrained to whisper, "My Lord, and my God!"

NOTES AND QUOTES

NOTES TO INTRODUCTION:

1. *Evangelical faith* — Charles Hodge of Princeton, one of the foremost evangelical theologians, thus summarised the "Evangelical System": "(1) That all men, in consequence of the fall of Adam, are in a helpless state of sin and misery; (2) that the Eternal Son of God, having assumed our nature, and having been made under the law, has brought in everlasting righteousness; (3) that this righteousness, with all the benefits of redemption, is freely offered to all men; (4) that it is by faith in Christ that we become united to Him, and that He dwells in us by His Spirit; (5) that all who, by the power of the Spirit of God, are thus united to Christ by faith, are partakers of justification, adoption, and sanctification, together with all the benefits which do, here and hereafter, either accompany or flow from them; (6) that union with the visible Church and participation of the Sacraments are not the indispensable conditions of our union with Christ; neither are they the means of communicating, in the first instance, His benefits and grace, but rather the appointed means by which our union with Christ is acknowledged, and from time to time strengthened and renewed." Language and emphases of 100 years ago do not disqualify that statement for today.

2. *The centrality of individual experience* — The declaration of Helwys, pioneer of British Baptist evangelicals, in 1612 against the interference of the Crown in spiritual issues — "men's religion to God is betwixt God and themselves: the King shall not answer for it, neither may the King be judge between God and Man" — is significantly echoed by Simeon, leader of Anglican evangelicals two centuries later, concerned about too great emphasis upon the institutional Church: "Religion, in its first rise in the heart, is a personal matter between God and a man's own soul. A man, desirous of obtaining mercy from God, and peace in his own conscience, reads the scriptures in order to find out the way of salvation and marks with special care those passages which assure him of acceptance with God through the merits and mediation of our Lord Jesus Christ. For a considerable time it is his own eternal welfare which engrosses all his attention, and almost exclusively occupies his mind. . .".

223

The chief strength, and the chief weakness, of evangelicalism are there authoritatively expressed.

3. *Homily or composition?* "Only occasionally [do] words occur that remind us this is not an address but a letter", says Guthrie. But 1:4; 2:7, 8, 12, 13 (bis), 14 (bis), 21, 26; 5:13 hardly justify the "only occasionally"; while the thought is so concentrated, the threads of allusion and implication so finely drawn, that as an address it would be highly indigestible. The point deserves argument only when it is made excuse for dismissing lightly the supposed incoherence and rambling of an old man — an appalling misconception. Bultmann's theories of the editing of an earlier document (1:5b-10) and the addition of an appendix (5:14-21), may be seen in Guthrie: the unity of 1 John as we have it, whatever its oral or literary history, should be sufficiently obvious from the exposition offered.

4. *Authorship, date, relation of Epistle and Gospel, provenance*: A. M. Hunter summarises the "general opinion" that all three epistles are by the same hand and were written in Asia near the end of the first century, possibly "the Elder" (2 John 1; 3 John 1) was the "Presbyter" (=Elder) John who may have been "a sort of bishop" in Ephesus, the mother-Church of Asia; "the real question is whether 1 John is by the author of the Fourth Gospel."

The letter is cited as by John "the Lord's disciple", writer of the Fourth Gospel, by Irenaeus (Gaul, about 181/9 A.D.), and similarly by Clement of Alexandria (190-210), Tertullian (N. Africa, 195-220) and Origen (Caesarea, 185-254) — a view accepted almost without challenge for sixteen centuries. "The Elder" is named as author of 2/3 John, and referred to by Papias (about 130), (according to Irenaeus): "If ever any man came who had been a follower of the elders, I would enquire about the sayings of the elders; what Andrew said, or Peter, or Philip, or Thomas, or James, or John, or Matthew, or any other of the Lord's disciples; and what Aristion says, and John the Elder, who are disciples of the Lord. For I did not consider that I got so much profit from the contents of books as from the utterances of a living and abiding voice". Eusebius read this as distinguishing two Johns, apostle and Elder (note also "what John said", "what John says"), and this distinction has been widely accepted (Bernard, Macgregor, Clogg, Dodd, McNeile-Williams). F. L. Cross, however, says that there is a growing tendency among scholars to deny that Papias countenances any second John at all other than John the apostle, and Plummer long ago made fun of John's "double", holding that apostle and Elder were one, with evidence drawn from Papias' use of "elder" for Andrew, Peter, etc., from the silence as to two Johns of Irenaeus, Polycrates, and Dionysius of Alexandria, and from some inconsistencies in Eusebius. Macgregor leaves little room for doubt that John the Elder was bishop of Ephesus before 100 A.D., but was the apostle also the Elder?

It was once argued, from certain scattered references, that Mark 10:35 had been fulfilled and John the apostle martyred by Jews before 70 A.D.; but Bernard criticised the argument severely; Macgregor and C. K. Barrett remain doubtful; Guthrie asks if the Fathers were likely to confuse the two Johns, to which the answer must be that tradition certainly did so, as this argument, Eusebius, and perhaps Irenaeus, prove.

Guthrie also remarks of 1:1-4, "In no more vivid way could the writer indicate that he was an eye-witness": but Papias and Irenaeus make the point especially that "John the Elder" was a disciple of the Lord — many were eye-witnesses without being apostles. In any case, the witness here claimed (in the plural, compare 4:6, 9, and 14) is not that of the writer alone but of the corporate inheriting Church. The fact that the Church accepted the letter as apostolic has no more weight here than in the case of Hebrews. Law argues that the opening verses must imply an eye-witness and thinks the theory of apostolic authorship holds the field; his other argument, that the writer was of so distinctive eminence and recognised authority that it was unnecessary to declare his identity, might be valid for an entirely loyal audience: but John is addressing those who challenge the original version of the gospel, and *for them* the assertion of apostolic authority, if the writer could make it, seems inevitable.

Neil Alexander rests upon Macgregor's argument for John the Elder of Ephesus, who had been a disciple of the Lord. Dodd thinks the author a disciple of the Evangelist. C. K. Barrett suggests John the apostle *may* have been the original teacher of apocalyptic at Ephesus, and John the Seer (author of Revelation), John the Evangelist, and John of the epistle may have been his (three) pupils. Bernard's exhaustive investigation ends with the opinion that the Gospel and the epistles were by John the Elder.

All argument about authorship involves of course the relation of the epistle to the Fourth Gospel. Law presents pages of detailed stylistic and theological similarities, finds good reasons for all the admitted differences, plausibly explains the changes of emphasis in doctrine, and turns the argument from these differences into evidence *against* an imitator of the Evangelist as author of the epistle: no mere imitator would show such independence of the master he was copying! Brooke lists 53 parallels in phraseology and adds numerous coincidences of grammar, style and thought: "In the whole of the First Epistle there is hardly a thought not found in the Gospel". Examining exhaustively the differences alleged, Brooke concludes that there are no adequate reasons for setting aside the traditional view of common authorship — at some interval of time. C. H. Dodd, again, specifies the linguistic differences between the two works (fewer compound words in the epistle, fewer particles, conjunctions, etc., absence of Semitisms, forty or so expressions of the epistle absent from the Gospel, and so on), and the theological differences (the outlook of the epistle less Hebraic in thought and language; Hellenistic ideas like *chrism*, seed, "God is light", and others have freer play; the eschatology is more primitive, and so is the exposition of the cross; the doctrine of the Spirit is nearer to the early popular view than to the Fourth Gospel's developed thought), and decides against common authorship. E. F. Scott says the divergences in its teaching, all the more remarkable because of the general resemblance, "are strong proof that it was written by a different author at a later date".

McNeile-Williams think that the criticisms of Dodd's argument by W. F. Howard and by Wilson allow the conclusion that the verdict reached after careful linguistic analysis by Charles and Brooke, that the Fourth Gospel and all three epistles were penned by the same person, has not been overthrown. Hunter calls Howard's reply to Dodd "masterly". Guthrie too discounts Dodd's evidence as inconclusive, and thinks that

225

the view that the differences exclude common authorship would not need discussion but for Dodd's advocacy. Neil Alexander thinks common authorship at least highly probable, presenting counter-arguments to Dodd's and stressing that the more elementary emphases of the epistle on the cross, eschatology, and the Spirit accord with its set purpose, to re-call the readers to the beginnings. Clogg, following Stanton, decides for unity of authorship; Moffatt held that "while the writer of the epistle lived and moved within the circle in which the Fourth Gospel originated, he had an individuality and purpose of his own". C. K. Barrett thinks the author of the epistle less profound than the Evangelist. Bernard holds to one author for both books.

Hunter's "most scholars" in favour of common authorship might there-fore be questioned: close relationship is obvious, but either the similarities are due to common milieu and the differences to different authors within the same circle, or the similarities are due to common authorship and the difference to varied purpose, occasion and form. The experts disagreeing, the inexpert can only suspend judgement.

A long argument as to which came earliest is now generally settled in favour of the priority of the Gospel. Plummer held that references to the Gospel are scattered thickly over the whole epistle (examples are the reiteration of the new commandment, the obscure references to "blood and water", the echoes of John 17 in the closing verses, and a few less obvious instances). Brooke examines the question with his usual thoroughness and concludes the epistle came later to render more plain and practical the high themes of the Gospel; the introduction of the epistle summarises the Prologue and some of the main themes of the Gospel; the Gospel, also, has the popular eschatology, while the spiritualis-ing of Antichrist in the epistle recalls the spiritualising of the Advent in the Gospel. Dodd thinks Brooke conclusive for the priority of the Gos-pel, and Neil Alexander agrees — "the epistle is a summary, not a first sketch, of the Gospel"; Law is persuasive that the epistle certainly presupposes acquaintance with the substance of the Gospel, and is probably later than the written Gospel too. Guthrie thinks the balance of evidence slightly in favour of this view; Hunter, that the epistle is full of echoes of the Gospel.

It has been argued that the epistle was an accompanying note intended to introduce and expound the Gospel (which it scarcely does!); an earlier product whose message was later expanded in the Gospel (the Gospel's prologue, form, and purpose — 20:31, contrast 1 John 5:13 — do not bear this out: the Gospel stands firmly on its own feet); an appendix to the Gospel, possibly by the authors of John 21; and a wholly in-dependent product from within the same school of Christian thought.

As to date, John of Ephesus flourished, according to Irenaeus (in Eusebius H. E. iii 23) into Trajan's time (98-117). The earliest trace of 1 John in other writings is in Polycarp's epistle to the Philippians 115 (Clogg, Bruce), 125-130 (Dodd), 135 (Harrison), "immediately after Ignatius' martyrdom" (Brooke; i.e., about 115); Polycarp quotes 4:3 almost verbally. Dodd places 1 John in 96-110, because of the absence of any persecution (i.e. before the situation reflected by Ignatius, and after the Domitian repression); if John the Elder is the author, the date would be pre-Domitianic. From the absence of persecution, the climate of thought, and the relation to the Fourth Gospel, Guthrie names 90-95, and on the some grounds Neil Alexander chooses 96. Law places it following the Gospel "after an appreciable interval"; Barclay "a little after 100".

The nature of the peril confronted, the association with Revelation, the similar trends of thought at Colosse, and the fact that the epistle first "emerges in the province of Asia, is there first quoted extensively, and attributed to John of Ephesus by Irenaeus, a native of that province" all suggest Ephesus and the Christian communities of Asia as the area of origin. Lightfoot, alone, suggested Corinth; the address *ad Parthos* (or variations), understood as "to the Parthians (Babylonia)", used by Cassiodorus and Augustine, is discussed and dismissed as "mere mistake" by Barclay (following Brooke, following Zahn).

5. *Gnosticism: Cerinthianism*: The summary description of Gnostic teaching offered here rests upon Alexander (Neil), Barclay, Brooke, Bruce (*The Spreading Flame*), Caird (G.B., *The Apostolic Age*), Cross (F. L., editor, *Dictionary of the Christian Church; The Early Christian Fathers*), Dodd, Guthrie, Gore, Hasler, Huther, Law, Mackintosh (H. R., *Person of Christ*), Moffatt (*Introduction to the New Testament*), Plummer, Scott (E.F., *The Fourth Gospel*), and Westcott.

Ancient authorities are cited in the following order:

Basilides, in Irenaeus, *Adversus Haereses* I xxiv 4.

Saturnius, in the same, xxiv 1.

Ignatius, *ad Smyrnaeans* 6:2.

Basilides as above, I xxiv 5.

Saturnius as above, I xxiv 2.

Leucian, *Acts of John*, par. 93 (in M. R. James *Apocryphal New Testament*, 1926, p. 252); see *On Docetism*, below.

Ignatius, *ad Smyrnaeans*, 3:2, *ad Eph.* 7:2, *ad Trall.* ix, x.

Gospel of Peter, Fragment I, verse 19 (M. R. James, as above, p. 91).

For the story of John and Cerinthus at Ephesus, Irenaeus, *Adv. Haer.* III iii 4.

Bettenson: *Documents of the Christian Church*, Oxford University Press (World's Classics) Edition, p. 52.

On Gnostic "infiltration" into pre-Christian Judaism, G. B. Caird remarks, "The Gnostic heresy at Colosse seems to have been a mixture of Jewish and pagan ideas"; Acts tells of Jews who practised magic (13: 6, 19:13f.); the Samaritans had their Simon Magus, long afterwards held to be the father of Gnosticism; divine names from the LXX (Hypsistra, Sabaoth) occur in pagan usage, and there are other traces of Judaist influence in the Hermetic literature.

On the moral neutralism ascribed to some Gnostics, Law cites Titus 1:10, 16, 2 Timothy 3:1-7, 2 Peter 2:12-22, Jude verses 4, 7-19, and Revelation 2:14, 15, 20; and quotes Irenaeus (*Adv. Haer.* I vi 2): "They [the 'spiritual' Gnostics] affirm that good moral conduct is necessary for *us* [i.e., for ordinary Christians] but they themselves will unquestionably be saved, not from moral conduct, but because they are by nature spiritual. For, as the material are incapable of receiving salvation, so the spiritual are incapable of receiving corruption whatever moral conduct they may practice. . . . Hence the most perfect among them perform all forbidden things without any scruple, and some of them, obeying the lusts of the flesh even to satiety, say that carnal things are repaid by carnal and

227

spiritual things by spiritual". So, Hippolytus (*Refutatio* VI xiv) of the followers of Simon Magus: "They even congratulate themselves upon this indiscriminate intercourse, asserting that this is perfect love. For [they would have us believe] they are not overcome by the supposed vice, because they have been redeemed. . . . They do whatsoever they please as persons free, for they allege that they are saved by grace"; and Clement (*Strom.* II xx, III i, iv), of the Nicolaitans: "They quote an adage of Nicolaus, which they pervert, 'that the flesh must be abused': abandoning themselves to pleasure like goats . . . they lead a life of self-indulgence"; "These quotations I have adduced in reproof of the Basilidians, who do not live rightly, either as having power to sin because of their perfection, or as being altogether assured by nature of future salvation, although they sin now, because they are by dignity of nature the elect"; and of the Prodicians, "They say they are by nature children of the supreme God, but abusing that nobility and liberty they live as they choose, and they choose lasciviously; judging that they are bound by no law as 'lords of the sabbath' and as belonging to a kind of superior race, a royal seed. And the law, they say, is not written for kings".

Of Cerinthianism, Caius of Rome is quoted for the extremely sensual millenial hopes which Cerinthus fostered, and Dionysius of Alexandria (circa 260) for the view that he was a voluptuary, wholly sensual, similar to (Brooke says "successor of", according to Hippolytus) Carpocrates, whose disciples "preached a licentious ethic" and in whom, says Law, "Gnostic antinomianism reached its unblushing climax". Some of the charges of gross immorality doubtless lose nothing in the telling from the indignation of Christians at Gnostic Christology, but even so the vehemence would stultify itself if wholly untruthful, and as Law remarks "such quotations might be indefinitely multiplied".

On Docetism, the "phantasm" theory by which Gnostics sought to evade a true incarnation is generally called "Docetism" (from *dokeō,* to seem), but there is a narrower usage (Christ's body a phantasm) and a wider usage (any theory which makes incarnation only apparent, including Cerinthianism) of the term, which leads to an unreal argument whether 1 John did or did not have "Docetism" in mind: it depends entirely on the definition given to the term.

Typical Docetic views are: "The Unborn and Unnamed Father . . . sent his First-begotten Mind (and this is he they call Christ) for the freeing of them that believe in him from those who made the world. And he appeared to the nations of them as a man on the earth, and performed deeds of virtue. Wherefore he suffered not, but a certain Simon, a Cyrenian, was impressed to bear his cross for him; and Simon was crucified in ignorance and error, having being transfigured by him that men should suppose him to be Jesus, while Jesus himself took on the appearance of Simon and stood by and mocked. . . . If any therefore acknowledge the crucified, he is still a slave and subject to the power of them that made our bodies: but he that denies him is freed from them, and recognises the ordering of the Unborn Father" (Basilides, in Irenaeus, *Adv. Haer.* I xxiv 4). "I, then, when I saw him suffer . . . fled unto the Mount of Olives, weeping at that which had befallen. And when he was crucified . . . darkness came. . . . And my Lord standing in the midst of the cave and enlightening it said, John, unto the multitude below in Jerusalem

I am being crucified and pierced with lances and reeds and gall and vinegar is given me to drink. But unto thee I speak . . . I put it into thy mind to come up into this mountain. . . . And he showed me a cross of light set up. . . . And the Lord Himself I beheld above the cross not having any shape but only a voice. . . . But this is not the cross of wood which thou wilt see when thou goest down hence, neither am I he that is on the cross. . . . Nothing therefore of the things which they will say of me have I suffered. . . . And so speak I, separating off the manhood. . ." (Leucian, *Acts of John*, par. 97-101, M. R. James, *Apocryphal New Testament*, pp. 254-56).

On Cerinthianism as target of 1 John, Westcott, Huther, Guthrie ("may be behind the epistle"), Law, Neil Alexander ("the best one-word diagnosis"), Clogg, Moffatt, Brooke ("most probable view"), and Gore support this interpretation of the teaching opposed. Brooke discusses the views of Clemen and Wurm that 2:22f. limits the doctrinal differences between John and the seceders to Christology, views on the Father being no issue — which would exclude Cerinthianism — and replies that John's argument that those who hold not the Son, who alone reveals the Father, leave themselves without knowledge of the Father also, has far more point against the Gnostic and Cerinthian claim that the enlightened possess superior knowledge of the "Unknown" Father, knowledge not attainable by the average Christian. Brooke however, like Clemen and Wurm, includes Judaism among the opposition John faces, mainly because the denial confronted is denial that "Jesus is the Christ", supported by the conflict with Jews in the Fourth Gospel and the disillusionment Jews must have suffered in 70 A.D. Dodd points out that Jewish deniers of the Messiahship of Jesus would not have been once members of the apostolic Churches, as the seceders certainly were (2: 19, 4:1) — and so Huther, Westcott, Guthrie, Law.

The teaching of Cerinthus about Christ is summarised by Irenaeus (*Adv. Haer.* I xxvi 1): "A certain Cerinthus also in Asia taught that the world was not made by the first God, but by a certain Virtue far separated and removed from the Principality which is above all things, a Virtue which knows not the God over all. He added that Jesus was not born of a virgin but was the son of Joseph and Mary, like other men, but superior to all others in justice, prudence, and wisdom. And that after his baptism Christ descended upon him in the form of a dove, from that Principality which is above all things; and that then he revealed the Unknown Father, and performed deeds of virtue, but that in the end Christ flew back, leaving Jesus, and Jesus suffered and rose again, but Christ remained impassible, being by nature spiritual". Brooke finds the evidence of Hippolytus on Cerinthus' teaching (so far as it can be recovered from Epiphanius, Philaster, and pseudo-Tertullian) "in substantial agreement" with that of Irenaeus.

NOTES TO PART ONE:

1. *Analysis of 1 John* — Elaborate attempts at analysis are made by Law, Plummer, Dodd, Westcott, and indeed by most commentators. Neil Alexander's impresses as much as any, just because it does not attempt to be too neat. Plummer remarks that "probably few commentators have satisfied themselves with their own analysis of this epistle: still fewer have satisfied other people"; and Brooke adds, "Perhaps the attempt should be abandoned as useless". Not all coherent writing yields to logical dissection; love-letters, for example, make their point by other means, and so does lyrical poetry; why should not meditation, even when informed with polemic? In the present instance, studied delicacy of approach and deliberate indefiniteness of allusion to prevalent controversy help to obscure John's method of argument even where he is in fact hitting the nail most squarely on the head! To appreciate this, attention needs to be paid more to John's style than to skeletal analysis. We are content with paragraphs.

2. *John's style* — This is regularly described as "spiral", but crab-like would be an equally appropriate adjective. Any impression that the letter is "the rambling prattle of an old man", mere "aphoristic meditations", a disconnected muddle of pious reflection and warning, will not survive any intelligent reading, while "the diligent reader or expositor finds it more difficult to detach any single sentence, without loss to the general meaning, than in any other writing of the New Testament" (W. Alexander). Plummer well says: "St. John's divisions are seldom made with a broad line across the text. The parts dovetail into one another and intermingle in a way that at times looks like confusion. Wherever we may place the dividing line we find similar thoughts on each side of it . . . the transition is gentle and gradual, but when it is over we find ourselves on new ground. . . . Like the doublings of the Maeander near which he lived, the progress of the apostle at times looks like retrogression . . . but the progress is unmistakable when the whole field is surveyed". Perhaps the best example of this "dovetailing" is seen at 2:18-25, where, after the most tactful preparation, the direct accusation of heresy is at last made, and no less than eight ideas already lightly touched upon are suddenly seen to be immediately relevant. And this mark of John's style is everywhere: he interweaves thought so closely and skilfully that any analysis must miss some interconnection. Neil Alexander aptly points to phrases which act like "swingdoors" — ushering the readers into a new section while swinging their minds also back to something already said: examples are "born of him", 2:29, " of the truth", 3:19, "the Spirit which he has given", 3:24, "nor he who does not love his brother", 3:10. It is this feature, the intense logical inter-connectedness of what seem to be separate aphorisms, that makes analysis of some "ground-scheme" unprofitable. It is significant how often commentators (Law is an example) rearrange John's epistle in order to expound it under summarising headings. Our "argument" introducing each separate section to illustrate

its place in the whole provides some atonement for dismembering into twenty-one distinct paragraphs one of the most closely integrated discussions in all literature.

NOTES ON 1:1-3:

The opening sentence — The interpretation offered of the long and tangled opening sentence is a summary of the profound thoughts which it enshrines, but how this meaning stands related to the structure of the sentence is an insoluble problem. The translators' invention of a parenthesis, and the apparent assertion about one "thing" (neuter) that it was from the beginning seen, heard, and handled, and "concerning" the word of life, illustrate the difficulties. Huther reviews eleven ways of construing the sentence; Brooke, with the oldest Greek commentators, supplies an object to the main verb "the message or mystery which was from the beginning . . . we proclaim". A subsidiary problem is the meaning of the phrase, "word of life".

"The Word of Life" — "The Word of . . ." is generally followed by a definition of the word's subject (or content) — word of the kingdom, word of reconciliation, word of salvation, word of the cross. But "of life", in the phrases "Bread of life," "way of life," "water of life," "light of life" (?), means life-giving, life-sustaining. And thirdly, the word of God is itself frequently said to be a living word, living and powerful (Hebrews 4: 12), a seed within the soul (Luke 8:11), a semen giving birth to life within the soul (1 Peter 1:23), a life-giving principle engrafted, implanted (James 1:21), fruitful and growing (Colossians 1:5, 6). If either of these precedents be followed, the phrase "word of life" may mean "the word about life", "the word which gives life" or "the living word" — in either case, the gospel. So Bennett (citing parallel in Philippians 2:16), Law (citing Matthew 13:19, Acts 20:32, 2 Corinthians 5:19) and Neil Alexander (who adds Acts 5:20, John 6:68). In support it is argued (for example by Westcott) that it is impossible to refer "that which" to Christ, and it is expressly said to be "concerning the word of life": what was from the beginning therefore is the revelation concerning the word of life, gradually realised through patriarchs, prophets, lawgivers, and Christ. C. H. Dodd draws a hairline distinction between the "theme" of the announcement ("concerning the word of life") and the "contents" of the announcement ("that which was from the beginning"), emphasises the neuter pronoun and the use of "word of life" elsewhere as the "life-giving word", the gospel, and concludes that the author intends to say his theme is the gospel, and that he is to state what has always been true about it, and what has been attested upon the immediate evidence of the senses.

This interpretation, however, makes nothing of the strongly emphasised evidence of the senses, nor of the contrast between "was in the beginning" and "was manifested unto us". Plummer thus argues that the words "seen, heard, handled" are fatal to the idea that what was from the beginning was a doctrine or revelation or message. They inevitably suggest Jesus Himself, especially as risen (Luke 24:39, John 20:27 — Brooke thinks this doubtful). Plummer therefore holds "the Word of life" is the Logos, and that the introduction deliberately echoes the Prologue to the Fourth Gospel. Law also assumes that Gospel and epistle must mean the same by the term "word", and holds that the second verse requires the reference to Christ Himself. That the readers possessed copies of John's Gospel must not of course be simply assumed: and the phrase "Logos of life" is nowhere used of Jesus: John 1:1 plus John 1:4 could explain it (if the RSV margin at 1:4 be ignored). "That which . . . concerning the Logos of life . . . that which we saw and heard . . ." still appears incoherent.

The fact is that of no one thing can all the statements be true — that it existed from the beginning before being manifested, that it demands a neuter pronoun, that it was seen, heard, and handled, and that it was "concerning" the word of life. Hence Law — usually so logical and consistent — says the subject is the Logos and proceeds to expound as though it were "the life", though yet again he says "what we declare is a certain truth about the Logos" — which is what Westcott said! Plummer too contends for the meaning "Christ — the Logos" but adds that it is "the life" that is the emphatic idea in "Word of life". Huther thinks the life itself was from the beginning, was manifested and experienced, and the neuter pronoun ("life" is feminine) is due to its being an abstract and general idea.

The writer has obviously changed horses in mid-sentence. "That . . . which we have heard . . . concerning the word . . . we proclaim . . . . This is the message" (1:5) seems of necessity to presuppose some form of statement, truth, message, and the "from the beginning" emphasises that it is the original, apostolic form of Christian teaching. Yet this message was itself not only heard but seen, embodied, incarnated, in Jesus: so the words "which we have heard" touch off in the writer's mind the fuller experiences of seeing, pondering, handling this message incarnate. The first subject therefore appears to be the gospel (neuter) or an entirely vague idea roughly corresponding to "the apostolic message", but this is at once identified in the most concrete way with Him in whom it was first perfectly expressed. At once, however, the writer's thought fastens upon Jesus as the embodiment not merely of a message but of the eternal divine life itself — and this far more adequate idea rushes in by way of parenthesis to define the message incarnate in Jesus. What we have in Christ is not only a message concerning a living word but the life itself: this is the main theme of the epistle, and finds incontrovertible assertion in 5:11. Verse 3 gathers up both subjects, the truth embodied in Christ and the life incarnate in Him, as what the apostolic authorities proclaimed.

Dodd's footnote remark, "The emphasis is upon the unchanged, original content of the gospel, over against novel forms of doctrine", is of great importance. The apostolic message is not abstract philosophical speculation but the verifiable historical embodiment of an eternal life — a contrast of the utmost significance for the situation John faces: yet he does not so state it as to provoke immediate opposition, but rather insinuates the sounder historical basis of the apostolic version of Christianity by means of a broken and incoherent sentence. The tentative uncertainty of his grammar is quite deliberate!

The collective witness — That personal eye-witness of the life of Jesus lies behind the emphatic assertions of 1:1-3 need not be doubted, but the use of the plural pronoun, and the wider implications of the statements, must be considered. Law very strongly, and very rightly, opposes any interpretation which equates the "hearing, seeing, handling" with faith-mysticism, which writer, readers, and Gnostics alike could claim. First-hand, physical experience of the real incarnation of Christ is plainly affirmed: yet this is not the possession of the first generation only, but of all who accept their testimony and by entering into the meaning of the historical events prove their power in spiritual experience. The plural "we" in 4:9, 14, and 5:19, 20 (contrast singular in 2:1, 7, 12, etc.) clearly means "all believers"; perhaps "we, Christians of an older generation" is specially implied in 1:1-3 (McNeile-Williams); certainly the writer speaks from within the apostolic circle — "He will hand on to his readers what he and his fellows have seen and heard, that they too, though they have not seen, may believe and share his joy" (Brooke). The "we" of first-hand apostolic testimony "is at once swallowed up in a 'we' which can be no narrower in scope than the whole membership of the Church . . . (verses 3, 7, as in 4:14 and throughout 4:6-19) . . . . Even if the language is that of an eye-witness, he speaks not exclusively for himself or for a restricted group, but for the whole Church to which the apostolic witness belongs by virtue of its (fellowship) . . . over against the world which . . . has no knowledge of the incarnate Son" (Dodd). The proclaiming of this witness was done in the general evangelistic and pastoral life of the Church; "these things we write" refers to the contents of the epistle, thus affirmed at the outset to be in strict accord with that apostolic message.

NOTES ON 1:3, 4:

Koinonia — It is worthwhile to retain the unfamiliar word in order to emphasise the unique quality of Christian community or fellowship; words like brotherhood, guild, society, fraternity, and even community, fellowship, are inadequate. Dodd's discussion of *koinonia*, like Westcott's exhaustive additional note on Eternal Life in Johannine Teaching, are compulsory reading for students of 1 John 1:1-4.

"Our joy/your joy" — These are equally supported readings in 1:4. Moffatt, NEB, RSV (text), Dodd, Plummer, Neil Alexander, Brooke (hesitantly), Law ("it is not easy to decide"), and Westcott ("positive decision is impossible") choose "our joy"; Barclay adheres, with RSV (margin) to "your joy". It is easier to see why copyists should change an original "our" into "your", especially because of the clear echo of John 15:11, than *vice versa;* as Law says, "our joy" here is the finer, more apostolic sense (1 Thessalonians 3:8, Philippians 2:2) but it certainly includes also the joy of readers adhering to, or returning to, the apostolic circle. (NEB: "that the joy of us all may be complete").

NOTES ON 1:5, 6:

God is Light — Dodd finds synoptic support for the message "heard from Him" concerning light, in the picture of one who lives and moves in the light (Luke 11:34-36) linked with Matthew 5:8, 48.

"We lie" — The distinction between "we lie" and "he is a liar" (2:4) — if there is one — would seem to be that to assert fellowship with the Light and walk in darkness is plainly to assert what cannot be; it is to

declare what is certainly false, whether mistakenly, ignorantly, or foolishly: to claim to know God and yet to disobey is nearer to hypocrisy, the practice of falsehood in actions and conduct. The one expression nails the statement as falsehood; the other condemns the character as deceitful and self-deceiving.

Doing truth — Barclay strikingly lists possible attitudes to truth: suppressing the truth (Romans 1:18), obeying the truth (Galatians 5:7), walking according to the truth (3 John 4), resisting the truth (2 Timothy 3:8), wandering from the truth (James 5:19). To these should be added knowing the truth (1 John 2:21), being made free by truth (John 8:32), established in the truth (2 Peter 1:12), being of the truth (1 John 3:19), having truth in us (1 John 1:8), to do the truth, or live according to the truth (1 John 1:6). It is necessary to remember this wide moral and experiential reference of the idea, if emphasis on truth is not to be wrongly conceived on merely intellectualist lines. "In truth, truly, true", has still further extensions of meaning: see note on 5:18-20.

NOTES ON 1:7—2:2:

As He is in the light — Huther: "That God is in the light is the same as this, that God is light; that which is the nature of God is also the element of His life". Westcott: "Light is God's garment. . . . The realm of truth and purity in which He is completely corresponds to His own nature". G. S. Barrett contrasts our walking "backwards and forwards" in light, and God's abiding steadfastly there. Brooke, Plummer also understand the phrase of God; Neil Alexander notes our "walking by grace where God is by nature". The suspicion remains that some strain of meaning is necessary to understand how God Himself is set "in" light in any sense in which we also can walk in it — which is John's point. Has not John's indeterminate use of pronouns misled here? and does not the appeal throughout to the imitation of Christ — to purify as He is pure, to walk as He walked, to be in the world as He is in the world — suggest here also that we should walk in the light as Jesus walked, and is in, the light?

Sins, sin, cleansing — Law holds that "the judicial view of sin characterises the whole paragraph"; ethical interpretation is groundless; from the propitiatory power ascribed to Christ's blood it follows that "sin" is regarded primarily as guilt; in 1:8 the judicial sense is unmistakable. It may be doubted if the ethical interpretation of *anything* in 1 John can be groundless: even if a "judicial" view is "primary", John would never admit its divorce from ethics. John 9:41, 15:22, 24, and 19:11 certainly show the Johannine usage of sin=guilt, stain; and the reference to "blood", together with the whole assumption that sin banishes from the divine fellowship, and the climax in "Advocate", make it certain that the judicial view of sin underlies the whole argument. Nevertheless, John distinguishes *sin* as the principle or spring of wrongdoing, and *sins* as the separate manifestations of that principle; he does also add cleansing from the unrighteous character to forgiveness of the separate acts; and he keeps a present tense which suggests a continual (ethical) cleansing "from sin itself" (Huther). John sees sin as essentially lawlessness (1 John 3:4), the violation of the divine order of life; as individual selfishness; as social "hatred"; and as disobedience to the divine command to. love: it is hard to suppose he could speak of a cleansing which did not mean, besides forgiveness, the actual removal of what needed to be forgiven. Since none confesses sin until he has ceased to love it, purification is implied in John's condition for pardon. Plummer remarks, as results of our confession, absolution from punishment and freedom from pollution: "forgiveness is the averting of God's wrath (?), the cleansing is the beginning of holiness".

On 1:8 Neil Alexander rejects "we are not guilty" because (he says) the same word in verse 7 means "sinfulness . . . principle of sin": the seceders' claim was that they were past the sphere of sinfulness altogether. But in verse 7, that from which *Christ's blood* cleanses must be guilt or stain "primarily", and John might not deny that Christians are beyond the ruling *principle* of sin (1 John 5:18): he does emphatically deny that they are beyond responsibility for the sins they do commit.

Confession — For the usage of the word implying acknowledgement to other people, as well as to God, see 2:23, 4:2, 3, 15, John 1:20, 9:22, 12:42, Romans 10:9, Matthew 3:6, Mark 1:5, James 5:16, and elsewhere. The place of confession in Jewish baptism, in John's (Matthew 3:6), and verses like Acts 2:38, 22:16, 1 Corinthians 6:9-11, make it almost certain that general confession of sin accompanied apostolic baptism. For the biblical value of confession, note Psalm 51, Psalm 32:5, Proverbs 28:13. Plummer held that confession to Him that is faithful and true, and to the "selves" we otherwise lead astray, is all that is meant! But acknowledgement to those wronged, with restitution where possible, is essential to true repentance, and so to sincere confession. On the supreme importance attached to this acknowledgement before men, especially to confession of Christ before men, see notes on *Confessing Christ*, on 2:18-25.

If we say — On the seceders' attitudes towards sin, see Note 5 to Introduction.

Our common fellowship . . . with Him — Westcott: "The supposition that 'we have fellowship one with another' means we with God and God with us is against the apostolic form of language, and also against the general form of John's argument, for he takes the fellowship of Christians as the visible sign and correlative of fellowship with God (4:7, 12)". This is to offer as a reason the point needing to be proved. The nearer verse 6 and the whole theme of the passage point to the meaning "fellowship with God"; but Bennett, Huther argue for "fellowship of Christians with Christians"; so does Plummer, who cites another reading, old as the second century, as evidence of the desire to make this verse the exact antithesis of the preceding one; Brooke likewise, adding that the writer follows his usual custom of carrying the expected antithesis one step further, namely that fellowship among Christians is based upon, and the realisation of, fellowship with God; and Law also says that to understand as fellowship with God, as Augustine, Calvin, is inadmissible. Nevertheless it is essential to the coherence of the passage, and to the meaning of the next phrase, that the idea of fellowship with God who is light remain the fundamental one. John has already emphasised his desire to promote fellowship among Christians, and stressed that this is a common fellowship with the Father: doubtless this motive shapes his language here. To be out of fellowship with God, through sin, is to be out of fellowship with each other, *and vice versa.*

Expiation — On 1:7, 2:2 — "one of the greatest verses on the work of Christ in the New Testament" — and 4:10, see Essay 5, "Evangelicals and the Cross".

Advocate — Westcott and Brooke both review the history and usage of the word "Paraclete" in much detail, and conclude for the juridical meaning, Advocate. Law says the active meaning "Comforter" is nowhere tenable, the word being by formation passive, and capable of no other sense than "one called in to aid the caller". Vincent Taylor, however, and Barclay support the meaning "Comforter, Strengthener", — the latter citing Genesis 37:35, Isaiah 61:2, Matthew 5:4. The Greek commentators so understood the word also. In the present passage, however, Barclay decides for "one who lends his presence for his friends", and Taylor for "Intercessor, Advocate". Dodd says the root meaning, "one called in", yields the most general sense, "helper, supporter", but popularly, and in religious usage, "a friend called in to support a party to a law-suit or the defendent in a criminal trial, an advocate — with men or God".

NOTES ON 2:3-6:

"By this" — The use of *this is, these things, in this, on this account,* with or without *and,* to link together a statement and a reflecton, is a feature of John's style. It is sometimes debatable whether *this* refers to what has just been said (as at 4:6) or to what is about to be said (as at 4:2). Brooke lists 16 instances where the reference is to what follows, and seven where the reference is, at least probably, to what precedes, and concludes that only the context can decide in each case.

We know Him — Westcott discusses fully but inconclusively whether "I know him" refers to Christ (as is suggested by the preceding verses, by John 14:15, and by the naming of God explicitly in 1 John 2:5 when the Father is meant), or to God the Father, to whom the commandments are usually referred in this epistle (3:22, 24; 5:2, 3), and who is generally referred to by this pronoun whereas another is used (in Greek) in verse 6 for Christ. On the other hand, John is evidently commenting upon a claim of his opponents, and a claim to know *God* would not distinguish them from many sects and groups, both Judaist and pagan: whereas a claim to possess better understanding of *Christ* than the novice-Christians of the apostolic groups possessed was the whole pride of Gnosticism generally.

Love for God — Bennett understands "in him truly love for God is perfected" as "the Christian's love toward God attaining full growth, becoming mature", as indeed the RSV translation necessitates. The original has, however, "the love of God". Moffatt, Dodd agree with RSV; Plummer says this is the common usage of "love of God" in this epistle (2:15, 3:17, 4:12, 5:3); only in 4:9 does the genitive mean the love of God for man. Brooke sides with this view, but recalls that for John, love for God is always the response to God's love for man. Westcott, however, adheres strongly to the interpretation "the love God gives", becoming now an active divine power perfected in the man who (by obedience) receives it, appealing to 4:9 and 3:1 as controlling John's thought of divine love perfected by being communicated to man and through man to the brethren. Law somewhat similarly holds that the "love of God" is neither God's love to us nor ours to Him, separately considered, but that which unites both . . . the love which is the nature of God and which is the nature also of those who are begotten of Him. In us divine love is perfected when it reaches its goal in loving action on our part. Even on these latter two views, however, it is love which is (now, at any rate) our attitude towards God which is intended in 2:5.

Knowledge and mysticism — Barrett says "those Gnostic teachers at Ephesus declared intellectual enlightenment to be everything; initiates into the hidden mysteries of knowledge were by that fact alone possessors of divine life." Law remarks Bousett's opinion that *gnosis* signified not so much a higher intellectual knowledge as initiation into the secret and sacramental mysteries of the Gnostic sects — "secret knowledge of deep things". Dodd traces the basic Gnostic concept first to the intellectualism of the Greeks, which in Plato's doctrine of eternal "forms" or "ideas" resident in heaven and contemplated by pure reason was already approaching mysticism; secondly to the non-rational knowledge of the "Mysteries", perceived in "divine silence and the annihilation of all senses," the ideal of religious life — a knowledge of God which is salvation makes man perfect and immortal like the gods, indeed makes man himself a god. In the Old Testament, knowledge of God is likewise the religious aim: but it is knowledge of God's character and will in order to obey and please Him (Jeremiah 9:24, 31:34, 24:7, 22:16). For the Fourth Gospel, "this is eternal life . . . to know Thee, the only real God"; while Matthew (11:27) and Luke (10:22) speak of the Son's unique knowledge of the Father, to be shared with men. But the manifestation of God is ever promised, not to the intellectual but to those who love and who keep Christ's words (John 14:15f.).

Abide in Him — Plummer understands this to mean "abide in God", in spite of the Fourth Gospel's familiar phrase, the usage in 1 John 2:28 and 3:6, and the end of the present sentence. Westcott too has to support his view that "I know Him" = God, with "abide in Him" = God, in spite of "the same way in which he walked".

NOTES ON 2:7-11:

Old - new — Law laconically says of 2:7-11, "These verses have been found susceptible of a bewildering variety of interpretations", and a review of opinions fully substantiates the bewilderment. Law himself holds that 2 John 5 proves that the "old" commandment = the "new" = "Love one another" (John 13:34) — too familiar to need quoting ("the well-known precept of Christ" — Dodd). A: It is old (i) as being no novel addition to the reader's present knowledge of the gospel (Gore, Bennett, Westcott, Plummer, Dodd, Neil Alexander); (ii) as the natural law of humanity (Law cites the self-sacrificing care of the tigress for her whelps, the mother bird for her nestlings); (iii) because it was in the Old Testament already (Brooke, Barclay, and partly Neil Alexander — old in this sense "for Judaist readers"). B: it is new (i) as never obsolete, always fresh, living, constantly unfolding fuller meaning (Law, Gore); (ii) supremely so when embodied in Christ, as "all things are made new in Christianity" (Dodd) because Christ called it new and made it new and because it is the commandment for the new age (Neil Alexander); (iii) and as being placed in a new light by the teaching and example of Christ (Law); it was new when Christ first enunciated it, and is still new for non-believers (Westcott).

Multiplied explanations lack conviction. A(iii) assumes the Judaist strain in Cerinthianism, to make it relevant to John's readers: and like A(ii) it flatly contradicts John 13:34 — the assumed basis of the passage. B(i) likewise is certainly not the meaning of John 13:34. Further: (1) The strong disclaimer of 7a is inexplicable if in fact it defends a commandment which, when it appears in 9-11, turns out to be one of the most familiar and authoritative words of Jesus — so familiar as not to need quoting. (Only Brooke attempts to explain 7a as heightening the contrast with the newer teaching which places knowledge higher than love, which is not the contrast John makes.) (2) The adversative force of "yet", "on the other hand", "all the same", "for all that" (so Westcott: "a new line of argument or reflection, starting afresh"; Abott-Smith: "in turn", "on the other hand" as Luke 6:42 [untranslated], 1 Corinthians 12:21 ["on the contrary"], 2 Corinthians 10:7, and Law adds John 16:28), makes *a turn of thought,* a shift to something not at first intended, set in opposition to what is first said; it is not exhausted by the contrast of "old since you knew the gospel" with "new as set forth by Christ". If the same commandment were in mind throughout, we would expect "yet the commandment I speak of is new, also, . . ." or "yet this is a new commandment that I write of . . .". (3) The initial impression of verse 7 is a defence of what has been written, not an elaborate and complicated introduction of what is yet to come in 9-11. To make it anticipatory of 9-11 is to destroy the coherence of 2:3-11.

If the identity of the old and new commandments be given up (and if 2 John 5 is an echo of the language of 1 John 2 but does not necessarily control or limit its meaning), then full value can be given to the defensive tone and the adversative force by taking "old commandment" as = all the foregoing, i.e., the moral imperative inherent in all genuine experience of God, of knowing Christ, of abiding in Him. Indeed, John expressly says, "This is the very word which you had from the beginning". The coherence with the foregoing which this establishes is further strengthened by the echo in 7 of the point made in verse 4, to which Dodd draws attention. For this moral imperative John needfully disclaims any novelty — too many are elaborating the original gospel already, with new notions of their own! Yet the very phrase "no new commandment" immediately recalls, for writer and readers alike, perhaps by simple word-association, the "new commandment" of treasured memory, and John turns "on the other hand" to yet another example of his main theme, yet another test of genuine spiritual experience. The exposition in 9-11 of this "new commandment" leaves the reference back to John 13: 34 (as taught in the Johannine Churches if not already penned in the Fourth Gospel) beyond doubt. (The omission of the superb argument "as I have loved you" suggests that appeal is *not* here being made to the written Gospel.)

True in Him and in you — 8b has not been satisfactorily explained on any interpretation. Plummer thinks the *commandment* was shown to

238

be true in Him (by example of it) and in them (by their endeavour to follow it); Westcott paraphrases beyond recognition: the commandment is seen to correspond more closely than we first realised with the facts of Christ's life and death, and with Christian experience. Attempts to explain how a *commandment* can be true or false, by substituting "realised in Him" or "actual", for "true, real", demonstrate embarrassment rather than assurance; nor can the Greek phrase be referred to "commandment" without violence to Greek genders. R. Law says it is "not the law itself but the fact that it is a new and living law, which is true in Him and you"; "the newness was realised in Him" (Moffatt) because He lived in the love of the Father and laid down His life for men; it was realised also in them because they were in the new order (Dodd). So Brooke also. Yet it is difficult to see precisely what this "newness realised in Him" means, or how "true" $=$ "realised".

If "which is true in Him and in you" is a parenthesis commenting upon the *assertion* that the commandment is new, then we have another example (as in 1:1) of the neuter relative pronoun used for an unexpressed abstraction. The assertion that the commandment is new is not an invention of John — he is extremely sensitive to any suggestion that like the opponents he is propounding novel ideas. The assertion of its newness is true "in Him" — for so we had it from Him, Jesus so described it; the assertion that it is new is true also for the readers, although 60 years have passed, for the new age is still only slowly coming to be as the darkness is passing. ("Because the darkness is passing" is taken by Law with "I write" — John reminds of the new commandment because the Gospel Day advances; Westcott thinks this interpretation "improbable"; Dodd takes the phrase with "you" — the newness of the commandment was realised in them because they were of the new order; better, the commandment was still new for them because the new order was still in process of coming to be.)

Darkness - light — Neil Alexander appositely cites on verse 8, 1 Corinthians 10:11 which describes the apostolic Christians as those upon whom the ends of the ages have come, with the comment "the 'ends' are the overlapping ends of the two ages into which the Jews divided the whole of time. The Christian era is the winding up of 'this present age' and the start of the 'age to come'". Hebrews 6:5, Mark 1:15, Galatians 4:4 and in another connection Hebrews 9:26 all reflect this conception. Similarly C. H. Dodd, who suggests that for John as for Paul the two ages of Jewish thought become the realms of light and darkness for Hellenism. "The darkness is being 'withdrawn' as a curtain from the face of the world, and the light is beginning 'already' to have free course" (Westcott). Since it is God's new age, and God is light, the new age is necessarily one of light and Christians are "sons of light" (1 Thessalonians 5:4-8, Ephesians 5:8-14), yet the darkness of the world-order passes only slowly, and Christians must therefore shine as lights in a shadowed world (Philippians 2:15). This is John's thought also: the changeover, certainly begun, proceeds slowly.

In it/in Him — There is no cause of stumbling in it (the light), so RSV, Moffatt, John 11:9f.; but "in him" RSV margin, Neil Alexander ("no internal stumblingblock of contradictory light-profession and dark-practice"). Law says: "The stumblingblock is conceived, not as a tempta-

239

tion that a man puts in another's way (Haupt) but that in his own disposition which is a source of temptation to himself (Rothe). There is nothing in love to entrap into sin". (This last is surely an intrusive thought here.) Better, perhaps, there is no stumblingblock to fellowship, nothing to occasion offence, in the man who loves his brother. "Want of love is the most prolific source of offence" (Westcott). John's thought might, however, be quite general.

Love - hate — "The ominous 'He who says he is in the light and hates his brother' points unmistakably to the Gnostic, who glorying in his superior enlightenment despised the claims and neglected the duties of brotherly love" (Law); "the loveless intellectualism which the writer clearly regarded as one of the worst dangers in the teaching and example of his opponents" (Brooke). See Introduction iv (iv) on Gnostic loveless-ness. Brooke remarks that the writer does not deal with the intermediate states between love and hatred, writing as prophet and not casuist; West-cott too regards sympathy and hatred as mutually exclusive; Barclay re-cites the variations of antipathy — treating men as negligible, with con-tempt, as nuisances, as enemies. But is not John thinking rather of the wilful withdrawal of fellowship from fellow-Christians, denying worship, prayer, the Lord's Table, to other believers, because of spiritual pride and a spurious claim to superiority — and is that not literally *hateful?*

"Brother" — The word commonly means in the New Testament, "fellow Christian", as 1 John 5:16, 3 John 3, 5, 10, John 20:17, 21:23, Acts 9:30, 11:1, 15:23, etc. In Matthew 5:22, Luke 6:41, James 4:11 it may have wider meaning; though Westcott says that "there is, as far as it appears, no case where a fellow-man, as man, is called a 'brother' in the New Testament". Abbott-Smith says the word is used in the papyri "of members of a pagan religious community". In 2 Peter 1, brotherly-affec-tion (inter-Christian loyalty) is deliberately named among the successive steps in the development of Christian character towards the wider, un-limited "love". The occasion for 1 John suggests John has the more limited meaning in mind.

NOTES ON 2:12-14:

I am writing: I write (= I have written, aorist) — The first phrase re-fers to the epistle in course of preparation, the second to the part al-ready penned (Brooke); Huther, Barclay, "I am writing" = the passage now being penned, "I have written" = the whole of the foregoing. Plum-mer pertinently asks if John would say he wrote the whole letter for certain reasons and then add he wrote part for much the same reason! Law (and apparently Gore) suppose an interruption in composition between "I am writing" and "I wrote" — a desperate explanation! Most think a reference to a former epistle or to the Fourth Gospel improbable, be-cause of the reasons John gives. The "epistolary aorist" which transfers the writer to the circumstances of the reader perusing the letter, does not explain the *change* of tense. Most probably the repetition is for empha-sis, and the variety merely to avoid monotony, to add a certain impressive-ness of style — not to be taken too seriously.

Little children/children — Two Greek words, one in 2:1, 12, 29; 3:7, 18; 4:4, 5:21, and the other in 2:13c, 18; 3:7(?), the former deriving from a word signifying "born one" and emphasising parentage and consequent community of nature; the latter from a word which emphasises age — "young child" — though used colloquially in familiar address ("lads", "you fellows"). Brooke, Law, Dodd think the difference again should not be stressed; the second word does, however, suggest the child's need of moral training in 1 Corinthians 14:20. The form of address is full of both seniority and affection: and "born ones" has a special appositeness to the argument ensuing concerning knowledge of the Father (verses 13, 22f.). To suppose that "children" here, or in 5:18, any more than in Galatians 4:19 or Luke 10:21, means child-members of the Church would not occur to anyone not searching desperately for scriptural arguments to defend a theory or support a practice! It would be as reasonable to suppose that "fathers" means only those male Church members who have children, and that the women-members are totally ignored!

Children: fathers: young men — Brooke holds that throughout "little children" = the whole society to which the author writes; it is "now generally recognised that the most satisfactory interpretation" takes fathers and young men as sub-divisions of the whole society of children of God. "A triple division, in which fathers are the middle term, could only be accepted as a last necessity." So Plummer, who cites Titus 2:1-8, Westcott (who thinks "fathers" combines age with eminence and office in the Church), Law, Huther; the divisions of thought might well be partly reflected in age-groupings. Dodd, however, finds two sequences of three aphorisms, and the arrangement probably not much more than a rhetorical figure, since the privileges mentioned belong to all Christians, but emphasis and variety are secured by so distributing them. Barclay: "These blessings are not the blessings of any one age, but of the Christian life". Plummer, Dodd following Augustine, Gore citing Matthew 18:3, Psalm 119:100, and Barclay with hesitations think there may be an implication that the Christian life of all has analogies with the innocence of youth, the strength of life's prime, the experience of full maturity. But if true, this does not mean that the *characteristic* blessing of youth may not be victory in moral conflict, and that of age the accumulated wisdom of experience.

That/because — Whether John writes "that" their sins are forgiven, or "because" their sins are forgiven (etc.) is not clear from the Greek. Rothe says " 'that', so making each sentence a pithy restatement of the purpose, or the essential content, of the epistle". RSV, Westcott, Plummer, Law, Brooke, Huther reject this: 2:21 seems to make the intention, "Not to inform but to remind", unquestionable.

For His sake — Greek: "on account of His name". Brooke: "the name always stands for that which is implied by the name", Ezekiel 20:8, 9, and 36:22. It is because Christ is what He is, and has done what He has done, that they are forgiven. So Acts 3:16.

Forgiveness, knowledge, victory — C. H. Dodd very effectively isolates in prophecies of the New Age (announced in verse 8) the three constant notes of forgiveness, knowledge of God, and spiritual victory which John here makes the essence of Christian experience, for example Isaiah 11:1-9, 52:3-6, Jeremiah 31:31-34, ("quoted at length in Hebrews 8:8-12 as, so to speak, the programme of the Christian dispensation"), Romans 8:31-39, 1 Corinthians 1:8-2:16, John 1:29, 12:31.

The Evil One — To John, as to Jesus, and to all the New Testament writers, the moral struggle is against personal forces of evil, living spirits antagonistic to the Holy Spirit: "Darkness has its prince" (John 12:31, 14:30, 16:11; compare 1 John 3:12, 5:18, 19, Matthew 13:19, John 17:15, Ephesians 6:16).

NOTES ON 2:15-17:

The world — In the present passage, this is the sphere in which the passing darkness has ruled; the crystallisation, so to speak, of sensual lust, external show, and boastful pride; opposed at every point to "the Father", and "on the way out". To this forbidding cluster of ideas John adds others (as at 5:19) — see discussion in Essay 3. Dodd defines "world" as human society in so far as it is organised on wrong principles and characterised by base desires, false values, and egoism. Barclay: "nothing other than pagan society, with its false values and its false standards and its false gods". Westcott more philosophically — the order of finite being regarded as apart from God; Brooke — the whole created system considered as apart from God and opposed to God (similarly Plummer); Huther — mankind, fallen away from God and of hostile disposition towards Him, together with all that it lives for and has made its own. Plainly too much is being said in some of these paraphrases of John: the Christian doctrine of creation — including man — must not be denied. Law takes world as "the mass of unbelieving and unspiritual men — the social organism of evil. . . . Do not court the intimacy and the favour of the unchristian world around you, do not take its customs for your laws, nor adopt its ideals, nor covet its prizes, nor seek fellowship with its life".

All that is in the world — Plummer refutes ingenious attempts to make the three vices John names cover the whole field of human sinfulness; but he records with less criticism the parallel sometimes drawn with the temptation of Eve — "When the woman saw that the tree was good for food (the lust of the flesh), and that it was pleasant to the eyes (lust of the eyes), and that it was to be desired to make one wise (the pride of life), she took of the fruit thereof. . .". The lust of the flesh has been understood as that indulgence in physical appetite which results in sloth, sensuality, and intemperance (Hasler), lust for wealth and inordinate enjoyment (Huther), the hunger of the godlike soul deprived of its proper nutriment and flying to the body for a substitute, compelling it to devour "so many more of the husks as will satisfy the starving prodigal within and make a swine's paradise for his comfort" (Law, quoting Bushnell). The lust of the eyes includes "every sort of wrongful gratification of which sight is the instrument, and also the desire to be seen, to outshine in personal display" (Hasler), sinful desire excited by the view of attractive objects (Bennett), the tendency to be captivated by outward show ("the eyes' desire", Dodd), the spirit which can see nothing without desiring to acquire it and having acquired it flaunts it in the face of men (Barclay), idle and prurient curiosity, exhibitions of the circus and the amphitheatre — "this it is that works in spectacles, in theatres, in sacraments of the devil, in magical arts, in witchcraft, none other than curiosity" (Plummer, quoting Augustine), covetousness and love of mere

material splendour, vulgar display, pomp and luxury, excitements of
theatre, arena, race course, the cult of the physically beautiful, the novelty
of intellectual sensation in science and art, when these are severed from
spiritual ends and made the object of man's devotion (Law), the desire of
seeing unseemly things and the sinful pleasure which the sight of them
affords (Huther). Matthew 5:28 and 29 are relevant. The pride of life,
or vainglory, is taken to mean acquisitiveness and pride in possession
(Hasler), pride in the whole course of human life in relation to the
seen and temporal — to live without looking up to God in dependence
and submission, to live looking down on one's fellow men (Law). John's
own terseness remains more plain, and pertinent.

The world passes — Huther and Law connect the passing of the world
with the last hour of the advent hope and the transition from darkness
to light. Huther says 1 Corinthians 7:31 was written with similar feeling. So Neil Alexander: "It was so late — John in A.D. 96 believed that
the days had run out, that it was 11 p.m. on Domesday Eve. . .". This
may be so, but the final words suggest John had also in mind something
near to *sic transit gloria mundi*.

NOTES ON 2:18-25:

Antichrist — so also in 2:22, 4:3, 2 John 7; it means "one who,
assuming the guise of Christ, opposes Christ" (Westcott), a development
of the pseudo-Christs of Matthew 24:24, Mark 13:22 (so Bennett) in
so far as the pseudo-Christ is simply a pretender to the messianic office,
whereas Antichrist proposes to do or preserve what Christ did while
denying Him (Westcott); a kind of diabolic parody of God's Messiah
(Dodd); the opposition Christ (Huther). Jewish apocalyptic taught that
the messianic kingdom would be preceded by spiritual declension:
apostolic teaching carried this further with warning of anti-Christ
tendencies as forerunners of the End (Matthew 24:5, 24, Mark 13:22,
John 5:43, Acts 20:30, 2 Thessalonians 3:3, 1 Timothy 4:1, 2 Timothy
3) Antichrist is here called "the Liar" as though this were a familiar title
— "The False One". Usurping to oppose appears to be the basic thought:
Barclay equates the idea with the incarnation of the devil and evil,
but he relates it also to the ancient Babylonian and Hebrew dualism,
to the "anti-God" activities of Antiochus Epiphanes (about 168
B.C.), Caligula, and Nero, as the incarnation of opposition to divine
truth, and concludes, "the fact is that Antichrist is not so much a person
as a principle". This is certainly John's use of the term: so approximately
Dodd, Westcott; Plummer discusses exhaustively and finds that for John
as for Paul, Antichrist was a person rather than a prevalent opinion or
tendency. Brooke reviews the history of myths of conflict between gods and
monsters, good and evil, as the basis of the later expectation. He thinks
John simply spiritualises, if he does not altogether depersonalise, the
popular conception, for his immediate purpose. Law regards John as
correcting the Antichrist expectation in that everything really signified by
the current belief was already being realised in the false teachers:
"many antichrists" is a tacit superseding of the earlier conception. In
2:18, one would think the earlier expectation first affirmed and then
used metaphorically to define a position.

The last hour — Barclay, Westcott, Law rehearse Bible references to the last hour (Genesis 49:1, Isaiah 2:2, Micah 4:1, Jeremiah 23:20, 30:24, 48:47, and the apocalyptic "Day of the Lord"). Barclay shows that the phrase usually means a period of ending and beginning, of judgement or salvation according as a man shall choose. Westcott thinks a last hour means a period of critical change; Plummer argues at length against mediating interpretations and shows clearly that John shared the advent beliefs of his age, expected Christ's return in a very short time, and was mistaken. Brooke too sees the last hour as the last period of the interval between the first and the second comings of Christ.

"Gone out" — It is evident that the seceders had received Christian training and membership. For schismatic sects at the end of the first century, compare Revelation 2:6, 14, 15, 20; I Timothy 1:19, 20. Paul had earlier said, with severe irony, "there must be factions among you, in order that those who are genuine among you may be recognised". Barclay says the phrase in 19 can mean "none of them are from us", but inclines to the interpretation "all who are in the Church do not really belong to the Church" ("Membership is no guarantee that a man belongs to Christ and not to Antichrist" — Dodd; "external membership is no proof of inward union" — Brooke). Compare Acts 20:30 (of Ephesus). Plummer thinks two ideas lie together — "not really of us", "not all professing Christians are really of us". Westcott, regarding the "all" as an afterthought, paraphrases "they are not, no not in any case however fair their pretensions may be, of us". Brooke notes that John's word suggests they were not excommunicated: it was necessary to show that none of them were truly members of the Body; Huther and others, troubled by the order of words, obtain the sense: "that all who seem to be of us are not of us" — outwardly belonging to the Church does not guarantee Christian life. Law denies any grammatical difficulty and gives strong grounds for the Greek idiom involved (e.g. 2:2, 3:15), translating "all of them are not of us" = not any of them are of us.

You know — On the illuminating *chrism* see on 2:26-27. Westcott explains "ye know all things" (so verse 27, John 14:26 and 16:23) as "ye have potentially complete and certain knowledge = no false teaching can deceive you if you are faithful to yourselves". The two oldest MSS have "you all know", as RSV ("you know everything" — RSV margin): Neil Alexander takes this as "saving knowledge is for *every* man", countering the heretics' claim that such knowledge was for the favoured and advanced few: so Law ("not the prerogative of an intellectual elite . . . on either reading . . . repudiation of the esoteric pretensions of Gnosticism"), and Dodd. In reply to the same boast, Paul wrote Colossians 1:28: compare also 1 Thessalonians 4:9, Romans 15:14, 15. John carefully avoids saying that the anointing "teaches you everything"; "teaches concerning everything" suggests instead a spiritual intuition concerning the truth or falsehood of doctrines put forward.

Confessing Christ — With this phrase the first clear indication is given of the offence of the seceding groups — the denial of the uniqueness and divinity of Jesus of Nazareth as Son or Christ: see Introduction, (iv) "Source of the Trouble, especially pp. 20, 21; (iii) p. 17. "Denieth . . . confesseth" recalls Matthew 10:32f., but on the importance of the confession of Christ's Lordship as the basis of Church membership, and consequently a necessary feature of Christian baptism, see Matthew 16:16-18 (Mark 8:27f. and 38), Matthew 10:32, 33 and 7:21, Luke 6:46 and 12:8; Acts 2:36, 21, 38; 3:37, 38; 8:16, 22:16, 15:17, 9:14, 8:37, Romans 10:9, 10, Philippians 2:10, 11, Hebrews 3:1, 4:14, 10:23, I Timothy 6:13, James 2:7, Revelation 3:5. So "baptism into the Name of the Lord, Jesus" distinguished Christian from other baptisms, and calling on the Name of the Lord, or having "that worthy Name" called upon you, was part of the rite. The same evaluation of public acknowledgement of the Lordship (Christhood) of Jesus underlies the prominence in the New Testament of the story of Peter's denial — told four times, the warning that preceded it also recorded, separately, four times, with three further references to Peter's reinstatement, and all in contrast to Peter's "great confession".

NOTES ON 2:26-29:

Anointing — The word *chrisma* may mean a ritual anointing with oil, the oil itself, or the solemn unction which the ritual signifies. The verb "to anoint" was familiar in Christian circles — Old Testament kings, priests, and prophets were anointed as symbol of their office and authority; so Messiah was to be anointed (Luke 4:18, Acts 10:38), and (here) all Christians. The noun, *chrism* = "anointing" was equally familiar in Gnostic teaching, and John's emphatic "you (too) have an anointing" (20 and 27) alludes to this. Dodd and Barclay cite Hippolytus: "We above all men are Christians, 'chrismed' with speechless chrism"; Plummer says John puts Antichrist with his antichrists beside Christ with His christs — you have a christing, the antichrists have not.

Whatever may be thought of this unfamiliar language, the unction or anointing in 20 and 27 may be (i) an actual ritual anointing such as later accompanied baptism (perhaps introduced because of this verse): so Plummer, Huther, Bengel; but this is surely the last thing John would contrast with the Gnostic claim. (ii) The anointing of Christians with the Holy Spirit, as of Jesus at His baptism (Acts 10:38, Matthew 3:16; see for the anointing of Christians 2 Corinthians 1:22; Ephesians 1:13 is close in meaning but a different word is used; for the Spirit given at baptism see Acts 19:1-7, 8:17, 1:5, 2:38, 1 Corinthians 6:11, 12; 12:13, and Titus 3:5). This is parallel to the Johannine conception of the Spirit of Truth teaching all truth — John 14:16, 17, 26 and 16:13f. So Brooke (the Spirit given at baptism), Gore (at Confirmation), Hasler, Plummer, Huther (probably the Spirit communicated by the preaching of the gospel). (iii) The heretical *chrism* being knowledge, the orthodox *chrism* must likewise be a body of teaching "as an indwelling, living, continuous teaching power", the gospel heard from the beginning (Dodd). Barclay (the instruction received on entering the Church) rests this view on the coincidence of 24 and 27 (though he thinks we need not choose between (ii) and (iii). Dodd cites a usage of Ignatius, contrasting (though in other words) the anointing of true knowledge (*gnosis*) with false, and concludes that the *chrism* which confers true knowledge of God and is also a prophylactic against the poison of false teaching is the word of

God, the gospel, as communicated in the rule of faith to catechumens and confessed in baptism. This avoids the subjectivism of an appeal to individual inspiration (so in 4:1-6); the interior testimony of the Holy Spirit is confirmation of the datum in the gospel.

The difference is mainly of emphasis. Law had said much the same, speaking of "the living witness which they had in themselves — the Spirit God had given them, who both set the seal of immediate conviction upon the Truth itself and enabled them unfailingly to distinguish it from all its counterfeits. . . . The distinctive feature is that the testimony of the Spirit is regarded as a 'teaching' given to the Church objectively through those ('prophets and teachers') who were the organs of a special inspiration. . . . It is not regarded as superseding the word, but as concurrent and co-operate with it". Since the seceders had been leaders and presumably teachers in the apostolic groups, the appeal to special persons would hardly be cogent: the anointing would appear to be the Holy Spirit of Truth, through whom the gospel first came to them, by whom it was authenticated in their experience (compare 1 Corinthians 2:4, 5), and who now led them into all truth: not the word apart from the Spirit (anointing with the word is a strange conception, and not easily opposed to that which the Gnostics claimed); but neither the Spirit apart from the word which He teaches and authenticates.

In it/in Him — In Greek, identical phrases (compare 2:10): but the closing words of 28 make "in Him" the obvious translation, while 27 clearly means "abide in what was taught you", in what the anointing teaches, as 2:14, and twice in 2:24, (and John 8:31). Repetition of "abide in Him" in 27, 28 would be jejune, whereas 24b lays precise foundation for the more telling point — "just as it taught you, abide in that; even more, little children, abide in Him". Neil Alexander, Huther, Plummer, Brooke hold to "in Him" twice; so Westcott, but remarking that "in it" appears most natural, and Augustine's Latin so read; Law also, but only because "the purpose of all the Spirit's work is the union of the believer with Christ". This does nothing to make the repetition of the last words of 27 in 28 any more meaningful!

He is righteous — The phrase here, in 2:1, 3:7, and thrice in Acts (3:14, 7:52, 22:14), strongly suggests that this title was current in wide circles, and John could probably assume that the seceders would accord at least this much to Jesus, and so (by John's implication, at any rate) to God. In 1:9, God is "righteous", and Huther and others discuss whether God is meant here also. Born of God is certainly much more familiar than born of Christ (3:9, 4:7, 5:1, 4, 18) — though a few argue that the latter idea is not impossible; Law thinks it "quite impossible". A change of reference within the one verse is not inconceivable: "strict grammar is violated, as not uncommonly in John" (Neil Alexander).

Confidence — There are no less than 28 references in the New Testament to the boldness of spirit exhibited by the Church or required from it, of which perhaps the most significant are: Acts 4:13, 29, 31; 9:8, 27, 29; 13:4, 6; 14:3, 18:26, 26:26, 2 Corinthians 3:12, Ephesians 6:19, Philippians 1:20, 1 Thessalonians 2:2. It includes beside freedom of address and speech, born of mutual confidence, "joyous abandon . . . fear-free . . . glad fearlessness" (Neil Alexander).

246

NOTES ON 3:1-3:

Love — Plummer remarks that "love" occurs in 2:29-5:12 sixteen
times as a noun, twenty-five times as a verb, and five times in the word
"beloved" — 46 times in 57 verses!

Father-children — On the family-metaphor, see for example Matthew
6:26, etc., Matthew 6:9, Luke 11:11-13, 1 John 2:8-11, etc., Hebrews
12:5f., Matthew 5:45, 48, Ephesians 4:32-5:1, Luke 15:11f., Romans
8:23, Matthew 21:28, Romans 8:29, John 14:1-3. John uses "children ($=$
'those born') of God" (1 John 3:9, 4:7, 5:1, 2, 4, 18, and 2:29) rather
than Paul's "sons" ($=$ those of accepted status — as "heirs" — whether
through birth or adoption). Plummer: Paul gives the legal, John the
natural side, of the filial relation. Dodd thinks that in Johannine circles
"Son of God" was reserved for "the only-begotten Son", and "children"
for believers. Westcott assembles the Johannine references to "born of God"
and usefully summarises: "the initial fact of the communication of the
divine life is expressed by 'to be born of God'; the essential connection
existing in virtue of this quickening is expressed by 'to be of (out of)
God'; in view of this connection the believer becomes and is a child
of God". To these should be added that this relationship is only in
evidence when the child resembles the Father, reflecting the image of the
Son (John 8:42-47, 1 John 3:9, 10). "Natural birth . . . relates us all
as creatures to the life-giving Creator. But there is another birth, entirely
of God's gift and initiative" (Neil Alexander): this occurs when men
accept (by believing upon) Jesus as Christ (John 1:12, 3:1-8f., 1 John
5:1f.; see also Galatians 3:26). Alexander compares being "in the kingdom" and "in Christ" as likewise not natural states but states of grace into
which God has called some; and holds, with Dodd, that John uses the
description "born of God" because "it was an expression used, and in
our author's opinion misused, by the false teachers. . . . The antecedents
of the idea of regeneration lie not within Judaism but in Hellenistic
thought". But this latter statement needs qualification. What Hellenistic
Mystery Religions regarded as essentially an initiation into profounder
secrets of *knowledge,* John held to be the sharing of a divine *life,* communicated through Christ and issuing in Christlike character and behaviour — the family likeness of all the children of God. Behind John's
language and thought lie ideas like "They shall be called sons of God"
(Matthew 5:9, 45, etc.), and even more the insistence of Jesus that men
can enter the kingdom of God only by becoming like little children
(Matthew 18:1-4, 19:14) — a clear, authoritative linking of conversion
with "rebirth" which sufficiently explains John 3:1-8. Behind this again
lies Jewish baptism of proselytes, of which it was said, "Whoever brings
a heathen near to God and converts him, is as though he created him",
and the newly baptised is "a child of one day", "new-born" — phrases
which lay ready to hand to be filled out with meanings probably much
deeper than Judaism intended. Bernard well says that "to say that believers are begotten of God is only to stretch a little further the
metaphor involved in Our Father, which art in heaven . . ."; and W. F.
Howard commented that John puts Mark 10:15, Luke 18:17, Matthew
18:3-4 into phraseology appropriate to his characters (in John 3): "the

moral regeneration which Jesus demanded is here translated into another region of thought".

World did not know Him — "The majority of commentators understand 'God': the world does not recognise the children because it does not recognize the Father whose they are and whom they resemble. It seems clear to me, nevertheless, that the reference is to Christ, who is not yet manifested to the world (2:28, 3:2, with other examples of usage)" — Law, and so Dodd. The past tense would seem to place the reference to Christ beyond argument.

If (when) . . . appear — The Greek particle "implies no doubt as to the fact, but shows that the results of the fact are more important than the time" (Plummer). So here, as in 2:28, the misleading "if" gives places to "when" in RSV; compare John 12:32, 14:3.

When He appears — could be "when it appears", answering "it does not yet appear". Plummer thinks it "rather violent" to change subject in mid-sentence; "like Him" would then mean "like the Father", "see Him" means "see God" — which seems to confuse the passage. The echo of 2:28 and the end of 3:3 really fix the meaning as "when Christ appears . . . like Christ . . . see Christ". Brooke says John uses the word "manifested" eighteen times, and in twelve Christ is the subject; Westcott argues strongly that the passage requires this; Huther recites authorities and holds it erroneous to say "when He shall appear" because of the immediately preceding phrases, but he then adds, "It is self-evident that this revelation will take place [when Christ appears]". Law thinks Christ's manifestation is the central thought of the passage.

Like Him, for we shall see Him — Westcott says the argument could run either, "We shall see God, and therefore, since this is possible, we must be like Him", or "We shall see God and in that presence we shall reflect His glory and be transformed into His likeness". Both thoughts are scriptural: we see that which we have the sympathetic power of seeing, and gain greater power of seeing (gaining greater sympathy) by the exercise of the power we have. Plummer prefers, "We shall be like Him because . . . we shall see Him", citing 2 Corinthians 3:18. Huther argues that the certain hope of the Christian is that he shall see God, and this includes the certainty of being like God, for "God can only be seen by him who is like Him". Law remarks that the whole tenor of New Testament teaching demands that the object of vision and assimilation be Christ, and cites the close parallel in Colossians 3:4; "appear", "pure", and "see" are words more appropriately used of Christ than of the Father. Dodd sees little difference involved, since for Johannine thought to see Jesus is to see the Father: "the Fourth Gospel expounds the whole ministry of Jesus Christ as the realisation of the hope of the vision of God and His glory". John's insistence that no man has seen God, that the Only-begotten has made Him known, that when any cries, "Show us the Father", the answer is Christ, and the close parallel in Colossians 3:4, still more exact in 2 Corinthians 3:18, all point to "Christ" in the present passage; further evidence for the contention that "Christlikeness is the supreme goal of the Christian on every page of the New Testament, implied in almost every statement of Christian experience", may be seen in the present author's *Into the Same Image* (1957).

NOTES ON 3:4-10:

To take away sins — Huther discusses "to take away" as meaning "to cleanse by His blood", sacrificially, but concludes from LXX and context as well as Johannine usage, that "remove" is the meaning here. "To take away sins" corresponds to "cleansing from all sin" in 1:7, and signifies the whole extent of the redemptive activity of Christ — forgiveness and sanctification (so Lucke); Westcott adds a third element, "to destroy the work of the devil". "The world can be saved only by the abolition of sin: to this end all Christ was and taught and did, by life, death, and resurrection . . . was directed" (Law).

No one who abides in Him sins — But earnest Christians do sin! To evade the dilemma, it is customary to hold that for sound pedagogic reasons — to leave the readers in no possible doubt of the seriousness of the issue — John deliberately sharpens the antithesis between perfect Christian and non-Christian, allowing no intermediate position. Another solution presses the present continuous "does not practice, continually, habitually, intentionally, with specious self-justifying arguments, the ways of sin", so allowing accidental "falling" into occasional sins as exceptions to the general direction of Christian life. Either way, John states the ideal which holds, indisputably, for all who claim to be Christian: failures to live up to this must be seen for what they are — failures deserving judgement. Dodd thinks readers would not grasp the subtle tense-distinction; the expectation of a sinless messianic people (Enoch 5:8, Jubilees 5:12) would lead them to suppose John meant actual sinlessness. The apparent contradiction of 1:8f. is due to the different problems being dealt with — there, the complacency of those who think themselves already perfect in virtue, here the moral indifference of those who hold virtue does not matter so long as you are enlightened. Brooke is content to say that the statement is made absolutely, without reference to the modifications necessary when it is applied to individual cases, but cites Augustine and Bede for the necessary qualification — "In so far as he remains in Him, to that extent he does not sin", adding later, "this fact that he has been begotten of God excludes the possibility of his committing sin, as an expression of his true character, though actual sins may and do occur, in so far as he fails from weakness to realise his true character". Brooke also remarks: "The writer speaks in the absolute language of the prophet rather than with the circumspection of the casuist". Law discusses very fully. He finds the assertion "not only of the inadmissibility in principle, but the non-existence in fact, of sin in the regenerate life, one of the crucial difficulties in the exposition of the epistle". He contends the point is missed when "to do sin" is assumed to mean "to sin habitually", for it is not the frequency which is in view, but the fact that Being is to be tested and known by Doing, the inward spiritual nature by the outward conduct. Law opposes 3:6, 9; 5:18 with 2:1, 5:16 and with Christian experience; he rejects the view that John is exhibiting an abstract ideal; or that "remain in Him" is to be pressed (Augustine), as no explanation of 3:6b; or that "to do sin" means simply a life of unbroken and impenitent sin; or that — on the lines of Romans 7:20 — "a Christian does not do sin, he suffers it" (Besser), for John is here expressly repudiating the attempt to distinguish between a man and his deeds;

he rejects also Westcott's "As long as the relationship with God is real, sinful acts are but accidents; they do not touch the essence of the man's being"; and Rothe's ascription of sin to infirmity rather that to the regenerate man's proper self, because John's argument is that a man cannot so repudiate his acts of sin. Law's own solution lies in the controversial situation: John's unqualified assertions are just vigorous contradictions of other assertions of equally unqualified falsity, namely the Gnostic assertions of the indifference of morality to the truly "spiritual". John's language is not that of "calm and measured statement but of vehement polemic". Huther is at first content to say "of course, it is not the physical but no doubt the moral impossibility of sinning that is described", but later he adds: John represents abiding in Christ and sinning as irreconcilable opposites; he does not mean that the believing Christian does not sin any more — for in 1:8-10, 2:1f., 3:3 he emphasises that sin still demands confession, forgiveness, intercession and self-purification. The Christian, as child of God, bears the contradiction in himself: he still actually sins, and yet is free from sin, has broken with it, is in his inmost nature in decided opposition to it, yet he finds it in himself, deals with it, and so discovers its power over him decreasing. So it is no longer sin, but opposition to sin, that determines his conduct. "Hatred of sin is the common mark of the children of God, love of sin the common property of the children of the devil" (Besser); "If I do what I do not want, it is no longer I that do it. . ." (Paul). Plummer likewise speaks of "that internal contradiction of which everyone who is endeavoring to do right is conscious", adding that not sin but the opposition to sin is the ruling principle of Christian living. Law is probably right in stressing the polemical situation, wrong in suggesting some betrayal of meaning by vehemence; against the Gnostic moral neutralism John argues cogently the theological impossibility that children of God through Christ should tolerate sin: it is unthinkable. But *as with every other theological principle* of the faith — the love that meets all needs, the power that can convert the world, the sufficiency of grace for perfect holiness, the certainty that prayer is answered — the task remains for the Christian to live up to what he assuredly believes. Plummer (on verse 9) says "it is a moral impossibility for a child of God to sin" — and cites, for "cannot = moral impossibility", John 5:30, 6:44, 65; 7:7, 8:43, 12:39, 14:17, and perhaps 1 John 4:20. So Neil Alexander: "The Christian cannot, without creating an impossible moral contradiction, deliberately and consistently sin". And this is worth saying, because of Gnostic and other antinomian tendencies in evangelicalism.

He who does right is righteous — The impression is irresistible that 3:7 has some relation to the problem that faced Paul to expound justification by faith in terms that did not undermine moral obligation; for John, Paul, and James alike faced a Judaism which laid all emphasis on achieving righteousness before God. To be "accounted righteous" (justified) by faith appeared to make unnecessary, or unevangelical, the effort to *be* righteous in fact. Dodd, Neil Alexander appear to support this interpretation of John's words; Huther says there is no reference to justification, but nevertheless understands "to do righteous" as signifying the action, and "to be righteous" as signifying the state — (which latter must be "before God", that is, justified). Luke 18:9-14 strongly suggests the whole question was far from confined to Pauline circles.

God's nature abides in him — Moffatt renders "for the offspring (= seed) of God remain in Him"; Genesis 17:9, Luke 1:55, John 8:33, Galatians 3:16, 29 illustrate the thought; Dodd says this yields "an excellent sense, closely parallel to verse 6; Neil Alexander thinks the fact that this makes John tautologous need not tell against its probability — an unjust remark. On the other side, Dodd cites Gnostic parallels for the idea of rebirth by the implanting of the "true good", suggesting in John's thought a divine principle from which the new nature of the child of God is produced. From the absence of the article, and the parallelism of the statements, Dodd argues a preference for this interpretation, citing James 1:18, 1 Peter 1:23-25, John 1:12, Luke 8:11 as the basis in "the authentic Christian tradition" for John's use of Gnostic concepts of an implanted divine seed. Brooke thinks that to make "seed of God" a collective for all God's children, parallel to "seed of Abraham", makes grammar and sense more difficult. Law: "As the seed of physical generation stamps upon the offspring an ineffaceable character, and nothing in after years can alter the inherited basis of life, so does the germ of spiritual life from the spiritual Father set the impress of a permanent organic character upon the God-begotten. . . . The Christian life, in its inmost, eternal essence . . . is a life of perfect righteousness; that is, under present conditions, a life of continual opposition to sin and of victory over it. . . . Unquestionably, the seed is here the new life-principle implanted by the divine begetting". Huther takes *seed* as the divine element of which the new man is produced; Westcott, "the principle of life which He has given continues to be the ruling principle of the believer's growth . . . . The germ of the new life is that out of which the mature man will in due time be developed". The verses Dodd cites, especially 1 Peter 1:23, help to persuade Westcott, Dodd, Barclay that the seed, or the instrument by which the divine element is conveyed, is the Word of God (compare 2:24). This rests on Bede, Augustine. Brooke, Plummer think this hardly in accord with Johannine teaching, in which the Spirit is the author of the new birth (John 3). In the present passage John probably means the divine life, from God — implying here nothing of its means or occasion.

Notes on 3:11-18:

Not like Cain — (1) John's explanation of the murder is "hardly justified by the spare and puzzling account" in Genesis 4:1-16, but it is not less satisfactory than those of Philo, of Hebrews 11:4, or the comment of Jude 11. The sacrificial language (see below), obscurities, and textual condition of the story raise suspicion of subsequent pious editing; possibly the original purpose was a protest against human sacrifice. "The ancient writer of the story evidently wished to teach that animal sacrifice alone was pleasing to God" (Gunkel, Skinner), but no reason for the preference of Abel is now given in Genesis. In Hebrews the gifts differentiate the men (Strahan says, the spirit in which they were offered, the disposition of the worshipper — "By faith Abel offered a more excellent sacrifice than Cain . . ."); in Philo, it is the manner of the offering — Cain delaying several days, and offering fruits and not firstfruits. In John, it is the whole character of the men. William Alexander remarks that it is characteristic of the historical spirit of John that he does not entangle himself with the luxuriant upgrowth of wild fable in which traditional Judaism has ever enveloped the simple narrative, and Plummer notes that Jewish and Christian literature use Abel as a prototype of the good and Cain of the wicked. Law says, "John sets before us the two figures . . . as prototypes of hate and love", adding that Cain slew his brother because his own works were evil and his brother's righteous whereas Christ's works were righteous and His brethren's evil, and yet He took on Himself their evil deeds. This juxtaposition of Cain's sacrifice of his brother with Christ's sacrifice of Himself is the more tempting because the word for "slay" originally meant "to cut the throat", especially of a sacrificial victim (compare its use in Revelation, of slaying a victim; Brooke says that in LXX its most frequent use is sacrificial). Huther thinks the word does not necessarily imply martyrdom or sacrifice, but that John's use of the story needs explanation. The contrast of Cain and Christ, illustrating that of love and hate between brethren, and the association of hate and death, as proving absence of life from God, with the overtone of the (world's) jealousy of the godly, provide sufficient explanation. In addition to the story, and the linking of hate with murder in the Sermon on the Mount, Dodd finds also that the sudden introduction of *murder* is easier to understand if it is seen that all the leading ideas of this passage are echoes of those in John 8:37-47.

(2) But another polemic purpose may underlie John's illustration. The Cainites were a Gnostic sect (Irenaeus, *Adv. Haer.* 1:31) — "one of the oldest forms of Gnosticism known to us" (Plummer), who regarded the creator of matter as himself evil, and so exalted all who withstood him — Cain, Korah, the men of Sodom, and Iscariot; the revolt of Adam and Eve was a righteous outcry against tyranny, inspired by the serpent, bringer of enlightenment, which may explain the Cainites' association with the Ophites (serpent-worshippers). Ethically their views were similar (according to Irenaeus) to those of Carpocrates (see Notes to Introduction, 5: Gnosticism — On Moral Neutralism ascribed to some Gnostics). All the prohibitions of the Old Testament were reversed. Plummer thinks it impossible that the monstrous system of the Cainites was formulated as early as the first century, but "the first beginnings of it were there, and it is by no means impossible that 1 John 3:10-12 was written as a condemnation of the principles on which Cainite doctrine was built". This seems too strong: rather, the illustration is chosen to press the point of love — life/hatred — death, but carried a topical aptness that lent it peculiar edge. Other scholars (Pfleiderer, F. L. Cross) think Cainism may have been pre-Christian (compare Philo's *de Posteritate Caini*).

To love in word — Plummer takes somewhat differently as "to have that affection which is genuine so far as it goes but is so weak that it never gets further than affectionate words — love opposed not to truth but to loving acts". "To love with the tongue", on the other hand, is to profess an affection one does not feel — hypocrisy, opposed to truth. Law rejects this double contrast — "sincere good wishes contrasted with good deeds, hollow phrases contrasted with sincerity": "with the tongue" is mere-

ly a contemptuous synonym of "in word" and expresses forcibly how
cheap such love is.

NOTES ON 3:19-24:

By this — Dodd tries hard to take as referring to what follows, in
John's more usual manner, but finds the result obscure and abrupt; he
appeals to 4:6 as a parallel, and concludes that "this" = loving in
deed and in truth. So Huther, Plummer, Westcott, Brooke (while thinking there is much to be said for the other view); Law says the phrase
is used retrospectively here only in the epistle.

Reassure — Either "convince, persuade (that)" or "win over by persuasion"; "talk over" is Dodd's suggestion, and he thinks "reassure" a
possible extension of meaning, though one for which it is difficult to find
an exact parallel. Westcott cites Matthew 28:14 and 2 Maccabees 4:45,
and finds "persuading our heart that God is greater" does *not* follow
from sincere love of the brethren, and that attempts to supply what we are
persuaded of leave too much to be understood. He therefore prefers
the meaning "assure" — "we shall still and tranquillise the fears and misgivings of our heart", in the sense "we shall assure our heart, whereinso-
ever our heart condemn us, because God is greater" — a sense "which
falls in completely with the context and flows naturally from the Greek. . . .
The context requires that this sovereignty shall be regarded under the
aspect of love as exercised for the calming of human doubts. . . . God,
who is greater than the heart, forgives us all on which the heart sadly
dwells". Brooke acquiesces with some reluctance, while thinking "we
persuade our heart (that we are of the truth)" is a more natural meaning
of the Greek. Law, citing Plummer, points out that "persuade our heart
before Him" (viz., that we are of the truth) amounts to the same thing
as *reassure;* but he then argues as Westcott (above) for "pacify, assure",
urging that our sincere love of the brethren does *not* persuade us that
God is greater. Plummer suggests "persuade our heart that it need not
condemn us" — which is again very near to *reassure.* The interpretation
here adopted is supported by Dodd, Westcott, Brooke ("the aim of the
whole passage is surely to give assurance, and not to strike terror";
the alternative makes the connection between 19 and 20 impossible to
explain), Law, Barclay, and Neil Alexander. Plummer says, "We must
not give 'God is greater' a one-sided interpretation, either 'more merciful'
or 'more strict'. It means that He is a more perfect Judge than our
heart can be. It is the difference between conscience and omniscience".

Hereby — probably refers to what follows, the gift of the Spirit,
though John writes not "hereby we know . . . by the Spirit", but "herein
we know . . . from the Spirit". Brooke thinks 4:13 makes this meaning
almost necessary. Westcott and others think the "hereby" looks back to
the love and obedience which assure the Christian of divine fellowship,
but this would merely repeat 24a ("purely tautological" — Law; and it
leaves the Spirit out of account altogether). Law thinks the un-
grammatical "in this we know out of the Spirit" is due to the use of a
formula-phrase ("in this . . . know") in which the force of "in" is
scarcely felt. Huther thinks "hereby" means "by the Spirit", the
Source of the knowledge that God abides in us — to which Law replies

that John tests Spirit by deeds and not deeds by Spirit. "Undoubtedly the meaning is not that the Spirit is the source of a subjective assurance that God dwelleth in us, but that the Spirit gives objective evidence of this by prompting the confession that Jesus is the Christ". So verse 2 of the next paragraph makes clear.

NOTES ON 4:1-6:

Test the spirits — Ecstatic speaking with strange tongues and inspired prophecy were familiar in apostolic days (see Acts 2 [?], 13:1, 21:9, 11: 28, 1 Corinthians 12:28f., and chapter 14), while "discerning of spirits" was itself a "spiritual gift" (1 Corinthians 12:10); 1 Thessalonians 5:19-21 illustrates the same need. Barclay, Bennett, Westcott, Brooke, and Neil Alexander all quote Didache 11:8, "Not every one who speaks in a spirit is a prophet; he is only a prophet if he walks in the ways of the Lord", alongside John's insistence that he is only a prophet if he speaks the truth concerning Christ. The false prophet is more than a false teacher in that he claims direct inspiration. In 1 Corinthians 14, men uttering unintelligible sounds under the compulsion of the Spirit would, if no interpretation were available, give the impression of madness (verses 2, 23, 27); even the prophets, speaking plainly, did not wait one for another! Barclay excellently describes the general background: a universe thronged with spirits and demon-powers — a haunted world: the divine Spirit visibly given at baptism with tongues and other manifestations: the ministry not yet professionalised, nor the exuberance of life organised out of the Church: the dangers of self-hypnotism or charlatanism as to spirit-possession. Dodd, in describing inspired prophecy in the apostolic Church, notes Paul's insistence on the prophets' control over their own "spirits" and the need that listeners exercise their own critical judgement on what the prophets say (1 Corinthians 14:32, 29); and adds that prophecy's importance outlasted that of the other "abnormal" gifts, though at the same time prophets remained subordinate to apostles, and true had to be distinguished from false. Law stresses that the possession of the Spirit was (here) an objective matter, a public sign; but he adds that "the Spirit, throughout these passages, is regarded simply as the inspirer of the True Confession of Jesus". Plummer mentions "those extraordinary and supernatural powers which at various periods of the Church's history persons have claimed to possess . . . no guarantee of the possession of truth!". John certainly believed in many evil spirits, but "every spirit that confesses Jesus come in the flesh" cannot refer to evil spirits; John seems to mean "every moving spirit behind various sects and teachings" (so, approximately, Gore). Law: "The spirits on either side are many and yet have one head and represent one character — the spirit of truth and the spirit of error. It is not to be assumed (as by Huther: 'The spirits of the prophets themselves interpenetrated by the spirit of truth or the spirit of error') that the plurality of spirits consists in nothing more than the manifestations of the one personal 'spirit, as these are diversified by the individuality of the human 'medium' — that the spirits are simply the prophets themselves as the inspired organs of the spirit. . . . On the contrary, all that we learn from the New Testament points to the Spirit of truth and the spirit of error acting upon men through a hierarchy of

subordinate spiritual agents" (1 Corinthians 12:10, 14:12, 32; "more re-
motely" Matthew 18:10, Hebrews 1:14, Revelation 1:4, 3:1; 22:6). On
the other side, abundance of spiritualistic manifestations seems to have
been characteristic of the heretical sects (2 Thessalonians 2:9, 1 Timothy
4:1, Revelation 16:13f.). Westcott, very briefly, seems to point in this
direction for John's meaning. Yet it must be confessed that the angel-
references seem too remote to explain John, and the 1 Corinthians cita-
tions scarcely justify the novel theory of a hierarchy of spiritual agencies
subordinate to the Holy Spirit (1 Corinthians 12:11 seems expressly to
exclude it). John appears simply to mean that every so-called "spirit" —
source of inspiration — must be judged by its confession.

Confesses — see notes on 2:18-25, and for the exquisite precision of
the confession here defined, the closing paragraphs of Introduction.

"Separates" Jesus is the reading which stood in the text (3) of Irenaeus,
Origen, and Clement. Neil Alexander thinks it probably crept in to make
the condemnation apply more clearly to some Cerinthian-style heresy of
their time. The received text could equally well have arisen from verse 2.
Plummer says the reading can scarcely be genuine for it is not found in
a single Greek manuscript, nor in any version except the Vulgate, (and
Polycarp's quotation is in its present form). "Separates" would evidently
mean "the divine from the human — divides the one divine-human Person"
(Westcott). Gore thinks it so difficult and so significant a reading that
he is disposed to believe it original, as expressing exactly what Cerinthus
did. Brooke: an explanatory gloss; Westcott also rejects: the phrase "divides Jesus" uses the name in a "comprehensive sense" which is unscriptural.

He who is not of God does not listen . . . . — Dodd and Neil Alexander
suggest that, taken alone, this idea would inhibit missionary activity
among indifferent or hostile hearers, Dodd adding that, oversimplifying,
"John has expressed himself somewhat incautiously". If so, it is a rare
lapse. Both scholars introduce here the idea of predestination. But (as
Dodd fairly says) the division of men by the gospel into hearers and
rejectors was a fact of evangelistic experience; John here has also in mind
those who appeared to "hear" but now deliberately prefer some other
message. Doubtless "we can but say with Dodd 'For ultimate reasons . . .
which we cannot penetrate' " some men believe and others do not: but
"predilection" is nearer the truth than "predestination". Some are of God,
and come to the light; others are "of the world", and "love darkness"
and will not hear.

NOTES ON 4:7-12:

Division at verse 12 (RSV) is very debatable, even for 1 John. But
it does appear that verse 11 effectively echoes verse 7 so as to suggest completeness of one thought-paragraph, while verse 12 provides another
swing-door — into a corridor of doors!

God is love — In Hellenistic religion, Neil Alexander acutely remarks,
"God being passionless could not love man"; nor, for that matter, could
the "Passionless Impersonality" of some modern thought. Gore: "The
ancient philosophers were so obsessed with the desire to deny to God
not merely everything carnal, but everything that belongs to the emotional nature of man, that the religion of the Bible — the religion of the

incarnation — can never in this respect find itself at home with them. There is nothing about God in the philosophers which will compare with Isaiah's 'In all their afflictions He was afflicted . . . in His love and in His pity He redeemed them' ". C. H. Dodd contrasts at length the Hebrew conception of God as the living, acting One whose nature is revealed in His activity, and the typically Hellenist abstract conception of Deity as absolute Being, timeless, changeless, unmoved, the negation of all that belongs to sensible experience — though some feeling is evidenced for a less abstract, nearer to Judaist, concept. The Hebrew-Christian concept, and especially the Johannine here, assumes the personality of God — "we cannot be loved by an abstraction".

Knows God — Love is the test of the knowledge of God, either as its indispensable condition ("like is known by like") or as its invariable consequence — the heart falling in love with love seen in God. Westcott stresses "sympathy", deriving one's spiritual being from God, as necessary to true recognition of God. Brooke evades the precise relation of knowledge, new birth, and love, as a question not present to John's mind, but he aptly quotes Odes of Solomon 3:3, 4: "I should not have known how to love the Lord if He had not loved me. For who is able to distinguish love, except the one that is loved?".

Manifest among us — Greek "in". "In our case" (RV margin), "among us" (RSV) are rejected by Westcott because the same preposition is used in 12 to express the presence of God *in* the Christian body. Plummer also prefers *in us*, citing John 9:3. Huther makes "in" = "to" ("as in verse 16 and John 9:3") and interprets as "the love of God to us has been manifested". Law argues emphatically for "toward us" here and in 16, with persuasive parallels; Brooke says if John meant this he would have written it, connects the manifesting with the purpose that men might live, and insists on "in us".

Only Son — In Luke 7:12, 8:42, 9:38 and Hebrews 11:17 "only begotten" denotes "an only child". So here Christ is He "beside whom His Father has none" (Huther). Westcott shows the same meaning in the LXX, together with "unique, alone, beloved", and follows the history of the word in post-New Testament times. Brooke, rather strangely, holds that the point of "only begotten" in the Johannine books is that "the one and only Son completely reproduces the nature and character of His Father, which is concentrated so to speak in one, and not divided up among many brethren". This idea may be present in John 1:14, less probably in John 1:18; it is hardly discernible in John 3:16, 18, or here, or in Luke, Hebrews.

No man has seen God — Huther and others deny that John here tilts at "seeing God" in polemical reference to the false teachers' claim to "see" God (i.e., know Him fully), as this would have been more definitely expressed, and the word "see" does not here refer to spiritual knowing. Yet such oblique reference to the opposing view is entirely in John's style, and the idea certainly comes in unexpectedly. Westcott, Huther: "Though no man hath seen God . . . yet God may be abiding in us, and the sign (or the reality) of this is present when we love one another". Law thinks this contrast of seeing and abiding is very abrupt; 4:20 is decisively in favour of "God is invisible, we cannot directly do Him any good — He has no need of our help; yet if we are begotten of God we have in us the same nature of love, and there is provision by which this nature may be manifested and exercised in us — If we love one another, God dwelleth in us". This seems over-subtle. Brooke makes the point that God's nature cannot be made visible to the eye, it is known in action — incarnation, atonement; so His presence in us is known in love. Dodd sets the reference to seeing God against the Platonic idea that the love of divine Beauty culminates in "beholding it" — the New Testament is notably reticent about the vision of God: here again it carries forward the thought of the Old Testament; in Hebrew religion hearing, not seeing, is the key to religious experience. Communion with God is a matter of hearing the word of the Lord, receiving the knowledge of His will, and ordering one's life according to it. Dodd quotes Luke 11:28 (thinks Matthew 5:8 refers to the age to come), and suggests that in Gospel and Epistle of John the direct mystical vision of God as the goal of religious aspiration in this life is set aside.

His love is perfected in us — Plummer: "Our love of Him is perfected in us"; His love to us is not perfected by our loving one another, and "the Love of God" in this epistle (2:5, 3:17, 5:3) commonly means man's love for God. But this yields a violent transition from the thought which has dominated the passage — it is that love that "God is" which provides the whole foundation of the argument. Westcott thinks neither God's love for man nor man's love for God suits the passage, and translates "His love" as the love which answers to God's nature and which He has imparted to us; Huther suggests "the love which is inherent in God". Westcott compares the perfection of the believer in love with the perfection of love in the believer (2:5, 4:17, 18). It is very difficult to give "love of God" a consistent meaning throughout the epistle: contrast 4:9 with 2:5, 15, 3:17. The variations of meaning are probably more apparent than real: for John, all love is of God, manifested as God's love toward us, communicated by God to us (3:1), and so becoming manifest again in our love for God and for the brethren. Our love is God's love in us. If this is true to John's meaning, then "perfected in love" can have all three shades of meaning: God's love reaching perfection in us, our love for God perfected in confidence and obedience, and our love for the brethren made complete and true. John's insistence on perfection in love doubtless contains a side-allusion not only to the lovelessness of Gnosticism but to the seceders' pride in their perfection in *knowledge*.

NOTES ON 4:13-19:

We have seen — Westcott: "The apostle does not speak of himself personally, but as representing the Church"; Law as emphatically denies this, because "it is the importance of the personal element in the vision and witness" that the pronoun stresses. This latter interpretation assumes eye-witness authorship, of course, but it also limits this ground of assurance to a very few (even in John's day), and distant believers, and makes the "we have seen" quite distinct from the "we know" of verse 16. This seems incoherent.

Whoever confesses — Baptism is plainly not mentioned in the passage! But the citation here again (compare 2:22, 23 and the Note on 2:18-25, "Confessing Christ") and the mention of Christ's baptism twelve verses later, justifies our assumption that the precise moment of the confession here referred to was the moment of baptism. It is of course the confession, rather than the rest of the primitive rite, that John here makes so significant. Neil Alexander remarks that verse 15 contains "almost certainly a citation of an ancient Church creed, as found in the Western reading of Acts 8:37".

In this — retrospectively, "that we dwell [together?] in love", may be supported by 4:12, by 2:5 in so far as "perfected" means fulfilled (accomplishing its end) in loving deeds, (so Law argues strongly that "perfected" always means proving reality by deeds), and by the plea that future confidence (at the Judgement) hardly proves love's present perfecting. So Neil Alexander; Plummer, Westcott: "In this = in our abiding in God". *In this* may, however, mean (prospectively) "in that we have confidence"; for John certainly thinks of Judgement as already begun (Huther); 4:18 supports this, and so does John's use of "that" definitively — John 15:8, 1 John 4:10. So, approximately, Brooke, Dodd, Huther. The argument from 4:18 seems more cogent than that from 4:12. Love is perfected in several ways, in whoever keeps God's word (2:5), whoever loves, God abiding in him (4:12), and here in whoever is fearless.

Perfected in us — Greek has "with us" (in verse 12, "in us"). Perhaps "love with us is perfected" (that is, love among us, our brotherly love), or "love is perfected in our case, with our co-operation, among us". Law thinks the unusual preposition was probably intended to emphasise that it is in the social relations of the Christian community that the divine life of love finds its fullest realisation; he holds that Westcott's "with our co-operation" (Brooke says this meaning is "possible") lays too great weight on a preposition, and introduces a thought foreign to the passage. Huther and Plummer: "Love . . . takes up its abode with us".

As He is, so are we in this world — almost defies relevant interpretation. That adopted follows Neil Alexander: this relationship (of Christ to God) is the archetype of ours with God; Jesus could never be thought to "fear" the Father. Brooke: we can look forward with confidence, knowing that as the exalted Christ abides in the Father's love so we abide in it, so far as that is possible under the conditions of our present existence in this world; Plummer: we do not fear God, because we are Christlike in love; Huther (rejecting six possible interpretations): if we live in love then we do not fear the Judgement because we are like Him and He cannot condemn us; Westcott, Dodd likewise think our imitation of Christ is the point, and Law persuasively appeals to this theme in 2:6, 3:3, 7, adding: "The heart of all Christ's doing and suffering was the intense longing to make Himself the channel through which the love of God might reach men. To this end He followed the path of love to the crowded city, to the wilderness, the cross and the grave. In Him love had its absolute fulfilment. And if we also seek to be channels through which the love of God reaches our fellowmen, then in our small measure and degree we are 'as He is', and love . . . has herein reached fulfilment in us, that we may have boldness in the day of judgement. Love will be on the judgement seat. Love will be before the judgement seat. And love cannot be condemned or disowned of love". Eloquent, but hardly exegesis. A great deal has to be read into John's six or nine words. In the end the "fulfilment of love" turns out to be not brotherly love but our confidence in the face of the judgement. In spite of the great names cited, it seems very doubtful if John would ever have said that our imitation of Christ gives us confidence before the Judgement, or make the claim "as He is so *are* we": his attitude is rather, "we purify ourselves . . . we *shall be* like Him when He appears". Yet sharing His attitude towards the Father is an element of imitation which is possible now, by grace. It haunts the mind that the reference to the Day of Judgement comes in very suddenly (2:28 is not exactly the Day of Judgement); that in Johannine thought the judgement "of this world" was at Calvary (John 12:31), and the judgement of hearts by the gospel's light proceeds already (John 3:17-19); and that Christians, like Christ, confront judgement "in this world" and need His fearlessness in face of it.

Fear hath torment — The last word occurs only here and at Matthew 25:46; RSV translates, "Fear has to do with punishment". Bennett remarks that fear is in itself a form of suffering, but that this hardly suits the context or the Greek; Neil Alexander says the Greek suggests the fearful pain of anticipated judgement as itself part of the punishment; Dodd merely mentions both interpretations.

We love — So AV (KJV), RV, RSV, NEB, Brooke, Moffatt, Dodd, Huther, Westcott; "Let us love", according to Vulgate, Luther, Rothe, Law (who thinks this "more pointed"). But the whole tenor of the passage requires statement, not appeal, and Law has to make the emphatic "we" into "as for us". Westcott notes the absence of "Beloved" (4:7) which we would expect in a hortatory clause. "Let us love men", and even "We love men", moreover, limit the meaning unduly: the contrast is between living in fear and living in love.

NOTES ON 4:20-5:3a:

Commandment from him — Plummer thinks "Him" = God, because Christ has not been mentioned for several verses, though he quotes Luke 10:27 as well as Deuteronomy 6:5 for the source. So Neil Alexander, following Brooke: "John seems to know traditional teaching such as Mark 12:28-31" while still taking "Him" = God. Dodd merely speaks of "the evangelical commandment"; Barclay thinks John has in mind the word of his Lord; Law that the commandment is from God, not expressly from Christ, though the reference is to Christ's new commandment; Westcott: "given by Christ but from God as its final source". Huther says "Him" means Christ because of the following reference to God, but perhaps it is safer to understand as "God"! The parallel in 3:23 — where the author of the commandment is certainly God — is balanced by 2:7f. where Christ's words are clearly in mind. But the substitution of "brother" for "neighbour", which makes the citation of Deuteronomy and the Mark-Luke parallels only partially appropriate, suggests reminiscence of the *new* commandment here, also.

Every one who believes — Law can say, "Belief is emphasised as the condition and test of life", but he argues, from the tenses in 5:1, that "the divine begetting is the antecedent, not the consequence, of the believing. . . . Christian belief, which is essentially the spiritual recognition of spiritual truth, is a function of the divine life as imparted to men". This Law supports with quotation of John 18:37, 10:26, 27; 17:6, 6:45, 65;

9:39, 3:18, 19 — not one of which touches the question, and he asserts some "Johannine predestination" in the sense that they discern the truth who are predisposed to do so, and the truth accordingly sifts men in judgement, as they have or have not capacity and predisposition to "receive Christ". This is true, but does not affect the point that until capacity and predisposition lead to actual faith, spiritual life and sonship do not begin. The only quotation that affects the point — John 11:52 — Law himself modifies by "at least *potentially* children of God". Brooke commends Law's words, though introducing them with John 1:12, which plainly contradicts this interpretation, and commenting that whether faith is cause or result of new birth is not present to the thought of the writer of 1 John. Westcott: "Brethren are united by a common divine Father. The human condition of this union is faith in Jesus as the Christ", though he adds that faith is here regarded simply as the sign of the life which has been given: nothing is said of the relation between human and divine, the faith of man and the seed of God, in the first quickening of life. On John 1:12 Westcott states that relation as: "It is of God to give, but men must use His gift, which faith appropriates . . . the initial act is at once a 'begetting' and a 'reception'". Hasler sufficiently comments, "Hath been begotten — the verb is used in the perfect tense to denote both the past completion of the act and also its abiding present result". Similarly Plummer. As to the importance and primacy of faith in the New Testament, "believe, belief" occurs in Acts eighteen times — 14:22, 27; 22:24, 26:20 are but examples; the Church is the company of "believers" (4:32, and six times altogether); and belief is the way to life (13:48). Paul's gospel is repeatedly defined in terms of faith: 1 Corinthians 15:1-11, 2 Thessalonians 2:13f., Romans 1:5, 16f., 3:21f., 5:1, 10:5-17; faith is counted for righteousness, receives the Spirit, is justified, "works by love", "avails" with God — the significant passages are innumerable. The sufficiency of faith in Christ alone to save is one of the major contentions of Paul's life. For Hebrews see 10:38, 11:1, 4; for 1 Peter see 1:5, 8, 9; 2:6, 7; 5:9. Compare the present writer's *Biblical Doctrine of Initiation,* pp. 180, 206f., 228f., 244f.

By this we know . . . — Law remarks that this verse has a significance apt to be overlooked; it is certainly apt to be confused! Bennett: we shall be sure of loving the brethren in the very best way when we love God so as to obey Him; Barclay: everyone who loves the father loves the child, and this is how we know that we must be loving the children of God, whenever we love God; Gore: you cannot know that you love the children of God, as being such, unless you love God, the Father of this new family (but why not?); Law: love to men is truly love only when it is rooted in and governed by love to God: piety without philanthropy is unreal, philanthropy without piety may be immoral . . . impotent to bestow the highest good; Brooke: "By this" points forward — we know we love the children when we love the Father — brushing aside the exceptional form "By this . . . whenever"; Westcott: it is equally true to say that he who loves God loves the children of God and that he who loves the children of God loves God: the effort to fulfil the commandment of God is the effort to do that which our brethren most desire to be done — itself the proof of love; Plummer: love to God and love to the brethren confirm and prove each other: either alone is not genuine; Huther: love to God and love to the brethren "mutually prove one another": he therefore who regards it as incumbent upon him to fulfil God's commandments possesses therein the evidence that he loves his brethren in reality. Unfortunately none of these interpretations accords at once with experience and with John's phrasing. The Pharisees' diligent attention to God's commandments did not produce or prove brotherly love; deep secular friendships do not prove loving obedience towards God. Certainly John means "Christian-brotherly" love, and that this arises from love towards God: but how we know we love the brethren by our obedience to God is not clear. We do not need proof of our feelings, and John would accept none except generous deeds and kindly acts. Dodd's solution is the only one which gives satisfactory sense without violence to the original words. He thinks "By this" does not refer to the following phrase "when we love God and keep his commandments", because this is not the usual order of thought in the epistle — to make love to God the evidence of love to men. We may add that it is not true to experience either. Instead, Dodd takes "By this" to refer to the preceding phrase "he who loves the parent loves the child": because of this (universal, unchallengeable principle), we know that whenever we love God and do His commandments we love and must love all fellow Christians, His children.

NOTES ON 5:3b-12:

This is the victory — Westcott appears to invert: This is our faith, "the embodiment of the victory that overcame the world" — which is not John's meaning but suggestively links the verse with John 16:33.

Came by water . . . — Moffatt has "came by water, blood, and Spirit" and Dodd, while admitting the text to be uncertain, thinks this reading, as well as being strongly attested by "those two excellent MSS the Sinaitic and the Alexandrine and some minor authorities", gives a good sequence of thought, which he illustrates from the Spirit's presence at Christ's baptism (Acts 10:38, 2:33, John 1:32-34) — the descent of the Spirit then being evidence of the Messiahship of Jesus. However, RV, RSV omit "and Spirit", Westcott ignores it, and so do most commentators.

The Spirit is the witness — Neither "the Spirit here is the spirit Christ committed to the Father at death" (Augustine), nor "the Spirit beareth witness that the Spirit is the truth" have found much support, mainly because neither yields an intelligible meaning in this context.

The witnesses — The words "in heaven, the Father, the Word, and the Holy Ghost, and these three are one. And there are three that bear witness in earth", which appeared in older versions at verses 6-8, are silently omitted by RV, RSV, NEB, Moffatt, because they were no part of the known text of 1 John until "quoted" by a Spanish heretic (died 385) from whose work the passage "gradually made its way into MSS of the Latin Vulgate. . . . There is no doubt whatever that the words are a spurious interpolation" (Dodd).

Witnesses . . . the water and the blood — Dodd points out that in John 19:34 the witness is that of an observer, not of the water and the blood; he thinks Johannine symbolism suggests the "real drink" (of John 6:54f.) and the "living water" (of John 4:14), but finds little help in the suggestion: "The Church possesses a counterpart to the baptism of Christ in the sacrament of baptism and a counterpart to His sacrificial death in the sacrament of the eucharist. But sacraments attest and confirm to believers the abiding effect of the life and death of Christ. It seems likely that our author is thinking of these two sacraments as providing a continuing witness to the truth of Christ's incarnation and redemptive death". Westcott finds the first reference of "coming by water and blood" in the cardinal events of Jesus' life, but stresses the echo of John 19:34 as indicating that Christ "henceforth became for men the source of blessing symbolised by the twofold stream. . . . Thus we are led to the ideas which underlie the two sacraments". Law says that "such expressions as the 'water' and the 'blood' are a kind of verbal shorthand intended merely to recall to his readers the exposition of those themes which they had heard from his lips". He declares that John 19:34 sheds no light, and he argues cogently that the first mention of the water and blood (verse 6) refers to the baptism and death of Christ in answer to the Cerinthian heresy, and the second mention (verse 8) provides "a natural transition from the historical realities to their permanent memorials, the Christian sacraments". The change of meaning between 6 and 8 is not an insurmountable objection in view of the extreme condensation of the whole passage; and to apply "the witness of the blood" to Calvary itself is altogether inadequate. Huther mentions ten main lines of interpretation, and decides firmly that the baptism and death of Jesus are intended in verse 6; he adheres to this meaning (rejecting any reference to the sacraments) for verse 8, holding that the baptism and death of Jesus are still witnessing through the Spirit in the Church — though not explaining in what way that would be convincing for the seceders. Gore explains by both Christ's birth and death and the Christian sacraments, holding it to be characteristic of St. John's mystical method that it should rest on outward facts and that his brooding soul should grow to see the inward meaning in the outward facts, passing from the record of past facts to present living witnesses in Spirit, baptism, eucharist. Barclay uses John 19:34 to illustrate the importance for John of water and blood "in connection with" Jesus as conveying an essential part of the meaning of the gospel: the witness of the water in Jesus' own baptism is maintained in Christian baptism, and in the eucharist is a continuing witness to the atoning power of the sacrifice of Jesus Christ. W. H. Bennett, comprehensively: "the water and the blood symbolise the events of Christ's life, and the features of His character; and also the cleansing, inspiration, and redemption which spring from His work. These also are a testimony to Christ". Plummer practically closes discussion, as to verse 6, by showing how water = Christ's baptism, blood = Christ's death, explains the order (contrast John 19:34), the prepositions (through, in) and the emphatic "not with the water only"; finding that both point "in a symbolic manner" to the two great sacraments, he aptly quotes Tertullian: "He had come by means of water and blood just as John had written; that He might be baptised by the water, glorified by the blood; to make us in like manner *called* by water, *chosen* by blood. These two baptisms He sent out from the wound in His pierced side, in order that they who believed in His blood might be bathed in the water; they who had been bathed in the water might likewise drink the blood" (*De Bapt.* xvi). Westcott, Brooke, Law, Neil Alexander all emphasise that "He who came (cometh)" is a messianic phrase which almost *requires* that "water and blood" (in verse 6) refer to historical events, the process of Messiah's coming among men in the baptism and the death. Brooke therefore thinks verse 6 refers to Christ's baptism and death and that "it is obvious" water and blood in verse 8 must mean the same — without explaining how then they still witness to Christ.

In himself — (verse 10): so Huther, Law, Moffatt, Dodd, RSV, Brooke, Plummer, Bennett, Neil Alexander; but RV, followed by G. S. Barrett, "in Him" — Christ's self-authentication to the believer — though (as Barrett says) in either case this witness is subjective, and within.

NOTES ON 5:13-17:

I write this — Huther, Brooke, Neil Alexander suggest 5:13 summarises only the preceding statements, but then it seems to have little point. Summarising the letter as a whole, the verse neatly parallels 1:3, 4 and introduces the final exhortations (RSV, Souter, G. S. Barrett, Plummer, Westcott). Law thinks the verse accurately defines the governing aim of the whole epistle, but contextually refers to 5:6-12. The sixfold "know" of 13-21 seems to bind the whole paragraph in thought if not in form. The parallel of 5:13 with John 20:31 does not make 14-21 as clearly an appendix as John 21 is; Neil Alexander thinks the final paragraph belongs to the substance of the epistle and concludes its argument; Plummer records the conjecture that 14-21 is by the same hand that added chapter 21 to the Gospel, but he argues from contents and diction and from patristic quotation that 14-21 has always been an intrinsic part of the letter. Dodd thinks 13 completes the epistle: "the rest is postscript".

A mortal sin — John's distinction between sin unto death and sin not unto death has been "the origin of infinite controversy . . . the source of the technical classification of sins as 'mortal' and 'venial' . . .". "Fatal" and "curable" would be nearer to John's meaning. Bennett usefully cites an analogy "by no means close" with Matthew 12:31, 32; Mark 3:29, Luke 12:10, and "a much more exact parallel" with Hebrews 6:4-6, and 10:26-29. "In Hebrews the fatal sin is deliberate and ostentatious apostasy from Christianity . . . here, a similar separation from the apostolic Church" (Holtzmann). Gore adds the parallel with 1 Corinthians 5:3-5. He also, like Barclay and Brooke, cites the Old Testament distinction between lesser sins of inadvertence and sins done with a high hand (Numbers 15:30, for example) for which sacrifice did not avail — a distinction which probably yielded through the LXX the form of John's phrasing. Westcott seems to think the sin unto death is such as is seen to separate a man from the divine society, the Body of Christ — hatred of his brother, for example: and that John does not in such case command intercession, but does not expressly exclude it. Westcott's note is mainly concerned with the Church's later use of John's distinction. Barclay, following Plummer, discusses six explanations of "sins unto death" — sins punishable by death, or visited by God with death, punishable by excommunication, post-baptismal sin, apostasy in days of persecution, or denial that Christ had come in the flesh — and concludes that John means sin persistent, delighted in, become fixed as the chosen way of life, sin "on the way to death because on the way to a state where the idea of repentance will not enter his head". Law says it is something committed by

263

Christians, recognisable by others, and that by which the fatal goal is reached — not (as Westcott and Plummer) that which tends toward the fatal goal but may not reach it. Law rightly urges that if only tendency were in question, not to pray concerning it would be unchristian. He concludes that the sin of final impenitence, such as marks the sin against the light of the Holy Spirit Himself, with apostasy from the faith, is what John means. Huther says no particular sin is in John's mind, but a species of sin which involves falling away from Christ, not "the act of inward rejection itself" (Ebrard) but open renunciation of Christ. Huther rejects the view that the anti-christian denial that Jesus is the Christ is "sin unto death", on the ground that if John meant this he would have expressed it definitely. But this is just what John has already done in 5:12b: John's vagueness has pastoral and charitable intention. Brooke thinks the sin implied is deliberate rejection of Christ and His claims.

Give him life — "He will ask and God will give him life" is the meaning of RSV, NEB, and hesitantly Westcott, Law, against Huther. Brooke says, "In virtue of his intercession . . . the Christian may be said to give life to his brother Christians"; this seems hardly a New Testament thought, though Plummer cites James: "He shall save a soul from death". The change from singular ("his brother" in verse 16) to plural ("life for those") is awkward, but Moffatt probably hits the meaning exactly: "life for him — for anyone who does not commit a deadly sin".

I do not say — Neil Alexander strangely speaks of "John's questioning of the apostate's right to the Church's intercessions" as "wrung out of him by the anguish to himself and the peril to the Church which such sinners were causing". He adds that the Church has since believed John's judgement harsh and wrong. This surely misses the whole point, which is to urge prayer for all sinning brethren, but without contradicting or withdrawing the inescapable dictum of 5:12b.

All unrighteousness is sin — The view of Brooke and others that John inserts this to show that "there is plenty of scope left for the exercise of brotherly intercession" seems a mildly rueful joke rather than exposition — and a joke in tasteless context. In a letter so concerned with rigorous definitions and unyielding distinctions of right and wrong, to close with an admission of varying grades of sin would seem very weak: John therefore roundly affirms again that "sin is sin" — although not all sin automatically forfeits eternal life as denying the Son must do.

NOTES ON 5:18-21:

He who was born of God keeps him(self) — RV, RSV understand "He who was born" as Christ, RSV departing from its custom to capitalise the pronoun in order to emphasise its interpretation; AV(KJV) follows some inferior manuscripts with "himself" making "He who was born of God" = the Christian; Huther, who dismisses the reading "him" (for "himself") as "only a clerical variation of the word", interprets as the self-preservation of the believer. Neil Alexander describes this as misled and misleading. "He who *was* born of God keeps him (that is begotten of God)" — compare John 17:12, 15: for the nearest parallel to "born of God" used of Christ, note the variant reading at John 1:13 ("Who was born") and "only-begotten Son" at John 3:16 and elsewhere. W. Alexander, Barclay, G. S.

264

Barrett, Gore accept "Jesus keeps him", the last-named citing John 14:30; Plummer remarks "on any other interpretation John's marked change of tense appears arbitrary and confusing" and with this Brooke agrees. If "himself" be the true reading, Brooke takes as "He who has experienced the new birth keeps himself" by the power of the new life from evil. But he thinks the reading "him" has strong claims (it is hard to see why an original "himself" should be changed to "him", easier to see why "him" might inadvertently become "himself"); he cites John 1:13 in Western text, 18:37, 17:15 and Revelation 3:10, with a glance at Psalm 2:7 "which has some claim to represent the true text in Luke 3:22", and emphasises the change of tense, concluding that the One born of God is Christ, who keeps all who are born of God. It could be added that "the evil one" almost requires this interpretation: Christians may keep themselves from evil, but need other help against "the evil one". It is said that "keep himself" is supported by "keep yourselves" in 21, though a different word is used, and repetition of the *same* thought is less likely in 1 John than addition of a slight variant — "He . . . keeps: keep yourselves". Dodd paraphrases as "the Son of God *par excellence,* the eldest Brother of the family (compare Romans 8:29) is there to preserve them". Westcott thinks it impossible to hold that the two phrases (in verse 18) mean the same thing; the mention of the great Adversary suggests the thought of the Son of God, and the difference between Christ and others "born of God" is illustrated in John 5:26. On the other side Law thinks the textual evidence between "him" and "himself" so close that exegesis has a right to speak: instances of the Christian keeping himself are as frequent in the New Testament as of God keeping the Christian; 1 John 3:3 is "almost identical"; for the change of tense compare 4:9, 10; John's purpose may be to warn against relying on what once was true but needs continual reassertion — being born of God (would John say this?); change of meaning in the phrase within one sentence is "very improbable" and there is nothing in the change which makes it intrinsically fitting; had he meant Christ he would certainly have written "the Son of God". Against Law, it may be asked, if the bare statement "the Christian, being born of God, keeps himself and the evil one does not touch him" is true, would the letter have been necessary?

Him who is true — AV (KJV) and RV (inserting "even") make this phrase mean Jesus, and the following words become the most explicit assertion of the deity of Christ in the New Testament (W. H. Bennett). But "his Son" suggests that "him who is true" means God, and "the true God" then means the Father, or the Godhead, parallel with John 17:3 (so Huther, Plummer, Westcott). Neil Alexander rejects the arguments that "even in His Son" in apposition to "him who is true" makes the latter mean Christ, and that both John and Paul speak of union with God, not with Christ; he finds a change of reference for "him that is true" awkward and unlikely, and concludes that John means "union with God through His Son". "This is the true God" then refers to "the previous subject as previously described" (that is, to God as revealed, or as true), citing Brooke who gives eight Johannine parallels. (Law thinks this is not tautologous, because of the addition "and eternal life".) Yet Alexander agrees with Dodd in broadening the final verse to recapitulate the letter: "All that he has been saying about God, how He is light, and love, how

265

He is revealed as the Father through His Son Jesus Christ, how He is faithful and just to forgive our sins, how He remains in us — all this is the true God!" This is somewhat confirmed by the apposition, "and eternal life". "This I have expounded of God is the real God, and this life I have described is life eternal." Or (Dodd): this (knowledge of) the real God is eternal life. Brooke discusses briefly the attempt to make "him who is true" = Christ, but argues that "in his Son" is not in apposition to "him who is true" but states the means by which Christians have fellowship with God. Plummer lists arguments in favour of the interpretation: "This [Jesus] is the true God" — Jesus is the nearest substantive, God has been already twice called true, Christ twice in the epistle (and also in the Gospel) is called the Life, and Athanasius' use of the verse. In favour of "This [the Father] is the true God" he argues: the Father is the principal subject of the context, the Father is the source of life, repetition is just in John's style, John 17:3 suggests the Father is here meant, and the warning against idols would confirm it. Law thinks it "unnatural" to suppose a change of meaning for "him who is true" in mid-sentence. Huther rehearses the dogmatic interests that have governed interpretation here, thinks grammar inconclusive, and that although "the life" seems more fitly to refer to Christ, "the true God" more naturally refers to "him who is true" and is not elsewhere ascribed to Christ; for John the source of life is God. The tautology is removed by 21; Huther rejects a reference to the whole line of thought. If it be accepted that the abrupt final warning is a deliberately contrived "punch-line" for a letter without signature, then "This is the true God and eternal life" is its necessary preparation, and admirably summarises the whole letter, as well as the immediately preceding affirmations. A new paragraph at "This is the true God" would excellently represent John's intention.

True — three times in these closing verses: (compare also note on 2:8). "True" means real, ideal, genuine, as opposed to spurious, counterfeit, frequently in John (for example John 1:9, 4:23, 33; 6:32, 7:28, 8:16, 15:1, 17:3, 19:35). A related Greek word means true to fact, opposed to lying, falsehood; but this word means true to the perfect conception of a thing, the "real thing", all it is supposed to be. Dodd, and Moffatt, translate "real" — Him who is the final reality — relating John's affirmation to the Platonic search for reality amid life's transitoriness and illusions. Neil Alexander draws upon LXX usage to prefer the meaning "genuine" (as opposed not to the unreal or illusionary, but to the false, the counterfeit: compare the phrases "a true friend", an "illusory" friend). Law gives the word here "its proper meaning . . . genuine, real, perfectly corresponding in fact to the idea its name expresses". Dodd well contrasts the *via negativa* method by which Greek thought approached the eternally real (denying step by step all that was actual, concrete, and temporal), and the way of historical and concrete manifestation by which John declares the real has become known and been experienced.

Idols — The root-word means that which is seen, appearance, external form (Luke 3:22, 9:29, John 5:37, 2 Corinthians 5:7); form, sort, kind (1 Thessalonians 5:22). The "idol" may be a phantom, image, likeness (in the mind), an idea or fancy; in LXX and New Testament, an image of a god, an idol to be worshipped (Acts 7:41, 1 Corinthians 12:2, Revelation 9:20), or the false god (or idol) worshipped in the image

(Acts 15:20, Romans 2:22, 1 Corinthians 8:4, 7; 10:19, 2 Corinthians 6:16, 1 Thessalonians 1:9 and here (so Abbott-Smith). The question is whether the insistence on "the true One" in the present passage indicates that the word "idol" refers to what is untrue, unreal, fancy, phantom, sham, or is to be taken of the literal images found in the shrines of Ephesus. W. H. Bennett takes literally and cites 1 Corinthians 10:14; the warning is a postscript additional to all the letter has said about heresy. Barclay refers to Plato for the meaning "illusions of this world as opposed to the unchangeable realities of eternity" and to the prophets for "counterfeit gods opposed to the true God", yet he understands John to warn against the manifold, elaborate and lascivious idolatries of Ephesus — which he powerfully describes. Neil Alexander appeals to the LXX to fix the meaning "false, counterfeit gods over against the one genuine God". The bogus gods constructed by the seceders' doctrine are foremost in John's mind, but wider still, the obligation to use the sure knowledge of the genuine as the touchstone of all that claims allegiance — all cults, ideas, and compromises inconsistent with the truth. G. S. Barrett takes the word literally, but spiritualises as money, ambition, amusements — the one interpretation we may be sure John did not intend! Gore says the epistle gives no hint of dangers of heathen idolatry: John warns against enthroning in the mind false ideas of God, something else than the real God, such as the epistle has ascribed to Antichrist. Plummer says the literal meaning lies to hand, is invariable in the New Testament, and the Gnostics held idolatry harmless; but, he proceeds, the warning against worship of the creature intensifies the message of the epistle — that Jesus is no creature but the Son of God and worthy of all worship, so bringing the thought close again to the real, genuine object of worship, the true God revealed in Christ over against all shams. Brooke makes the word refer to all false images men make for themselves, not those of Gnostics only, and probably not actual objects of pagan worship. Dodd thinks John warns against all contact with paganism, the Greek word "idol" always carrying the suggestion of unreality; but John means also all false or counterfeit notions of God, all God-substitutes. Westcott: "vain shadows which usurp His place"; he seems to take the word literally, but adds that in Paul (Colossians 3:5, Ephesians 5:5) idolatry has a wider meaning, and the context here also may require extension of the term. Law thinks a wider meaning reasonable provided the readers could understand it; absence of such warning elsewhere in the epistle could make that meaning more likely here — it was certainly necessary; "upon the whole it seems very doubtful that the apostle would describe the phantoms of Gnostic theology, not to say unreal professions of Christianity, as 'idols' ". Huther says, "If the warning is not to be regarded as a detached appendix foreign to the contents of the epistle . . . John certainly has in view . . . principally . . . the untrue mental images" of the false teachers leading the secession. Both "detached appendix" and oversubtle psychology seem very much out of place in 1 John. An exposition of tests for distinguishing true from false, genuine from counterfeit, fittingly ends with an appeal to beware *shams*: but as the shams in question are religious, and as the intellectual pretensions of the Gnostics made them contemptuous of the common people's love of idolatry, it was especially appropriate, and forceful, to choose for "shams" the loaded word "idols".

Essay 1 — Apart from books elsewhere listed, this review of modern discussion of religious authority rests heavily upon J. R. Nelson: *The Realm of Redemption,* chapter 4; "The Authority of the Bible", by Archbishop Ramsey, in *Peake's Commentary on the Bible* (1962); J. S. Whale: *The Protestant Tradition*; C. H. Dodd: *The Authority of the Bible*; Stephen Winward's chapter on "Scripture, Tradition and Baptism" in Gilmore (editor): *Christian Baptism.* W. R. Inge, *Faith and Its Psychology* (chapters 3-8), was also consulted.

Essay 2 — Reference is made to the general introduction to the "Library of Constructive Theology" series published by Nisbet and Co. under the editorship of W. R. Matthews and H. Wheeler Robinson.

Essay 3 — Two quotations from C. H. Dodd are taken from *The Gospel and Law of Christ,* the William Ainslie Memorial Lecture, 1946, published by Longmans Green and Co., page 7. The article by William Barclay on Graeco-Roman society appeared in the *Expository Times* (Edinburgh), LXXI, 9 (June 1960), 280-284.

Essay 4 — Carey's "An Enquiry into the Obligation of Christians to use means for the Conversion of the Heathen" was published in 1792; see also S. Pearce Carey: *William Carey,* 1923; Charles Hodge's sermon on the *Unity of the Church,* 1866, was reprinted in *Christianity Today,* May 26, 1958; evangelical opinion cited was gathered from various articles and booklets by Rev. Marcus Loane, Bishop co-adjutor in the Diocese of Sydney, Rev. Professor R. A. Finlayson, of Free Church College, Edinburgh, Rev. A. T. Houghton, Secretary of the Bible Churchmen's Missionary Society (in booklet published by World Dominion Press), Rev. Leith Samuel (in booklet published by the Evangelical Alliance), Rev. Paul Rees (in a book review), and from chapter 7 of J. R. Nelson: *The Realm of Redemption.*

Essay 5 — This is considerably indebted to Denney: *The Death of Christ;* Vincent Taylor: *Jesus and His Sacrifice* and *Atonement in New Testament Teaching;* A. M. Stibbs: the Tyndale New Testament Lecture, 1947, "The Meaning of the Word 'Blood' in Scripture" (published by the Tyndale Press, London) from which are taken quotations from Micklem, Quick, Behm, and one from Vincent Taylor. The meaning of the cross is expounded from many sides in the author's *Beneath the Cross of Jesus* (1959).

Essay 6 — Typical examples of 1 John's allusions to details of the Johannine record are: 5:6 = John 19:34; 3:5 = John 1:29; 3:20 = (in the context of reassuring shaken hearts) John 21:17; and 4:14

= John 4:42. Typical examples of 1 John's allusions to sayings of Jesus in Johannine idiom are: 1:3 = John 17:21; 1:4 = John 15:11, 16:24; 2:10, 11 = John 12:35; 2:18 = John 21:5; 2:25 = John 17:3; 2:27 = John 14:26; 3:13 = John 15:18; 3:22 = 8:29 (9:31); 3:23 = John 6:28, 29; 4:5 = John 15:19, 8:47, 3:31; 4:12 = John 1:18; 5:8-10 = John 8:17-18; 5:11, 12 = John 5:24, and much else (especially alluding to the Upper Room Discourse). Typical examples of 1 John's allusions to thoughts and phrases characteristic of the Fourth Gospel's style are: 1:1 = John 1:1, 4; 4:14 = John 1:14; 5:1, 2 = John 1:12, 13; etc.

SUBJECT INDEX

SUBJECT INDEX

Abiding, 48, 165, 218f, 237, 256, 258

Abstractions, 85, 89, 90, 92, 118, 120

"Advanced" Christianity, 16

Advent hope, 71, 73, 74, 76, 78f, 116, 133, 168, 212f, 219, 243f, 248

Advocate, 43, 44, 196f, 200f, 210, 214, 234, 236

Age (new, passing), 63, 73, 239

Agnosticism, 34, 214

Analysis of 1 John, 230

Anointing, 73f, 153, 162, 165, 167, (see: *Chrism*) 211, 218, 245

Antichrist, 16, 66, 67, 101f, 104, 172, 175, 190, 210, 243f, 264, 267

Assurance, 13, 46, 88, 91, 94f, 96, 99, 111, 112f, 114f, 118, 137, 168 170, 199, 253, 268

Atonement, 17, 18, 20, 91, 105, 108f. (see: Blood, Death 111, 115, of Christ, Sacrifice) 130, 140, 153, 191, 195, 200-202, 203, 204, 213, 215, 217, 257

Authorship, 14f, 224f, 247

Authority in religion, 145f, 209, 268
apostolic, 233
of epistle, 14

Backsliders, 131
(see: Love, Prayer)

Baptism, 73, 97, 102, 113f, 119, 126f, 128, 146f, 151, 185, 211, 218, 235, 245, 246f, 254, 257f, 261f

"Beginning", 151f, 155, 209, 218f
(see: History)

Belief, 97, 119, 121, 123-125, 126f, 159, 202, 217-219, 247, 250, 259f

Blindness, 51

Blood of Christ, 43, 196, 198-200, (see: Atonement, 202f, 235, 249, Death of Christ) 261, 268

Born again, of God, 74, 76-78, 105, 107, 109, 118, 124f, 137f, 161, 190, 214, 241, 247, 251, 256, 259, 264f

"Brother", 240

Bunyan, 112

"By this . . . " (etc.), 236, 253, 258, 261

Cain, Cainites, 88, 90, 94, 151, 175, 191, 251f

"Catholic" Christianity, 10

Cerinthianism, 21f, 214f, 227f, 238, 255, 262

Children of God, 81, 85, 87, 89, 118, 121, 124, 134, 212, 250, 260
"children", 240f

Gnostic Ethics, 19, 21, 39, 138
(see: Ethics)
Gnostic Lovelessness, 19, 92, 178f,
240, 257
Gnostic Popularity, 91, 103, 173f
"Great Awakening", 9, 11

Hatred, 51f, 90, 118, 191, 212, 240,
263
Heresy, 132, 135, 255
History, 108, 113, 115, 127, 129,
130, 146f, 152f, 158, 204, 210,
215, 217, 219f, 232, 266
Homily? 224
Hope, 76, 79, 159
(see: Advent)

Idols, 137, 266f
Imitation of Christ, 48f, 74, 78f,
87, 151, 167, 179f, 209, 218, 234,
248, 258f
Incarnation, 17-20, 84, 102, 104f,
108f, 111, 115, 126-129, 130, 139f,
153, 191, 195, 201, 203, 210,
214-216, 219f, 233, 256f, 262
Indwelling, 164f, 210
"in Christ", 48f, 164
Inspiration, 101f, 105, 150
Intercession, 134, 136, 201, 250,
(see: Prayer) 263f

Joy, 33, 116f, 160, 162, 191, 233
Judaism, 229, 238, 247, 250
Judgement, 106, 111, 116f, 133,
168, 212, 249, 258f, 260
Justification, 85, 217, 250, 260

Knowledge, 17f, 47f, 72, 91, 94,
107, 109, 137, 151, 161, 237,
241, 247, 256f, 260
Koinonia, 32f, 233

Last hour, 244
Lawlessness, 81, 84, 88, 176f, 234
Law-work, 170f, 207
Lie - Liar, 233f, 243
Life (see: Eternal Life)
Light, 34-36, 51, 53, 80, 107, 171f,
(see: Darkness) 201, 219, 233f,
239, 255
"Illumination" 71f, 161f, 168, 244
Light of the world, 72, 162

Walking in light, 36f, 39f, 41, 69,
161f, 191, 206f, 211, 239
Logic, 154
Lord's Supper (see: Supper)
Love, see: 257; then - 17, 19, 51f,
64, 88f, 91f, 105-111, 116f, 118f,
120f, 162, 163, 165, 199, 201,
205f, 209, 214, 218, 236f, 247,
252f, 255f, 258f, 260f
for brethren, 33, 65, 83, 89, 91,
95, 105, 109, 117, 119f, 133,
167, 177f, 191, 193, 207, 257
Luther, 114, 193f

Memories of Jesus, 147, 151f, 165,
209f, 211, 213, 268f
Mind of Christ, 155, 181
Montanism, 9, 11, 157
Moral Obligation, 177, 181, 207,
(see: Commandments) 250
Moral Indifference (see: Ethics)
Moravians, 11
Mystery Religions, 82, 126, 237, 247
Mysticism, 159f, 162, 166f, 209,
233, 237, 257

Name (of Christ), 60, 131, 159, 210,
213, 241, 245

Obedience, 47, 163, 166, 253
"Of God", 163f.
Old Testament, 151, 257
Outline of 1 John, 230
Overcoming (see: Victory)

Person of Christ, 17, 66, 97, 99, 111,
118, 123, 126, 130, 132, 150, 195,
202f, 209f, 214-216, 244, 255f
Postscript, 263, 267
Power, 100f
Prayer, 93, 96-98, 113, 131, 134-
(see: Intercession) 136, 160, 168,
177, 182, 191, 212, 264
Prayer for Backsliders, 178f, 193,
263f
Prophets — Christian and other,
101f, 127, 151, 153, 161, 254
Propitiation, 196f, 200-203, 205
(see: Expiation)
Purpose of epistle, 15f, 131

276